Reflections on Blaxploitation

Actors and Directors Speak

DAVID WALKER
ANDREW J. RAUSCH
CHRIS WATSON

THE SCARECROW PRESS, INC.
Lanham, Maryland • Toronto • Plymouth, UK
2009

SCARECROW PRESS, INC.

Published in the United States of America
by Scarecrow Press, Inc.
A wholly owned subsidary of
The Rowman & Littlefield Publishing Group, Inc.
4501 Forbes Boulevard, Suite 200, Lanham, Maryland 20706
www.scarecrowpress.com

Estover Road
Plymouth PL6 7PY
United Kingdom

British Library Cataloguing in Publication Information Available

Library of Congress Cataloging-in-Publication Data
Reflections on blaxploitation : actors and directors speak / [interviewers] David Walker, Andrew J. Rausch, Chris Watson.
    p. cm.
  Includes index.
  ISBN-13: 978-0-8108-6706-2 (cloth : alk. paper)
  ISBN-10: 0-8108-6706-0 (cloth : alk. paper)
  ISBN-13: 978-0-8108-6732-1 (ebook)
  ISBN-10: 0-8108-6732-X (ebook)
  1. Blaxploitation films–United States–History and criticism. 2. African Americans in motion pictures. 3. African American actors–Interviews. 4. African American motion picture producers and directors–Interviews. I. Walker, David. II. Rausch, Andrew J. III. Watson, Christopher.
  PN1995.9.N4R46 2009
  791.43'652996073–dc22   2008045841

∞™ The paper used in this publication meets the minimum requirements of American National Standard for Information Sciences—Permanence of Paper for Printed Library Materials, ANSI/NISO Z39.48-1992.
Manufactured in the United States of America.

To the many actors and filmmakers
from the blaxploitation era
who are no longer with us.

If you were to talk about a film that was made by Charles Bronson—*Death Wish*—and we called it "whitesploitation," you'd laugh. Why then don't we laugh when we take a film that's made by Jim Brown or Fred Williamson and we call that blaxploitation?

—Oscar Williams

Exploitation? Movies are exploitation. They are. But for some reason, they put the words black and exploitation together and brought those words to the film—to *our* film. They called the other action films with Humphrey Bogart and these other guys, they called those "B" movies. And they called us blaxploitation. It just seemed to have a bad connotation.

—Gloria Hendry

I never understood what it meant. Who was being exploited? Certainly not me. My checks cleared. And the people who worked for me, their checks cleared. So who the hell was being exploited? The people went to the show because they enjoyed what they were seeing.

—Fred Williamson

Contents

Introduction

David Walker

Big bad soul brothers and super sexy sisters, their afros picked to spherical perfection and their guns blazing, lit up the silver screen in a dynamic cinematic explosion that forever changed Hollywood. The time was 1970, and much of America—especially black America—was still dealing with the tumultuous times of the 1960s. Out of this era came a new breed of film that would completely change the way black people were presented in movies. In time, these films would be called "blaxploitation."

Audiences were mesmerized by these new films. Never before had black men and women appeared on screen in quite the same way. Even during the height of the "race films" and "black cast films" of the 1930s and 1940s, there had never been anything quite like blaxploitation. In *The Emperor Jones* (1933), Paul Robeson's character threatened a white man and was made to pay for this unthinkable sin. Forty years later, in *The Spook Who Sat by the Door* (1973), black militants led a revolution to overthrow the government in a violent fantasy that reflected much of the lingering rage from past decades. Although the anger and frustration of black America had long been suppressed or ignored in films, filmmakers of the 1970s drew from those feelings to create a new kind of entertainment.

Film historians and fans alike have long debated exactly which film launched the blaxploitation cycle. Some say it was Melvin Van Peebles's seminal independent film *Sweet Sweetback's Baadasssss Song* (1971), while others say it was director Gordon Parks's *Shaft* (1971), produced by MGM. The tremendous financial success of both films helped open the floodgates for the more than 200 films that are now considered blaxploitation, but the origins of the genre can be directly found in films like *In the Heat of the Night* (1967) and *Cotton Comes to Harlem* (1970), which is technically the closest to being the first blaxploitation film. As for the term itself, blaxploitation wasn't coined until 1972, most likely a direct result of the film *Superfly* (1972).

As difficult as it is to decide which film to credit with giving birth to blaxploitation, it is equally as difficult to figure out what blaxploitation really is, how long it lasted, and what films should bear that label. Is the term positive or negative? Can "blaxploitation" be used to describe films made before the term was coined, or after production ceased on most of the films? Since most of the films thought of as blaxploitation are action thrillers, does that mean that comedies or dramas are exempt from the label?

You could ask these and other questions of a dozen different people, and you're likely to hear a different answer every time. Some say that movies like *Cooley High* (1975) or *Lady Sings the Blues* (1972) are not blaxploitation, because they are "too good," or because they aren't action films. Some say that blaxploitation is a terrible word and horribly offensive, while others say it is a perfect way to describe films of that era. Some say that blaxploitation ended in the 1970s; others claim it is still alive.

The reality is that blaxploitation is neither positive nor negative; it simply is what it is. And what it is, first and foremost, is a genre of film that includes action, comedy, drama, romance, and even documentary—made and marketed to a predominantly black audience—as well as the era in which these films were made. The traditional blaxploitation film—if there really is such a thing—may have ended in the 1970s, but many movies similar to blaxploitation have come along in the decades that followed.

In understanding the blaxploitation era, it is important to understand the era that preceded it. The 1960s were a turbulent time in American history. The war being fought in Vietnam divided much of the country, as did the struggle for civil rights. Segregation was still the law of the land in the South, and the battle to change that and create a greater equality for all Americans was a struggle that did not come without sacrifice. This is especially true for black America, which saw the murder of leaders like Medgar Evers, Martin Luther King Jr., and Malcolm X.

Going into the 1970s, black America was in need of an escape from the brutal reality of the past decade. The films that came along during the early part of the 1970s provided just such an escape, creating a fantasy world on the big screen where black men and women were the heroes. But these films proved to be more than a cinematic catharsis; they also created a new mythology.

In a society inundated with pop culture icons that were white, the black heroes of the blaxploitation films provided a needed respite from characters like James Bond and cinematic icons like John Wayne. For arguably the first time since the invention of motion pictures, there were finally larger-than-life black heroes who saved the day, often by standing up to the dominant oppressor (a.k.a. whitey). And no matter how much negativity can be said about the blaxploitation era, the fact that it provided a generation with iconic heroes remains a significant truth.

The other truth about blaxploitation is that it helped save Hollywood. For the studios, which had been suffering financially for several years after a string of box office disappointments, blaxploitation represented a form of salvation. These were the days before suburban multiplex theaters. Most movie theaters were still located in the heart of the city. But after the massive migration of whites to the suburbs (known as "the great white flight"), those theaters became harder and harder to fill, because there were so few white people living in the inner city. Films like *Shaft* and *Foxy Brown* (1974) drew in black audiences and box office revenues that helped struggling studios stay afloat.

Blaxploitation films changed how black men and women were portrayed in films. Gone were the old negative stereotypes that had dominated films for over 70 years. Replacing them were new archetypes, including drug dealers, pimps, and hardened criminals. The new images were initially a welcome change for audiences, and the studios were more than happy to be making money, but the constant barrage of morally ambiguous anti-heroes soon led to a backlash. The films soon became a target of political watchdogs looking to earn a reputation. Critics of blaxploitation included organizations such as the NAACP and the Urban League. In fact, it is widely believed that the term blaxploitation was coined by a leader of the Los Angeles chapter of the NAACP.

By the mid-1970s, the popularity of blaxploitation was fading. As a genre, the films were seldom allowed to deviate from a standard model, which grew very old very quickly. Less money was being spent on bad rip-offs of movies that were already low budget, and the result was unwatchable trash like *The Guy from Harlem* (1977), which represent the bottom of the blaxploitation barrel. The political backlash that surrounded blaxploitation, and diminishing sales for a genre that had grown weak and tired, led to the "death" of blaxploitation. And of course, there was also the return of the "big picture"—films like *Jaws* (1975) and *Star Wars* (1977)—that made tons of money at the box office and played to audiences of all colors.

Though the number of black films had diminished considerably by the end of the 1970s, prompting many to believe the genre had died, nothing is ever that simple. The most obvious successors were Eddie Murphy's early films in the 1980s. A less obvious mutation of blaxploitation was hip-hop, which drew heavily from the mythology created by the films. And of course, the careers of many contemporary black actors and filmmakers can be traced directly back to the often disregarded films of the 1970s. John Singleton's *Boyz N the Hood* (1991) borrowed heavily from *Cooley High*. Keenan Ivory Wayans launched his directorial career with the blaxploitation spoof *I'm Gonna Git You Sucka* (1988). The films *Training Day* (2001) and *American Gangster* (2006), both starring Denzel Washington, are nothing if not expensive blaxploitation films. And the career of Will Smith, who has emerged as a major box office star, would not be what it is today if films like *Superfly* and *The Mack* (1973) had not changed everything.

The years have not always been kind to blaxploitation. It has been maligned, mocked, and misunderstood. As both a genre and an era, blaxploitation spawned well over 200 movies, grossed millions of dollars, launched many careers, and changed the face of pop culture forever. But somehow it has been largely ignored in the history books. Of the small handful of books that have examined blaxploitation films, most are now out of print. Furthermore, very few offered a look at blaxploitation from the people directly involved in the films.

This book is far from being the most indispensable guide to black films of the 1970s. It is, however, perhaps the most comprehensive collection of interviews with people who worked in front of and behind the camera on many blaxploitation films. Some of the people interviewed in this book are sadly no longer with us. But the contributions of all the interview participants—living and dead—remain a rich and integral part of film history.

CHAPTER 1

Ralph Bakshi

A publicity photograph of animator Ralph Bakshi from *The Lord of the Rings*.

Animator Ralph Bakshi began polishing his skills at the School of Industrial Art, where he graduated with an award in cartooning. He then began his storied career working for Terrytoons Studio, where he worked on such legendary cartoons as *Mighty Mouse, Heckle and Jeckle*, and *Deputy Dawg*. After the demise of Terrytoons, Bakshi landed on his feet when he was placed in charge of Paramount Pictures' animation division, Famous Studios, in 1967. The following year, Bakshi established his own studio, where he produced the animated *Spider-Man* television series until 1970, when he shifted gears and went to work in feature films.

Bakshi's first feature film, an adaptation of Robert Crumb's underground comic *Fritz the Cat* (1972), gained notoriety for being the first animated film to receive an X rating in the United States. Despite this rating, *Fritz the Cat* received positive reviews and went on to earn more than $100 million, becoming the first animated film to do so. Bakshi followed this success with *Heavy Traffic* (1973), which remains one of his most popular films. Bakshi's third film, *Coonskin* (1975), would ultimately become his most infamous. The film, often cited as the only animated blaxploitation picture ever produced, was accused of being racist. Because of this, *Coonskin* received negative press. It was picketed and even boycotted. As a result, Paramount Pictures dropped the film, and its theatrical run was limited. But the film wasn't really racist, and the passing of time has gained this once notorious film a fine reputation. Today, *Coonskin* is seen as one of Bakshi's finest and most daring films.

The groundbreaking animator's subsequent films include the fantastical *Wizards* (1977), the animated version of *The Lord of the Rings* (1978), and *Cool World* (1992).

ANDREW RAUSCH: *What about the political climate of the 1970s inspired you to make* Coonskin*?*

RALPH BAKSHI: I felt that animation could be better used to say the things I wanted to say in those days than live action, or at least in a different way. I was very much aware of what *Heavy Traffic* and *Fritz the Cat* had said socially and politically. So I knew exactly what I was trying to do, but I wasn't sure what kind of ground I was on. So the political climate then was very similar to the political climate now, only a little different. I sit here amazed with my mouth open. There was so much shit going on at the time that it was just incredible. A lot of good things were happening, too, but always the con artists would show up and preach some cause. Black revolutionaries were just taking money from organizations and not handing it out. There was so much bullshit going on, and so much idealism going on. So I certainly wanted to make a political cartoon about what I felt was going on, which was no different than the first two films I made.

Using the fact that I'm in animation and no one really knows what I'm doing in Hollywood, using the fact that black exploitation films were running rampant at the time . . . the body count on killing whites was very high in those films. The more whites you killed, the more money you make. So I knew that was going on. So really, I knew I could sell the film as a blaxploitation cartoon, which seemed unique, using the characters from Uncle Remus, which I personally love. As a young man I loved to read the Uncle Remus tales, and I found them hysterical in as much as they were black slaves dictating stories about how to get around white masters. Some of the stories were very oblique, and some of them were hysterical when you knew that the black guys were fighting their white masters.

There was this wise-ass rabbit . . . everything was a put-on. Even the dumb bear wasn't as dumb as you thought. So I loved those characters, and I knew they would be very commercial in Harlem. I'm telling you the truth. What I'm saying is that, as a salesman, I knew if I mentioned these three things, it would sound very commercial, very funny. And I knew I wasn't really going to make a very funny film. I knew already that I was going to discuss white racism, black racism against blacks, black racism against whites who controlled Harlem.

The amount of ground you can cover in an animated film is not that much. But I knew what I was going to discuss—what to me was very serious—could sound hysterical in the selling of it. I knew what issues I wanted to discuss with *Coonskin*, which was basically racism at all levels and different problems with our society. But I sold it as Brer Rabbit, Fox, and Bear go to Harlem, which sounded like a good blaxploitation film. So the truth of the matter is that I used the blaxploitation films. I wasn't making fun of the blaxploitation films so much as I was using it to sell my political film. The buyers would think that it was hysterically funny, and if I had made it funny, I probably would have made a fortune. [Laughs.] That original film was hysterical when you pitched it! But the making of it is when I made my movies. *Heavy Traffic* was very, very funny when I pitched it, too.

They eventually caught up to me, but what I did, and I'm admitting it, is I used the animation medium's never having done anything like this—the fact that it's always been funny and automatically these people looked at this as funny—and I used all of that to pitch funny pictures. That enabled me to go and make the kinds of pictures I wanted to make. I wasn't looking to turn anyone off. I was looking to basically see how I felt about certain things. So I used black exploitation to sell what they thought was going to be a black exploitation film.

AR: *What was Paramount's reaction when they saw the movie for the first time and saw what they actually had?*

RB: I've been both the world's luckiest guy and the world's unluckiest guy. The guy who bought the picture was Frank Yablans. He saw the picture and absolutely loved it. Yablans was a New Yorker and knew that the black people would love this film. He spoke quite honestly to me about a number of things, and he was very much behind this film. Then he gets fired the week I deliver the film to Paramount. Then comes his replacement, Barry Diller. Now Frank Yablans bought the movie and he greenlit it. So when Barry Diller came in, he didn't want any part of it because it was a controversial film from the get-go. So Barry washed his hands of it immediately and did not release it. And I can kind of understand that; I mean, he comes in to run a company, and he doesn't need this. Diller called the film's producer, Al Ruddy, and said, "Bakshi? What the hell is a Bakshi? What's going on here?" [Laughs.] So they started to part company. It was a bad break because Yablans could have turned it into a smash hit.

As it was, when it got released, they were all packed in the theaters. Most of the rappers today send me letters. You have to understand that all this rapping and this generation of hip-hop grew up on *Coonskin*. They're absolutely crazy about it. Some of the biggest rappers in the world want me to animate their stuff because of *Coonskin*. The problem with that is I don't typically agree with everything they're doing. [Laughs again.] I'm a pain in the ass.

So that's the story of *Coonskin*. It got a very bad release by a distribution company called Bryanston. It was very small. The film still gets played, it still runs all these years later when people look at it. I still get letters on it. I get college kids writing their dissertations—black kids in black schools and white kids writing about what the film really meant. The fallout of *Coonskin* is over with. It's been screened around the country. At a major retrospective in LA last year, it ran for three nights in a row and received a standing ovation. It's gotten a little bit of a push now. Everyone thought it was racist, but it's not. It keeps going. It was very well animated; it was one of my better animated films on a technical level.

So that was *Coonskin* to me.

AR: *Your producer, Albert Ruddy, also produced* The Godfather *(1972). Since you parody* The Godfather *in* Coonskin, *I was wondering what Ruddy's reaction was to this.*

RB: Al thought it was funny. Those were the moments the film got laughs. You have to understand that those were the moments I pitched in the room that made it sound like the film was going to be hysterical. Al loved the movie. He stood behind the movie the whole time. But what it sounded like in the meeting and what it was were two completely different things. They thought it was hysterical. Look at how ugly my Godfather was, living in the subway with this pus-filled head, right? That was all part of my initial pitch. My pitch to Al was this: "I got this Godfather like Brando trying to get these black rabbits." I carefully sold the attitude as funny because I knew they would never buy the other one. I knew exactly what I was doing, and that was why they got so mad at me when they finally caught up to me. I knew I had to con them because I had an opportunity that I would never have again. That's not heroic, but I really wanted to make these films, and I knew this was my opportunity because of *Fritz*. If I told them straight what I wanted to make, they would shoot me. [Chuckles.] I knew what I was doing as a young man much better than I do now.

AR: *How did the actors react to the material?*

RB: Loved it.

AR: *No apprehension whatsoever?*

RB: Not at all. The actors I hired . . . Look, it's the same thing as Obama running for president. They keep saying, "First black president." I keep saying, "That's an American running for president of the United States." What is this racist bullshit? Why is it every time some announcer or TV anchor talks about him they have to say "the black Obama"? This is an American running for president of the United States! There is no black issue here. So the people I hired for *Coonskin*, like Charles Gordone or Barry White, were basically the rappers of their day. They knew what the hell I was saying. I was right. You couldn't argue with what I was saying. It's maybe hard to take that black revolutionaries were taking the money and running, but I knew that and the black guys knew that. Everyone knew the Mafia ran Harlem. Everyone knew the cops were racist. What was I saying that was so wrong? Everyone knew the boxers worked for the Mafia. Everyone knew that drugs and prostitution were the big problem in Harlem. There wasn't anything that I was talking about that your average black man didn't know about. Now your average black middle class, or your average Jewish middle class, or your average white middle class had no idea what the hell I was talking about. But your question was about the black actors. Charles Gordone, who played Preacher Fox and did all the fox voices, won a Pulitzer for a play! The man was a major writer. This wasn't some guy off the street—this was a major American writer! And he won a Pulitzer Prize for *No Place to Be Somebody*, which was a great play. And he was so proud to do my movie! I couldn't believe it. Barry White said, "Right on, man. Right on."

I didn't have any problem with any of the black actors or getting any of the work done I had to get done. When the Miss America character was fucking over black guys, you should have heard the roaring in the recording room. She was saying, "I should have fucked them when I had the chance."

The whole controversy around the movie was a setup. They wanted to get controversy around a film that Paramount wanted to dump. That wasn't real. I got a letter from the NAACP saying that for a white man, I certainly knew a lot about black people. They said that *Coonskin* may be tough to take, but it was certainly very honest about the black/white relationship.

AR: *Could you tell me a little bit about the screening at the Museum of Modern Art? I understand that was quite interesting.*

RB: Right. That was the beginning. That was the setup. I'm screening the picture, and Al Sharpton and about 50 black guys are standing in the back of the screening. The screening starts and they start saying, "No white guys leave this audience at the end." They started to bang sticks. And this a true story; the museum has a tape of this. So people are freaking out, they're dying, everyone in the audience is really scared. Help me God to my kids this is a true story. The lights go on, and Sharpton comes walking down the aisle toward the stage. Of course I'm up there defending my film, right? He's walking and he turns around, and none of the guys are following him. None of the black guys are following him. Sharpton is furious and he says, "Why aren't you guys following?" And you could see they liked the movie! [Laughs.] I mean, you could *see* they got it. So Sharpton starts screaming at them, and then I start screaming at Sharpton. I said, "You fucking nigger middle-class sell-out! You fucking punk!" And I'm screaming at Sharpton, and one of the guys from the back of the room says to Sharpton, "Look, Al, either get up there and kill him or let him go! But we ain't coming." So at that point Sharpton stuttered and I ran out the back door. And it was over with. And everyone got up and left. They had sticks, they had bats, some of them had guns, but the black guys at the back of the theater *loved* that fucking movie. I'd bet on it. I'd bet my life on it. They were all supposed to walk down the three aisles, but they just stayed in the back. Sharpton could not get them to walk down the aisle to say that no one leaves. So I took that to start screaming at Sharpton because I was terrified. And I always learned the best defense is a good offense. You start scream-

BARRY WHITE and his men
are bustin'
out to win!
they'll stop the
man from
calling them
COONSKIN
"REMARKABLE, FUNNY AND ENTERTAINING!"
—Gene Shalit, NBC-TV
Albert S. Ruddy presents · A Film By Ralph Bakshi "COONSKIN" Starring Barry White · Charles Gordone
Scat Man Crothers · Philip Thomas · Produced by Albert S. Ruddy · Written and Directed by Ralph Bakshi
Technicolor® · A Bryanston Release
R RESTRICTED

ing at black guys . . . [Chuckles again.] It's all on tape because the museum was taping my conversation with the audience.

And this was the scariest moment. My mother was there, my mother-in-law was there! My sister was in the audience . . .

AR: *I read that Martin Scorsese caught another incident on film. Is that right?*

RB: That was funny. Thanks for reminding me. You keep bringing back great memories. The film was finished and the controversy had begun. Martin Scorsese was filming *Taxi Driver* (1976) in New York. He was driving around the city shooting second-unit stuff of crowds and just general insanity in the city that he could intercut into his film. And he shot a roll of the riot in front of the theater in *Coonskin*. He said, "Ralph, what kind of picture did you make?!" [Laughs.] He sent me footage of people fighting and pushing and screaming. And I'm just sitting there in California saying, "Oh my fucking God."

I had a good time, as you can see! [Laughs again.]

AR: *I found a quote where you once said,* "Coonskin *shows what white people think of blacks." Would you care to elaborate on that?*

RB: Look, there's a lot of soul-searching of my own in *Coonskin*. Being white, growing up and hanging around, I heard the racist remarks. I heard the attitudes. You grow up with guys in Brooklyn, you hear these things. You go to a bar, you hear the conversation. Growing up, I myself had certain fears that I exorcised in *Coonskin*. So the moment someone said the film was racist, all the white people stayed away. They just couldn't tell the difference. They couldn't go to this film and judge that it wasn't. The racists overall were white. So, as a white man, I exposed what I knew about the way white people felt about black people. That was another reason I wanted to make the movie. White people don't know where black people come from. That's why I say Obama is an American. He's not a black man. We basically perpetuate our racism by pointing out everyone's blackness and differences. How dare we point that out at this stage of our lives. Why is there a discussion about the first black this and the first black that? This has all been set up by racists simply to point out the fact that he's black. White people don't know how to act around black people. The minute that the racists get into the network loop of calling Obama black and making a point of this, it's picked up and it's carried. So everyone now knows that he's black. You know, don't vote for him. America and the media have no business discussing that issue. If I owned any of those media outlets, I would say he's to be discussed as an American running for office. And anyone who discusses his color is being fired. The racist spin doctors set it up, and then that's all you're getting. And then he's through. And that's what *Coonskin* was about. Like the guy in Texas who wanted to outlaw the word nigger, and basically all the black guys in town said they're going to get arrested. [Laughs.] All the black guys will end up getting arrested in this town for saying the word. It's all fucking madness.

This is all the roots of *Coonskin*. I could go on and on because here we are today and it's the same shit.

AR: *You mention that a lot of these things are still happening today.*

RB: It's all still happening.

AR: *Okay, with that in mind,* Coonskin *was largely misunderstood at the time of its release. But today it has a huge following and is recognized as a cult classic. To what would you attribute the change in perception toward the film?*

RB: Time will heal. When you're in the middle of something, you can't see the forest for the tree. It's been so long since *Coonskin* was released that now you can look at it and say, "Yeah, that's right. That's what happened." Poverty is still here. The ghetto is still the ghetto. Drugs are still everywhere. Racism is still rampant; just look at Hurricane Katrina. So what I'm saying is that, in retrospect, "Okay, this is true." As the film slowly shows and the word of mouth spreads, people see it and say, "Yeah, that's right." The film speaks for itself, which is what films are supposed to do. I wasn't lying. I may have told some truths that were unpleasant, but I never lied.

CHAPTER 2

Jim Brown

Former football star Jim Brown looking lean and mean in *Three the Hard Way*.

Arguably the greatest professional football player in history—perhaps even the greatest athlete, period—Hall of Famer Jim Brown dominated the National Football League in a way that few players have come close to before or since. Although Brown played pro football for only nine years, the mark he left on the game is indisputable. The intimidating fullback was the NFL record holder for both single season rushing (1,863) and career rushing (12,312) at the time of his 1966 retirement. He was also the all-time leader in rushing touchdowns (106), career touchdowns (126), and all-purpose yards (15,549). Brown was the first player in history to score 100 rushing touchdowns, doing so in only 93 games. He was voted to the Pro Bowl in each of his nine seasons, and never missed a single game due to injury. Several of his records, including yards per carry by a running back (5.2), still stand today.

Brown has also enjoyed a successful second career as an actor, first appearing on screen in the 1964 oater *Rio Conchos*. Three years later, Brown received critical acclaim for his turn in Robert Aldrich's war thriller *The Dirty Dozen* (1967). Brown continued acting, turning up in such films as *Ice Station Zebra* (1968), *Riot* (1969), and *100 Rifles* (1969). By the time the blaxploitation cycle kicked off in 1970, Brown was poised to become one of its biggest stars. His blaxploitation filmography includes *Slaughter* (1972), *Black Gunn* (1972), *Slaughter's Big Rip-Off* (1973), *The Slams* (1973), *Three the Hard Way* (1974), and *Take a Hard Ride* (1975).

Brown has since dabbled in directing and producing, and his subsequent film appearances include *Mars Attacks!* (1996), *He Got Game* (1998), *She Hate Me* (2004), the blaxploitation parody *I'm Gonna Git You Sucka* (1988), and Larry Cohen's *Original Gangstas* (1996).

DAVID WALKER: *I'd like to start off talking about you. It seems to me that you played a rather significant role in the evolution of the black action hero film. Let's talk a little bit about the historical relevance of your participation in Hollywood.*

JIM BROWN: I came along at a time when Hollywood wanted a black action hero. I was a football hero, and it was easy for them to make money off of me, and to give me the opportunity to use my dignity to bring in audiences. Not just black audiences, but white audiences also. I looked at it as an opportunity for me to break down taboos. To play roles that had never before been played by black actors. It really did not become a historical thing because people always felt that I was a football star. Basically I played every kind of role there was to play. Scripts that were written for human beings, I was able to get those scripts financed. Probably most important was that I did break the doors down, but I did it by getting financing for the films, because they financed the films on the fact that I was going to be a star.

DW: *Some people feel that you and Sidney Poitier, back in the 1960s, helped to change the way Americans viewed blacks. Do you think that your films, and the films of the 1970s, served to further the cause of civil rights?*

JB: Not really. Racism in America is throughout. There are racists and there are non-racists. Economics is pretty much universal. People really want to make money off of film. And the inclusion of black people in our society was not there. We were excluded from most things of value. Therefore Hollywood was really no different. But what they did was they took advantage of certain audiences that they discovered. They discovered that there was a lot of money in the black community, and they had what you might call special markets. I'll use special market instead of black exploitation. The trends of film usually went along with the producers in Hollywood who wanted to make money. And in a lot of cases, they could make money by using black actors. But then on the other hand, black producers who raised the money could make the film they wanted to make. So I would say there was racism, throughout this country and in the film industry, but on the other hand, things did not happen because of racism or a lack of racism. They happened because individual producers decided that there was a trend out there that they could make money. And they did not mind using certain individuals to help them make that money.

DW: *You referred to the "special market." That's the market that came to be known as blaxploitation. What does that word mean to you?*

JB: The word is basically irrelevant. It's a tag. It's like you have the Dream Team now. But it's irrelevant because there is no real dream team. It was something that would promote trickery, because whenever you sign a contract to play a role and make money, you're exploiting yourself. Nobody else is exploiting you. In a free enterprise system, you work and you get paid. You accept a particular role or you don't accept it. But there were no blacks who accepted these roles who were . . . blinded, or tied up, or forced. So the collaboration was of a producer that would pay you, and the fact that you would do a job; and the term blaxploitation came out. But you could say that James Cagney was white exploitation, or John Wayne, because they did action films, they made money, and they were major stars.

So it's a term that really has no real meaning except in those who are looking for some type of way of explaining history. But in America, it was very simple at that time. They found a black audience. The audience wanted to see some action, and the producers could film these films without putting up a lot of money. They kept changing black stars so they wouldn't have to pay anybody too much. And they made money. A lot of black people made money, because a lot of black people were included in it. So it has no great significance to me.

DW: *There was a lot of negative backlash that surrounded the black films of the 1970s. Groups like CORE, NAACP, and PUSH were all quick to condemn the films that were being made. What's your take on the whole situation?*

JB: Well, here's my evaluation of it. Most black organizations, and a lot of so-called black leaders and media people, deal with making their living through complaining about other people's economics. I'm a believer that if I have $100 million, I'm gonna hire who I want to, and I'm gonna make the film that I want to. And I can be called what I want. That's what freedom is all about. I never felt that anyone had to make the films that I liked. I only go to see the ones that I like.

The NAACP is obviously an organization that has thrived off of fighting against racism, and so have most of the black organizations and most of the black leaders. When you start talking about business, what the black community should have done is raise the money, make the films, distribute the films, put them in the exhibit halls, and make sure that the black audience went to see them. And that would have eliminated all of that.

I don't want to be a person that's always looking to complain. I've been very successful in America, on many levels. And the only reason I was successful is because I got up off my butt; I worked hard; I recognized where the doors were closed. I broke some of them down. Some of them I didn't break down, but I didn't wallow in complaining about where other people put their money. You're talking about a free enterprise system. You're talking about private capital. You're talking about venture capital. You're talking about a risk. So let's uplift this to an intelligent level and say that we, in America, as black folks, have the resources to produce, distribute, and go see what we want to see. Why don't we do that?

DW: *In some ways what you're saying sounds like what Fred Williamson and I discussed. We talked about forming a separate Hollywood, about becoming self-sufficient rather than self-reliant.*

JB: I totally agree with that. I'll give you three examples. In 1944, 1945, the Japanese were a defeated people. Now they're one of the strongest economic countries in the world, with tremendous power. The Jewish were probably the most persecuted people on earth, but now they're a tremendous power. Koreans are a new economic power in America. In the black community, they've created businesses that black folks couldn't create. And they all have the same formula: work with each other, become educated, control your resources, and then deal with others on an even playing field. In other words, if you have enough capital and you are successful, in America you can do whatever. Success is a journey, not a destination. We as a black community have to recognize ourselves in a positive way. We're our own worst enemies.

DW: *I think too many African American filmmakers are dependent on Hollywood for their funding.*

JB: Obviously no one is going to put themselves out of business by using their own money. [Laughs.] That isn't very smart. If I was in the good old boy system, why am I going to finance some other group of people that wasn't in my immediate family and make them more powerful than me? But even if I observed them, and I saw that they didn't use their resources properly or didn't have the kind of community that I wanted to emulate, then I would probably be driven, even if I was the most liberal person on earth, to not involve too many of them in what I was doing.

Now if I'm an overt racist, I'm going to hate everything that's black because it's black. See, it's not one monolithic block of white folks out there that's just plotting and afraid of black people. Black folks are afraid of black folks. And if we cannot utilize the economic power of our entertainers and athletes, in some kind of connected way, then why would Hollywood deliver us? We have it within our own community, among the Magic Johnsons and the Oprah Winfreys and the Dennis Rodmans, to do anything we want to do. But what we have is someone like Dennis Rodman, who is a very popular hero, and never talks about anything of substance that's based upon cultural development.

DW: *By your observation, how have things changed since you started in the film business?*

JB: You have Samuel L. Jackson. You have Denzel Washington and Wesley Snipes that are truly actors and stars. They're participating at the highest level, and that's an exalted area for any kind of culture. And that's a tremendous change. Denzel plays leading parts, and he has a following, and his films make money. You can't turn out an assembly line of black actors or anything like that.

Consider this: racism is in America. Now, once I say that, what can you do about it? Not sit around and discuss all these trends and all these things that other people are doing with their money, but produce something, once again, for ourselves. I think there's been tremendous advancement from the standpoint of five or six stars. I'm not saying that's enough, but hell, I think I've had every chance on the screen that I should have. I haven't been held back from the screen because I'm black. I've had a lot of chances. And if those audiences were breaking records to see me, I'm sure I'd be out there now. I think this is the only country this can ever happen in. I think Fred Williamson has been tremendously fortunate, because he worked hard, he used his mind, and he made a lot of films, and he's made money. I don't know how much more we should do. But I know there's a lot more we can do for ourselves.

DW: *As we wrap this up, I'd like to get your feelings on the contributions that you and your peers—Fred, Ron [O'Neal], Pam [Grier], Jim Kelly—I'd like to get your take on how your contributions have affected the careers of people like Wesley and Denzel and Will Smith.*

JB: Cold hominy grits. There's nothing worse than cold hominy grits. Let me give you this, as my final answer.

I helped Richard Pryor create Indigo Productions, a major production company, one of the biggest production companies in the business, according to the studios. We had the biggest offices. We had our parking lot. We could hire who we wanted to hire. We hired a lot of black folks. And we could develop the films we wanted to develop. Okay? He was black and I was black. I answered to nobody but him. And all he had to do was make a decision on what he wanted to. That's how bad they wanted him as an actor. So he turned that into a production company. And then he gave it away. That's the most significant story I know about Hollywood. And then he gave it away.

CHAPTER 3

Michael Campus

After a stint in the U.S. Army (he was stationed in Germany, where he was responsible for scheduling the nation's railway activity), Michael Campus went to work as an executive at CBS. In 1969, at the age of 34, Campus quit his job to pursue his lifelong goal of becoming a motion picture director. Campus then convinced a Las Vegas casino boss to finance his directorial debut. The casino manager forked over $100,000, which would ultimately result in Campus's first film, *Survival* (1970). The heavily improvised film was shot entirely in one location—a friend's home in Palm Springs—and was constructed around a screenplay penned by *Shaft* (1970) scribe John D. F. Black. This led to Campus's second feature, *ZPG*, or *Zero Population Growth* (1971). The film, which features the late great Oliver Reed, is a sociological study of a futuristic society in which human reproduction is outlawed.

In 1973, Campus crafted the film for which he is best known—the blaxploitation classic *The Mack*. Although Campus has stated many times—and states within this very interview—that he does not consider *The Mack* to be blaxploitation, the film is one of a handful of titles that are *always*, without fail, listed or mentioned as one of the most representational entries of the cycle. And, intentional or not, *The Mack's* influence on subsequent films in the blaxploitation canon cannot be ignored. The film, starring Max Julien, Richard Pryor, and Carol Speed, depicts the rise and fall of an Oakland hustler. The following year, Campus made his second black film, this time on the East Coast. This acclaimed film, *The Ed-*

ucation of Sonny Carson (1974), is a gritty biopic of gangster turned political activist Sonny Carson.

At the time of this interview, Campus was putting the finishing touches on the film *Thomas Kinkade's The Christmas Cottage* (2007), starring legendary actor Peter O'Toole. Next Campus hopes to write and produce a feature film about the making of *The Mack*.

ANDREW RAUSCH: *The term blaxploitation means a lot of different things to different people. As a filmmaker, does it offend you to have your work labeled as blaxploitation?*

MICHAEL CAMPUS: From the beginning, I have always stated that I believe that the label minimizes the accomplishments of the film. In my mind, you have to separate *The Mack* on one side and a lot of other films on the other side. Because *The Mack* was the only film of that era that was totally based on the truth. I lived in Oakland for two months under the wing of a man named Frank Ward, who kind of ran the Oakland underworld. It was because of Frank Ward that Richard Pryor, Max Julien, and I rewrote the original script. The original script was by a man named Bobby Poole, who wrote it in prison on toilet paper. His script was the basis of the film—kind of an early blueprint. It was by going to Oakland and living that life with Frank Ward that I got to really understand what was happening. The real story. So I have always resisted the label blaxploitation. It's not blaxploitation to me. It isn't. It wasn't. Unfortunately it got lumped into that category.

AR: *Blaxploitation has sort of become an all-encompassing term for anything that was black in the cinema in the 1970s.*

MC: You're right, and it's sad. There was some very good work. Now, it's true, there was also some very mediocre work, and there were a lot of people who jumped on the financial bandwagon and said, "Let's make a lot of money." Some of those films are pretty terrible. But there are also some very good films. Under this blanket, under this umbrella of blaxploitation, there was some very good work done.

And there was another key factor. That era provided opportunities for a lot of African Americans to act, to direct, to write, to work behind the camera. It was a great learning experience for a lot of people, and a lot of opportunities came out of this.

But again, I do feel that the terminology is completely wrong. I don't think it reflects what was really going on.

AR: The Mack *has also been labeled misogynistic by a lot of people. Do you feel that that's true, and is it possible to make a film like* The Mack *without being somewhat misogynistic?*

MC: Well, I think so. My private joke about *The Mack* has always been that this is a film about sex that has no sex in it. It's a film in which there literally are no sex scenes. This is a character study, and it's a character study not only of the man but of a very violent and turbulent world. And as such, I don't think it can be accurately labeled as being misogynistic or anything else. It just doesn't fit any category because it really is Frank Ward's story. It's a story of a man who lived and died—he got murdered at the end of the film—and it really is a reflection of all the things that were happening in Oakland at the time: the war between the Black Panthers and the black underworld; 50 percent unemployment for black people. This was a terrible time. It was a time of desperation, and fear, and unemployment, and despair. And the course that Frank

Actors Max Julien and Richard Pryor on the set of *The Mack.*

Ward and the Ward brothers took was one course. In their minds, it was the only way out. Obviously it wasn't. And Bobby Seale and Huey Newton and the Black Panthers were suggesting that there was a whole other way to rise above this. In fact, because of my interaction with them, Goldie's brother in *The Mack* speaks for the Black Panthers. His character reflects their way of thinking. Their belief in the war to drive the pimps and the pushers off the streets was a very strong theme of the picture—this war between the two sides over how best to save the black community.

AR: *I've heard that the Black Panthers were somehow involved with filming* The Mack. *What was the story behind this?*

MC: Well, you should probably know there is a film being prepared called *Making The Mack*, which is the story of a young white director [laughs] coming to Oakland to make this film. The whole concept is being discussed by the studios right now, with a young actor playing me, and a Eddie Murphy or a Jamie Foxx playing Richard Pryor.

But to answer your question, part of the war between the Wards and Bobby Seale and Huey Newton was because the Panthers came to us and said, "You can't operate in our territory." Every time I started the cameras, the chairs and glass bottles would come flying from the roof tops. We had to stop filming several times. And what became apparent was that we were not going to be in business unless we made a deal with the Panthers. So eventually my producer, Harvey Bernhard, who was the producer of the *Omen* series, made a deal with Huey, and Max and I made a deal with Bobby Seale, and they controlled the extras. The money literally went to the Black Panthers, and they portioned out the money to the extras. As you might know, at the end of the picture when all hell had broken loose in this war, Bobby Seale made it pretty clear to me that we were going to have the opening in Oakland with benefit to their cause. And Max and I agreed. We felt that was the only thing to do to keep the peace. So the opening of *The Mack* in Oakland—this so-called exploitation picture—was done for the benefit of the milk fund.

So again, it's not arrogance or ego that makes me separate *The Mack* from the other pictures. It's simply that we were different. We were the only picture that was based on a true story.

AR: The Mack *is one of the few films of the era that stays popular and continues to find a new fan base. To what would you attribute this?*

MC: I really believe that there are two factors. One, when the film opened that first night in Oakland, when the film came on, something happened that I had never seen before and have rarely seen since. Literally in the opening scene when Max Julien and Richard Pryor are in the shootout with the police, the audience got on their feet. I'm not talking about later in the film. From the first moment the film came on, the audience was on their feet. They were screaming, yelling, and talking to the characters. This was repeated all across the country. And this was at a time when there weren't that many so-called "black" theaters. We were in 17 cities and 22 theaters. That's all. But the fact is that somehow the audience totally related to what they saw on the screen. This was part of the Oakland that they knew and understood, and somebody was finally making something about their lives. Or at least a portion of their lives. They could see that these were things that were happening on their streets, in their homes, in their alleys, in their clubs.

When we went back to Oakland and were developing *Making The Mack* four or five years ago, Max Julien and I were treated like royalty. By the time we reached the airport, the word was out that we were there. And everywhere we went, we were mobbed. We went to a club, we were mobbed. We went to the hotel, we were mobbed. So there is something there that the population relates to that I don't even think occurs with films like *Shaft* (1971). That doesn't happen with those other films. So that's got to be reason one.

Max, by the way, was a crucial factor in this film. He wasn't just the lead actor. He was my sidekick, my soul mate on this film. He was very much a part of the film in every aspect, all the way. And that was a very unusual collaboration at that time. It was a director/actor/close friends relationship.

The second factor is the music. Everyone from Snoop to Dre to 50 Cent to Usher—you name it—kind of made this film an anthem of sorts. It always had this following. So I think the combination of the initial reaction and the spread of the lore about *The Mack* through music and people like Quentin Tarantino, who championed the film, had a great deal to do with it. Through the years, at times when the film was not intensely popular, it stayed alive through music. We sold 500,000 videocassettes before the arrival of DVDs and without any publicity. That's amazing.

AR: *A wide variety of hip-hop artists have sampled dialogue from both* The Mack *and* The Education of Sonny Carson. *What are your thoughts on the hip-hop community's embracing of these films?*

MC: It's a reflection of their honesty. Again, let's examine the canvas of *The Education of Sonny Carson*. I went to Bed-Stuy with Sonny Carson, who was one of the youngest people ever to be incarcerated in Sing Sing. He was in Sing Sing at age 16. And Sonny was already a legend in Bed-Stuy and lots of places in Brooklyn. And I went into the community and I interviewed 1,700 people, and actually used gang members, real people who had never acted before. I set up a table on the street in front of Sonny's headquarters in Bed-Stuy, and anybody who wanted to see me, I saw. So I think again, the thing that links *The Mack* and *Sonny Carson* is that they're both based on the total truth. I think people really understand the truth in there. Something comes through in those films. I hope it's my passion, but whatever you want to call it, the driving force behind those films is the truth. And people recognize that.

There was a moment when I was filming Rony Clanton as Sonny Carson being beaten up in the basement of a police station. And this had really happened—as had everything else in the film. I mean this was really a *true* story. And the cop involved beats Sonny half to death. It was a terrible beating that lasted about 30 minutes. On film it lasts about one minute. When I first screened the film out here in California, somebody in the audience jumped up and said, "How could you do that? How could you subject us to that?" It felt like it lasted forever. It didn't last forever—it lasted a minute. And Sonny said later to the audience, "If you had lived through what I lived through—if you had been subjected to that full 30 minutes that I went through—the theater would have been empty."

The film is the truth. That's why it's stayed popular through the years. That's why its following continues.

AR: *Very few films have been as honest and realistic in their depictions of street life as* The Mack *and* The Education of Sonny Carson *are. Why do you think there aren't more films like these?*

MC: I think there's a resistance right now to making films of substance. There is a small minority of people out there—there are the Brad Pitts and the George Clooneys—who really believe that film has to be a vehicle for change. I think overall there is a real lack of that right now. Maybe it's because the world we live in is filled with such terror and such fear that we're working in this whole escapist cycle. It's so difficult to wake up and turn on the news or pick up the newspaper because everything is so frightening. So people tend to turn in other directions to escape. I find that disap-

"The education of sonny carson"

pointing, because I think there are the George Clooneys and the Brad Pitts and the Angelina Jolies who really want their films and their fame to be a means of achieving change . . . to achieving a better world.

I am an outright, unabashed dreamer for peace, understanding, and love. That's what my new film, *The Christmas Cottage*, is about; it's about love and family. I think what I'm afraid of is that people do not wish to tackle the really tough subjects because they're afraid of turning audiences off. So instead, the films that are popular right now are *The Transformers* (2007), the *Die Hards*, *The Bourne Ultimatum* (2007). And I'm not saying these are bad films. These are well-made films. But don't we have a responsibility as artists to humanity, to the human race, to each other, to this country . . . to try to make the world a little better place? Again, I realize film companies have to make money, and that's the driving force, and everybody who writes, directs, or produces understands that, but shouldn't there be more films that really wear their hearts on their sleeves and talk to us about how to make this place better? I wish there were more. If you look at the top 20 films of the past year, can anyone name more than a couple of great lasting value? I don't think you can.

AR: *I find it interesting that two of the most unflinching and realistic depictions of urban life were directed by yourself, a white filmmaker. Would you care to comment on this?*

MC: There were some people when I was making *The Mack*, and even more so with *Sonny Carson*, who said, "What qualifies you to tell this story? Why isn't there an African American director doing this?"

I think you have to look at my childhood. I was born on the Upper West Side. I was the product of parents who were very left wing, parents who utterly believed in equality long before it was fashionable to do so. And the search for equality, for the expression of humanity became my mantra . . . the driving force of my life. My mother died, unfortunately, and never got a chance to see my films. But my father did, and he understood that that legacy—what my parents stood for in their beliefs—was a guiding factor in what I've done.

I think it came out of my outlook and my beliefs. I assume certain people would think my views are kind of a Pollyanna-like, overly idealistic statement about life. It's just that I understood very early in my life that black America was not getting a fair shake. The oppression of black America was overwhelming. And it's only been in the last 20 or 30 years that we've seen any real progress. And there's still so much that needs to be done.

There is no doubt in my mind that my two so-called black films are a reflection of my upbringing and the values that my parents instilled in me at a very young age.

CHAPTER 4

Steve Carver

Steve Carver studied fine arts and still photography at Cornell, Washington, Buffalo, and the University of Missouri before being invited to the American Film Institute. There he studied under such teachers as George Stevens Jr. and Czech filmmaker Frantisek Daniel, crafting his thesis film *A Tell-Tale Heart* (1971). He then met and went to work for legendary producer Roger Corman, crafting some of the most memorable exploitation pictures ever produced. Carver would ultimately direct 33 feature films, including *Big Bad Mama* (1974), *Capone* (1975), and *Lone Wolf McQuade* (1983), which he also produced. A listing of actors Carver has directed in his career is a virtual Who's Who in Hollywood: Angie Dickinson, Sylvester Stallone, Richard Roundtree, John Cassavetes, Warren Oates, Ben Gazzara, Art Carney, Chuck Norris, Christopher Lee, William Shatner, Donald Pleasence, Pam Grier, and many others.

Carver's first foray into blaxploitation was the 1974 action film *The Arena*, which reteamed Pam Grier and Margaret Markov of *Black Mama, White Mama* (1972). Carver then helmed a second blaxploitation feature— the controversial *Mandingo* (1975) follow-up *Drum* (1976). The film starred boxing legend Ken Norton, Pam Grier, Warren Oates, Isela Vega, and Yaphet Kotto.

CHRIS WATSON: *At the time you were making* Drum, *were you aware that you were making a type of revolutionary film?*

STEVE CARVER: No. You don't feel those things at the time. I took over from another director, and I was working for Dino De Laurentiis, who produced the picture. I had fun with the picture, but it was kind of weird with the "N" word—they said nigger every other word in the script. Norman Wexler was the screenwriter, and it was written very similar to the novel series on which it was based. It was never really looked at as a sensational thing . . . I got to work with Lucian Ballard, the Academy Award–winning cinematographer. I worked with Warren Oates. We had a great cast. It was an $18 million picture, which was the largest budget I'd worked with. So I didn't look at it as any kind of flagship in filmmaking. For me, it was just another great project.

CW: *Did you go to any of the screenings of* Drum*?*

SC: Yes. Actually I went with Kenny Norton to the Chinese when the film premiered there. Kenny was sitting next to me. We were sitting near the back so we could watch the audience. There was a group of kids about five rows up from us saying, "Kenny Norton . . . I could beat the shit out of him!" And so on. At the end of the film when the lights came on, they turned around and saw Kenny. And he just looked at them. They said, "Kenny Norton! We didn't really mean that!" [Laughs.] They turned white! I remember Kenny just bursting out in laughter when we got outside.

The film evoked a lot of feedback from the audience to the screen. I've seen that happen during a lot of my films, but this particular film . . . people were reacting to every single line of the film. A lot of that was very brutal. There was some publicity, and I remember reading that people were cutting the seats open with knives when *Drum* played in some theater chain. Apparently *Drum* held the record for most seats slashed after a screening. I don't know what that means, but I find it very interesting.

CW: *I've heard that Burt Kennedy was somehow involved with the production. What was his role on the film?*

SC: He was the original director. He shot footage that wound up being scrapped. I met with him because this was the first time I'd ever taken over for another director—especially someone of his stature. I liked his work, and I liked him. I actually went to him and said, "Listen, they assigned me to take over for you on this film. Is that okay?" He said, "Oh, yeah, that's fine." He said he'd never really liked the script. He'd liked Richard Fleisher's script for *Mandingo*, which was just a really fine script. He didn't think *Drum* was written very well, and he didn't care for the story. It was basically the same thing as the first film, but rehashed and told from a different point of view. (This was before it was rewritten.) So Kennedy said it was okay with him that I do it. So as far as his involvement with the production, it was zero after that.

CW: *You worked with Pam Grier on both* Drum *and* The Arena. *What was Grier like to work with?*

SC: She's great. On *The Arena*, I got her in a situation where she and Margaret Markov were gladiators pitted against each other. We shot it in Italy, and they had no problems working with the Italians and working on a production that was outside the safety net of working in Hollywood. They felt very comfortable and therefore made me feel very comfortable.

When Pam was assigned the role in *Drum*, I could have cut her—because of the rewriting. But I really enjoyed working with her, and she had a great attitude. I can't say enough about her. She had a great body . . . and probably still does. And she had no discomfort in regards to the nudity that was required.

She was great. I'd work with her again in a heartbeat.

Pam Grier as Mamawi in Steve Carver's film *The Arena*.

CW: Drum *starred Ken Norton, whose only significant role prior to this was in* Mandingo. *Did you have to work extensively with Norton, or did you find that he already had the natural chops?*

SC: It was in between. A little of each. The extensive work with him was to get him to emote, which is the usual thing. I've worked with a lot of sports personalities who became actors. And the problem is that, because of their stature, it's hard to get them to do things beyond their physicality and what they accept themselves as. Kenny was the World Champion and a big-time fighter, a formidable individual.

I'll tell you a story. This was the first time I worked with Kenny, the very first scene. He was supposed to be riding on a horse with Warren Oates. They're coming towards the camera. Kenny couldn't ride a horse, and I found out later on when I worked with him on other pictures that he also couldn't swim, he couldn't do this, he couldn't do that . . . all these things you would think an athlete would have the natural ability to do! But he didn't. So he was having problems with the horse. It was a very gentle horse. It used to be John Wayne's horse, or something or other. And this was a joke from the beginning, just with him trying to get on the horse. So here's this scene where he rides the horse towards the camera, a simple scene. He got off the horse after the take, and I guess he'd gotten really pissed off at me because of things I was yelling to him. And on the side of the road was a rock—a really big rock. He picked up that rock—and here I am standing with Lucien Ballard and the camera. He was a good 300 feet away, and he threw this sizable rock, and it rolled up to my feet. He threw it with the intention of saying, "I'm Ken Norton and you're the director." So from then on, I had a respect for him. And we eventually became very close friends.

In directing him, getting him to emote was the thing. Doing things that he wasn't as talented with or trained to do was tough. But there were other times where his clowning around, his ability to be a personality in front of the camera, and to be around other actors and to have a good time, was apparent and very useful in doing that picture. Because I had other actors who were very difficult. And because of Ken, we made it work. Not to the extent that we won Academy Awards or anything, but he was really a lot of fun to be around.

And, you know, I've subsequently made a number of pictures with him. And I found out a lot of things, like he couldn't swim when he'd said, "Yeah, I can swim!" I took him to Mexico to make this film called *Oceans of Fire* (1986). And the first time I told him to jump off the boat, he looked at me very seriously and said, "I can't swim!" [Laughs.] Funny stuff! He used to eat a dozen doughnuts every morning before the shoot. And here he was the champ and in great shape! He was great.

CW: *You mentioned the usage of the "N" word in* Drum. *As a white filmmaker, did you feel at all nervous about this?*

SC: Yes. I questioned the validity of using this word from the beginning, before we ever began rolling cameras. It was accurate to the novel. It was an integral part of the script. It's used almost every other word. During rehearsal, the black actors had no problems with it. Another actor would have to approach them and say, "Hey nigger!" And there was absolutely no reaction.

What happened, which I didn't know at the time—I had shot for three or four weeks before I realized this—there was always a representative of the NAACP on the set. And they would talk to various actors and ask them if they were comfortable with this word. It was being thrown at Kenny, it was being thrown at all of the actors. And they all were comfortable with it. It didn't mean anything to them at the time. And I actually received an award from the NAACP based on the fact that I was a sympathetic director, having cut the word several times. And I did. There was no need for dialogue where they just kept saying "hey nigger, hey nigger." I kept saying, "Why do we need to do this? Cut that. Cut that. Cut that." And apparently the guy was standing there and he overheard me saying all of this, and said, "That's the right way to do it." In editing, we actually chopped a few more of them out. It was just too much; too over the top. And it became, you know, excessive.

CW: *You worked with the legendary cameraman Lucien Ballard on that film. Ballard had worked with such greats as Henry Hathaway, Budd Boetticher, and Sam Peckinpah. What was Ballard like to work with, and how helpful was it to have a cinematographer with so much experience?*

SC: How helpful was it? Great. I learned a lot from Lucien. These were very complicated sets. I had to learn shooting in a complex setup. For instance, there was a lot of fire in some of the scenes. And in setting up cameras, safety, and setting up the effects of the fire, Lucien was a master. I mean, I learned a lot from him.

I was fortunate to have had skilled people where I needed them. I wouldn't have been able to physically work with the special effects people.

They were some of the best in Hollywood, and we had some very lethal circumstances in having the fire out in a wooded area. And we were shooting at a time in which fires were fairly prevalent. Having all the special effects people who were the very best in Hollywood, having Lucien behind the camera to ensure that the scenes looked the way they should . . . if you hire a cameraman who doesn't know what he's doing when he hooks up all those wires and lights, he can put a lot of people in danger. But Lucien was very conscious of all those things. And he had a great eye. He could see things exactly the way the camera would see them. He would literally tell me how a scene could be shot with special effects to achieve the effect we wanted. He was invaluable.

He was also one of my closest friends. I used to visit him all the time. I loved the guy, and I can't say enough good things about him. He was just great. He was the type of guy who would never step over the director and would never force his vision upon a director—and a lot of cameramen do. He would always offer me his opinion. He was a great teacher.

CW: Drum *featured several cast members from* Mandingo, *and was also adapted from a Kyle Onstatt novel by screenwriter Norman Wexler. Did the studio see the film as a sort of unofficial sequel when the film went into production?*

SC: I don't know because I wasn't there when the film went into production. When I took over the production, there was a problem between Paramount—they were originally supposed to be the distributor of the picture—and producer Dino De Laurentiis. So United Artists picked it up. There were a lot of politics. I have no idea if it was seen as a sequel. When I came on, it was simply *Drum*—not a sequel, but *Drum.* The script wasn't really in line with what Dino wanted, so we rewrote it. And I really didn't use *Mandingo* as a guide, you know, how this thing would work as a continuation and/or sequel. Actually, I like *Mandingo* so much that I tried to recreate some of the things they did—like the fight scenes. So it had some similarities, so maybe that helped make it appear as a sequel.

When you take over a picture—especially a picture like that, where you're inheriting a lot of problems—you don't think of things like that.

CW: *You mentioned rewrites. What was the screenwriting process once you came onboard the project?*

SC: The script was thrown to me—literally. And when I caught it, it looked like the yellow pages. And I knew it wasn't going to be filmed in that form. The script would have to go through a lot of changes. The timing we had to rewrite the script and prep for the picture kept getting chewed down. They kept saying, "We've gotta move up the shooting date." It was down to days. And I remember sitting there with Norman Wexler, who was so inebriated that I couldn't understand anything he had to say. I met with Wexler twice, and this resulted in absolutely no creative ideas or story alterations. So a new writer was hired, but his ideas were based on Dino De Laurentiis's ideas, which were based on contractual obligations to certain actors. It was one of those things where the story was a mess—it didn't gel—because of all these different puzzle pieces they had to shift around to satisfy various contractual obligations to actors, the former director, and to the studio. We had so little time to prepare and rewrite that some of the new pages would come in as I was shooting the scenes!

Here was this $18 million picture, and we were making it on the cuff. I had never had a single problem on a Corman picture . . . I had seen pictures with Roger Corman where they were literally writing it on the set, and yet this $18 million picture had more problems. It was very unnerving and amateur. That wasn't the way to do it, especially with all that talent and the budget of the production. They'd build sets, and then we wouldn't use them. Here's an example. When I took over the picture and went to look at the sets they were building at MGM, we were using 12 of the studio's 22 or so soundstages—I think they were using the rest for *King Kong* (1976). On those dozen stages, they had all these interior sets. And do you know how many of those sets we used? Maybe four. It was shocking.

CW: *You directed Yaphet Kotto. I've heard that Kotto is an incredibly prepared actor. What was he like to work with?*

SC: Yaphet's preparation is very "method," in nature. He would come up to me and say, "What's my motivation?" And Kenny would ridicule him for saying that, or for saying things that were synonymous with that. And then the whole crew started doing that. Yaphet became a real problem actor to work with. It's because of his "preparedness." An actor can prepare by knowing their lines, and researching their character, and working in depth with their role. That's one type of preparedness. But his type of preparedness was harping on "Why am I doing this?" After having read the script and accepted the role, why would an actor suddenly question particular aspects of a scene pertaining to his character? He really got on everybody's nerves.

I think a lot of it had to do with ego. Yaphet didn't like Kenny being treated like the star. Muhammad Ali came down to the set to pay homage to Kenny. Kenny had tremendous perks. Kenny had a Winnebago the size of my house! [Laughs.] And Yaphet didn't like that. He was very jealous. If something on the set was not to his liking—for instance, if a chair was not presented to him immediately between scenes—there was dialogue, and it was usually directed toward me. There was a time I wanted to strangle Yaphet, and I'm sure he felt the same way. He's a big guy. He could have easily done it. [Laughs.]

A lot of this was unnecessary. It was counterproductive to making the movie. When we had to shoot Yaphet, we had to rig him with bullet squibs. And in rigging him, there were wires that went back to the battery to activate them. Between takes, because he was hooked up to those wires, he wasn't allowed to go back to his trailer, which was half a mile from the set. It was a very complicated setup, so we couldn't take the time to put him in a car and get him back there to redo everything. It was just easier to do it on the set. But he demanded that they bring his Winnebago to the set. So they brought up his Winnebago, and so then Kenny brought up his. I spent a lot of time negotiating with Yaphet to get him to cooperate.

And when his character was killed, we had a dummy that was put in the scene with the fire. In between takes, actors, crew members, and even extras would go up to the dummy and kick it! You could say that Yaphet was influential in that. [Laughs.]

CHAPTER 5

Matt Cimber

Matt Cimber (real name Matteo Ottaviano) started his career as a theater director in the early 1960s. He directed numerous off-Broadway plays in New
York City by such noted writers as Tennessee Williams, F. Scott Fitzgerald,
and John Steinbeck. He then directed his future wife Jayne Mansfield in a
Broadway revival of *Bus Stop* (they would be married from 1964 to 1966,
just months before her death). He then made his cinematic directorial debut
with *Single Room Unfurnished* (1968), Mansfield's final film appearance.
Cimber followed this up with a handful of sexploitation films with titles such
as *Man and Wife* (1969) and *The Sensuous Female* (1970).

Cimber then directed *The Black Six* (1974), the first of three blaxploitation films he would helm. In an ingenious move, Cimber cast the
film with six National Football League stars as its leads. Next up for Cimber was the blaxploitation classic *The Candy Tangerine Man* (1975), which
stars John Daniels as a family man with a dual life as a pimp. Cimber's
third and final blaxploitation outing would be *Lady Cocoa* (1975), starring
Lola Falana and footballer "Mean" Joe Greene. The film would later be
listed among *Variety*'s top 100 highest domestic box office grossing films
made for less than $1 million.

Cimber's later directorial works include such films as *Butterfly* (1982),
starring Stacy Keach, Orson Welles, and Pia Zadora, and *A Time to Die*
(1982), which he cowrote with Mario Puzo. In 1986, Cimber created, produced, and sometimes directed *GLOW* (*Gorgeous Ladies of Wrestling*) for
television. He then began working on documentaries, producing films on
such subjects as Ronald Reagan, Malcolm X, and Richard Nixon.

In 2006, after a 22-year hiatus from directing feature films, Cimber returned to the director's chair for the Holocaust drama *Miriam*.

ANDREW RAUSCH: *Were you a fan of the blaxploitation films prior to making your own?*

MATT CIMBER: Not really. I mean, I'm a fan of all films actually. But I wouldn't say that I was specifically a fan of the genre. I had seen a couple of them. I saw *Sweet Sweetback's Baadasssss Song* (1971), and I thought that was very good.

AR: *How did you become involved with the genre?*

MC: Only because I had this idea of these great icons. You know, in the late 1960s and 1970s, the football players of color really started coming into their own. We had all these great icon type of characters, such as "Mean" Joe Greene and Willie Lanier. They became larger-than-life characters. I didn't set out to make a blaxploitation film. I set out to make a film that was based on the British poem "The Charge of the Light Brigade." And it was how these people fought for a cause and died for it. I thought about modernizing it: six guys coming home from Vietnam. They've seen enough blood and action. The irony is that they still have a war at home to fight. So that was basically where *The Black Six* originated.

And it opened in New York City to lines around the block. And of course it had this huge reaction. It was too bad that the theater distributors never could envision it in white theaters. They only saw it at black theaters. They didn't realize what heroes these guys were to everybody.

AR: *In terms of exploitation, I always found the casting of six NFL players to be rather ingenious. I mean, here you had six guys that already had their own built-in fan bases.*

MC: Yeah, and you needed six guys who were very rugged. And I liked the idea of getting guys who weren't slick actors. These guys had this spirit, and they put that spirit into the film. And that's why the film was successful.

AR: *Was it any more difficult directing what were essentially six amateur actors?*

MC: They all went along pretty good. There were a couple of things. Gene Washington was always sort of a doll. You've got to remember, these guys were all college graduates. They were all bright. They understood and took direction well. Yeah, we had some bumps along the way, but for the most part it all worked very well. They had a feel for what it was, and that was

the most important part. Gene Washington was the one who carried most of the dialogue, and he did a very good job.

AR: *Gene Washington called* The Black Six *the "first film to portray the black man as a pure hero." What are your thoughts on this?*

MC: Well, he's right. These are guys who weren't dope dealers. They weren't from the ghetto. They were just six guys who had had enough of war and blood, and they just wanted to get on their motorcycles and go see Colorado. And their motivations were pure. It was the camaraderie among them, just as it was in "The Charge of the Light Brigade." It was the camaraderie. They knew they were going into an impossible situation at the time, but they knew they had to do it because they had to leave their mark. And their cause was much greater than, you know, being a sensational dope dealer. Recently we've seen big black stars playing famous dope dealers, trying to make them look like they're something special. No, a dope dealer is a dope dealer. And these guys were not that. These guys were products of the sixties. Their sister tells them, "You're part of the revolution," and that's it. So I think that's what Gene is meaning—their cause was something honorable and important.

AR: *Okay, switching gears a little bit, I'd like to talk to you about* The Candy Tangerine Man. *What attracted you to that project?*

MC: *The Candy Tangerine Man* was a personal challenge of mine. I love trying to do the impossible. You know, how do you make a hero out of a pimp? Of course *The Candy Tangerine Man* is a tongue-in-cheek film, which is something I also like to do. It's a tongue-in-cheek film, man. The idea was that in the 1960s and coming into the 1970s, we had all these people talking about the black revolution. "Why don't these guys go and get jobs?" Well, nobody ever gave them any education. So the idea of *The Candy Tangerine Man* was that basically he chose this road to go—becoming a pimp—not because this was the way he necessarily wanted to go, but because that was the way to make money. Prostitution was something that existed, and he treated his girls a certain way and he had a great brain. He was very smart. So the idea was that he was leading this double life—that if you gave him a chance and an education, he'd probably be an executive of a company. Look how he runs his business, how he's got everything organized. He has a talent. So that was my quest there.

I used to see all these pimps on the Sunset Strip with the big fancy cars and the clothes. And sometimes I would talk to some of them. Maybe they weren't so literate . . . they didn't have great command of the English language; they had their own slang. But you wanna know something? They were clever and smart and they had good minds. And the problem with them was—at least in my mind—was that we never really dug into those minds to put them to good use. So that was the premise, and of course it was all tongue-in-cheek: the guy taking off these clothes and getting into this Chevy and he's a good family man. But he has this floating whorehouse going through Hollywood. He had this deal going, that deal going . . . I guess you'd call him a magnate in the business world. So that was basically the whole temptation of *The Candy Tangerine Man*.

Of course the picture became an enormous success. I still have people come up to me today and say, "You're the guy who made *The Candy Tangerine Man?*" [Laughs.] And I can't believe it. And LL Cool J's company called, and they want to buy the remake rights. Samuel L. Jackson goes on television and says it's still his favorite film. And it's because the film had that quirk where the guy is really a good guy.

AR: *I definitely believe that's what stands out about the film—the fact that he goes to work pimping like it's a regular nine-to-five job.*

The Baron (John Daniels) takes out his aggression on a heavy bag in *The Candy Tangerine Man*.

MC: Exactly. And my idea was, hey look, if you'd sent this guy to college, he could have been another Bill Gates. Who knows?

AR: *I've read that you used actual prostitutes in the making of the film. Is that right?*

MC: Yeah. We shot it all right there on the actual strip, and a lot of the girls were actual hookers. And the people are actual pimps who came and got into film. We also had some pimp wannabes. [Laughs.] And it really worked. I bought the car from a student at UCLA for $2,500 and put the machine guns in it, which was really a takeoff on all the crap that was going on in movies at that time.

AR: *I think the ambiance is one of the things that makes* The Candy Tangerine Man *special.*

MC: Yeah, it really does. The film really puts you there. It was one of the first films that were really shot in locations where it could have really happened. There are films shot on location, I know, but the locations are usually rigged for lighting and accessibility. But here we shot it where it happened, baby.

When I showed it to Barry White and asked him to do the music, he flipped for the film. He had a group called Smoke that he owned, and they ended up doing the music.

AR: *What was Barry White like to work with?*

MC: I didn't have much interaction with him really. All I did was go have a hamburger with him and show him the film. He said, "Hey man, I really dig this film. I'll get you the music." And that was it. I never gave him a dime, but he owned all the publishing.

AR: *I understand you had a conversation with Quentin Tarantino about* The Candy Tangerine Man *and some of these other films. How did that come about?*

MC: It was very nice. He came on the set of *Miriam*, the film I was doing, and he was talking to my crew, telling them how much of a fan of mine he was. He said he'd grown up on my films. He was telling me, "You know, Sam Jackson loves *The Candy Tangerine Man*, and my favorite movie of yours is *The Black Six*." He told me he'd watched it 20 times or something like that. And he was telling everybody around me what a great fan of mine he was.

Then there's this lady in Austin who owns a theater. She booked me in to a couple of festivals. And she said, "These directors all call up and ask to see films when they come down for the weekend as guests." And she said, "Your films are the most requested."

AR: *That's interesting.*

MC: That is. It's a very nice thing because, who the hell knew? I had a kid come up to me—this was very strange. I had a white kid—a postgraduate film student—come up to me in Spokane at a festival. He couldn't have been older than 22 or 23, and he said, "I just want to shake your hand. I want you to know that *The Black Six* changed my life." [Laughs.] I was a little flabbergasted. I mean, don't ask me how *The Black Six* could change the life of a white 23-year-old kid in 2007, but it was very flattering. He was very sincere. And it shocks me, this whole rejuvenation. It's very interesting.

AR: *What are your thoughts on the criticism regarding the violence in the film?*

MC: Well, you know, it's a violent world. By today's standards, the violence in that film would be a joke. You know what's funny? At the time, the MPAA [Motion Picture Association of America] wasn't screaming so much about the violence as they were about the girl pissing on the guy! They didn't like that golden shower stuff. You could show lots of bloodletting, lots of killing, he shoots the guy's hand off. You could do all of that, but boy, that girl pissing on that guy, to the women on the MPAA, that was disgusting, horrible, and should not be put on film.

AR: *Did you have to make many cuts to appease them?*

MC: Nope. I made the cuts to appease them, but then I put those scenes right back in the film. I knew none of them would go to check it out.

AR: *Your third blaxploitation film,* Lady Cocoa, *was one of the highest grossing low-budget films ever made. To what do you attribute its success?*

MC: Lola Falana was a hot number. She was hot, and I think in many markets it did creep into the white area. Also, you have to remember that Lola went on *The Tonight Show* with Johnny Carson to promote the film. And the picture was financed by Sammy Davis Jr. It had a lot of things going for it. It had a lot of advanced publicity because of her. And Sammy talked it up. It had a very good sendoff. And by the time that *Lady Cocoa* came out, Joe Greene was really hot. And of course he's one of the assassins in the film, along with me. That got lots of attention. So yeah, it did really well.

AR: *What are your thoughts today on the blaxploitation genre?*

MC: You know, the wonderful thing about working on these films—the so-called black films—was that here I had this huge pool of wonderful talent that wasn't being used by the industry and was willing to work for me for a price we could afford. And that, to me, was the greatest thing about all of it. These people were so talented. And they came on the set and they worked, and worked, and worked. It was fabulous.

AR: *At the time you were making these films, were you at all aware that you were a part of making history?*

MC: No. Not at all. I'm just a filmmaker. I don't make history, I just make films.

CHAPTER 6

Greydon Clark

Greydon Clark was born in 1943 in Niles, Michigan. He briefly attended Valparaiso University in Indiana. For a short time he lived on the East Coast before relocating to California with the hopes of becoming an actor. The would-be thespian supported himself by working as a door-to-door salesman while studying acting under John Morley. He then met schlock-meister Al Adamson by chance, and the two quickly became friends and collaborators. This partnership led to Clark's writing and appearing in two of Adamson's most infamous pictures, *Satan's Sadists* (1969) and *Dracula vs. Frankenstein* (1971).

Using his own money, Clark then financed his own directorial debut, *Mothers, Fathers, and Lovers* (1970). He followed this up with the blaxploitation film *The Bad Bunch* (1976), also known as *Nigger Lover*, which earned him enough money to finance his next project. Clark's third film as director would be a second blaxploitation film, *Black Shampoo* (1976), about a vengeful hairdresser named Mr. Jonathan.

Clark would ultimately direct more than 20 feature films, including *Satan's Cheerleaders* (1977) and *The Forbidden Dance* (1990).

ANDREW RAUSCH: *How did you get started in Hollywood?*

GREYDON CLARK: Well, I came to Los Angeles from a small town in the Midwest at the age of 22. I literally didn't know anyone west of the Mississippi. I came here young and dumb and inexperienced to be an actor. Since I didn't know anyone at all or have anyone even remotely in the entertainment industry, I had no idea how to get started. So I bought a book titled *The Young Actor's Guide to Hollywood*. In the book were two acting coaches, Jeff Corey and John Morley, and their phone numbers. So I went to see Jeff Corey. I didn't know who he was. I went to see him and we talked, and he seemed to think I had some potential. He said he was starting a class in something like four weeks. I thought to myself, four weeks? In four weeks I could be a star . . . I don't want to wait that long.

So I went to see the other guy. Instead of doing group sessions, he was doing individual sessions. This meant you could start whenever you wanted, so I decided to go with him. It was relatively inexpensive, which was good, since I didn't really have any money. He also did group sessions, and after three or four weeks with him, he invited me to attend.

After a couple of weeks, I met a girl there who said she was up for a role in a movie, and the director was interested in her on a personal basis. And she wasn't interested in him. So she asked if I would come down to her callback interview as a beard, pretending to be her boyfriend. I said, "Gee, I get to meet a director?" I didn't really even know what a director did. I'd never been on a movie set in my life. All I knew was the director's name was the last name on the screen before the movie started. So I went down with this girl and met the director, Al Adamson. And at that time, Al had only done one or two films prior to that. I was sitting in a hallway outside a very tiny office Al had, waiting for her to finish her interview. He got a call and I heard him say, "Yeah, I'm playing tonight. Are you going to?" Being eager and full of vim and vigor, I picked up on this and asked, "What do you play?" And he said he played basketball at the YMCA. So I said, "I play basketball." He asked if I was any good and I said, "I played in college, but I haven't played in a while." So he invited me, and Al and I became friends.

So Al made the film and the girl got the part. Since I had become friends with Al, I went with them to Utah to help make the film. We were coming back, and I naively asked, "So what's the next picture?" Al said he didn't know. He said he had 40 pages of a western script, but it needed to be rewritten and fleshed out. The only problem was that he had no money. So I said, "I'll rewrite it and you won't have to worry about paying me."

Well, somehow the script turned out pretty good. So good, in fact, that Robert Taylor signed on to appear in it. This was to be one of the first made-for-television movies and we were going to shoot it in Spain for about $300,000. I had written myself a great part, too. But then Robert Taylor got sick and was diagnosed with cancer, and the project fell apart.

So the film was never made, but it allowed me to get my foot in the door. I then wrote Al's next film, *Satan's Sadists*, which was a very big hit.

AR: *How did you get your start as a director?*

GC: I wrote a script on my own about a guy who comes back from Vietnam, and how he adjusts to society. And this was an anti-war picture, and so forth. But I didn't think it was the type of film that Al would do because it wasn't really as raw exploitation as what he was doing at that time. And I found a guy with $10,000 and decided to make the picture myself. So I made the picture, *Mothers, Fathers, and Lovers*, and appeared in it. And the picture turned out pretty good. It was kind of a social comedy. We had a minor release on it.

Based on that, I then made a second picture. This one was a blaxploitation picture called *The Bad Bunch*. I was always interested in politics. As a very young man, I was in a parade with Martin Luther King, and I'm very proud of that. I actually drove a car for Mr. King. So this picture, *The Bad Bunch*, was a very political picture.

AR: *I understand that* Mothers, Fathers, and Lovers *and* The Bad Bunch *share some scenes. Is that right?*

GC: They do, yes. I took about 20 minutes from *Mothers, Fathers, and Lovers* and incorporated it into *The Bad Bunch*. What happened is in *Mothers, Fathers, and Lovers*, the young man that I played was in Vietnam. He has a black buddy, and they're discussing politics. A shot rings out and his buddy is killed. So when he gets back to the United States, he goes down to Watts to see the father of the buddy who was killed, to pay his respects. And he and the younger brother of the soldier buddy who was killed get into a confrontation through a misunderstanding. Then there are white racist cops played by Aldo Ray and Jock Mahoney, and they beat up on the black kids. And the black kids mistakenly blame the white guy. It's really the confrontation between the liberal white do-gooder and a young black gang through a misunderstanding. And it ends rather dramatically. There's a lot of political stuff to it.

I remember I screened *The Bad Bunch* for MGM to try to make a distribution deal. And the first time I screened it, the guys loved it. They thought it was terrific. Then we screened again, and again, and again. Finally, after at least three or four screenings, the very first guy who had been championing the picture came to me and said, "You know, we at MGM just cannot release this picture. We think it's a good picture and we think it's gonna do well, but you can't have white cops harassing and beating up these innocent black kids and being so racist with their dialogue." The guy says to me, "My brother's a cop in New York City and I know this is the way it really is, but we can't show it."

So I released the picture myself. The picture did quite well. I've made 20 pictures so far, and this was my second film. And throughout my career, I've only really cared about how well the picture did in that I wanted it to do well enough that I could make another picture. So from that perspective, *The Bad Bunch* did very well. I had a few bucks in my pocket and I wanted to make another of what they called blaxploitation pictures. In those days, before home video, you could make a picture, and if it had certain exploitive elements to it, you could actually get it released theatrically throughout the United States. And at that time, pictures with African American leads were easily released theatrically.

The so-called blaxploitation pictures were really exploitation pictures— sex and violence and action and so forth. The only difference between those and the other exploitation pictures being made was that they featured African American actors. It was kind of about the black milieu, about black life. So I wanted to make one, but I didn't want to make one about a pimp or a cop or a detective or something of that nature. I actually wanted to do one that featured a successful African American businessman. That was kind of the extent of my thinking on it. I was trying to think of what to do, and publicity began on Warren Beatty's *Shampoo*. A light bulb went off in my head and I thought, Why don't I make *Black Shampoo*? Why don't I do a blaxploitation picture, and make the leading character a successful hairdresser in Beverly Hills?

So I sat down with my writing partner, Alvin Fast, and wrote *Black Shampoo*. And I had a few bucks—$50,000 is what the film cost to make—and I shot it in two weeks in 1975. I had to cast the movie, of course, and I saw a movie called *Candy Tangerine Man* (1975), where John Daniels played a pimp. John had a lot of charisma on film and I thought he'd be perfect for the lead in *Black Shampoo*. He was perfect, and I was fortunate enough to get him to do it. We had open casting for the rest of the parts, and Tanya Boyd, who plays the female lead, came in and gave a terrific reading. Again, I was lucky enough to have her do it. So we made the picture in the fall of 1975.

Black Shampoo is a crazy mixture of comedy, violence, and sex, but it works really well. The audience responds to it. I was amazed. We had a screening of it the other day in Los Angeles as part of Black History Month, and they asked me to come down and do a Q&A afterwards. This was the first time I had seen the picture on the big screen in more than 30 years. But the audience went crazy for it. It was actually the same reaction they had more than 30 years earlier whenever I would see it with an audience. They would hoot and holler and laugh and have a good time. They got with the story and seemed to like it very much.

AR: *Several of the actors used pseudonyms. Why is that?*

GC: Because it was a non-SAG film. It's actually the only of my films shot here in the United States that was a non-SAG film. Several of the actors were SAG, so they opted to not use their Screen Actors Guild names. They wanted to stay out of trouble with the union, so they used pseudonyms on the picture.

About a day before we were to begin filming, my cameraman got into an automobile accident. Nothing too serious, but he hit his head on the steering wheel and he looked terrible. But he assured me he was okay and we began filming. Within a couple of hours, the poor guy came to me in a lot of pain and said there was no way he could continue. I was about to panic, of course, because I was losing my director of photography. And on a low-budget picture, unlike a big-budget picture, the director of photography is also the camera operator. So he said, "Don't worry. Our gaffer can be the DP." I thought, Oh my God. What have I gotten myself into? I've always had a limited budget—not only limited in the amount that I had to spend, but limited in that whatever amount I had, that was literally all I had. There was no studio I could go to to say something had gone wrong and we needed more money. I had what I had, and I'd budgeted the picture to spend every dollar I had. So by then it was too late. I couldn't stop shooting.

Well, the gaffer, Dean Cundey, came over, and he had maybe shot one or two films. But he turned out to be terrific. Dean was great. On a two-week shoot, you're happy if most of it is in focus. You don't have take two or take three. But Dean was quick, he was good, and he was also very good with the crew. Dean and I wound up making four more films together after this one. I was very lucky. After *Black Shampoo*, I got to make one picture after another each year for 10 or 12 years straight. And I just kept rolling whatever money I made off picture one into picture two. So anyway, Dean and I worked together for four or five more years. During that time, he got a lot of work and eventually did *Halloween* (1978). He then eventually became cinematographer for Spielberg on a number of pictures, not the least of which was *Jurassic Park* (1993). And he did the *Back to the Future* movies with Bob Zemeckis.

Incidentally, he called me about 10 years after making *Black Shampoo*, just to say hello and reminisce about old times. This was after he'd done all these great movies. And I said, "Dean, what's it like to work on a *real* movie?" And he said, "It's the same. You know, you're always in a rush and you never know what you're doing. It's always pressure." I laughed and said, "Dean, come on. I think you've forgotten what it was like to do a two-week movie." And he said, "Yeah, I think you're right. It is different."

AR: *What kind of distribution did* Black Shampoo *have?*

GC: I originally planned to release it myself, because I had kind of a quasi-distribution company set up just to release my own pictures. But I decided to go ahead and screen it for Dimension Pictures. In those days, there were at least half a dozen truly independent distributors. Today most if not all "independent distributors" are divisions of multibillion-dollar corporations. But in those days—this was early 1976—there were truly independent distributors. There were people who owned their own companies, put

John Daniels plays Mr. Jonathan in
Greydon Clark's film *Black Shampoo*.

their own money on the table, and distributed pictures. And Dimension Pictures was one of these. It was really owned by two people, a man and a wife named Larry and Betty Wolner. They were an exploitation distributor. They were former theater owners in, I believe, New Orleans, and former partners of Roger Corman at New World.

I screened *Black Shampoo* for them, and they made me an offer that was advantageous for me. So I gave the picture to them for distribution, and they distributed it literally all over the world. We played in every major urban environment in the United States. And we played all over Europe and Asia and South America. The picture did well enough, again, that I was able to make another picture, which would be *Satan's Cheerleaders*. And from there, for the next 10 years or so, I made a picture a year.

I was very, very lucky, because today there's a very slight chance of ever getting a small picture into any type of theatrical release.

AR: *I've read that there are multiple versions of* Black Shampoo *floating around. What are the differences in those versions?*

GC: Well, there shouldn't be multiple versions. There was only one released. But the version we saw the other night at the screening for Black

History Month had one very short scene missing. I don't know if it was purposefully cut or what happened there. I don't even know where the print came from. But it was just a scene where Jonathan stops by to see one of his clients. He's in an upset mood because he's had something happen in the story that is distressing to him, and he stops by. It's a little out of character for him in that he is angry rather than being his normal charming self. But that's the only cut I'm aware of.

Now VCI has a DVD out of *Black Shampoo* that I did a commentary for a couple of years ago. That was literally the first time I'd seen the picture since it was released. And their version misses that same scene, although their version is very good and very clean. But somehow and somewhere somebody cut that scene without my knowledge. I was surprised that it wasn't there.

AR: *What do you feel is the legacy of* Black Shampoo *and the other films of the blaxploitation era?*

GC: The blaxploitation films paved the way for more mainstream participation by African Americans in front of and behind the camera. They also proved to the establishment that there was an audience for similarly themed films. Today, similar films are being made and distributed by major film organizations. They may not carry the name blaxploitation, but if you look carefully, they carry many of the themes we explored back in the day. African Americans are still underrepresented in the film industry, but progress is being made, and the early blaxploitation films certainly helped.

CHAPTER 7

Larry Cohen

With a career spanning five decades, screenwriter, producer, and director Larry Cohen has established himself as one of the most versatile and prolific individuals ever to work in the medium. He has written and directed pictures in nearly every genre conceivable, and his rather impressive filmography bears this out.

In 1970, Cohen made his directorial debut with the film *Bone*. Because he pulled a terrific performance out of leading man Yaphet Kotto, the studios saw him as a white director who could work well with black actors. Based on this, Cohen soon crafted a gangster film for Sammy Davis Jr. When the project fell apart, Cohen shot the film as a blaxploitation picture for American International Pictures. The resulting film, *Black Caesar* (1973)—a retooling of classic Warner Bros. gangster films such as *Little Caesar* (1930)—would ultimately be one of the finest films to emerge from the genre. The film would also solidify lead actor Fred Williamson's standing as one of the genre's greatest stars.

Despite the fact that *Black Caesar*'s protagonist, Tommy Gibbs, dies at the end of the film, the studio soon sent Cohen and Williamson back out to shoot a sequel, *Hell up in Harlem* (1973). This film would not be quite as solid as its predecessor, but it made a killing at the box office and would ultimately become one of the genre's most popular titles.

Cohen's other screenwriting credits include *The Return of the Magnificent Seven* (1966), *El Condor* (1970), *Phone Booth* (2002), and *Cellular* (2004). His directorial credits include *It's Alive!* (1974), *God Told Me To* (1977), *Best Seller* (1987), and the blaxploitation reunion film *Original*

Gangstas (1996). In addition, Cohen has written extensively for television and has even created the cult television series *Branded* and *The Invaders*.

ANDREW RAUSCH: *There has always been quite a bit of debate over the term blaxploitation. Some people find it offensive, while others, such as Quentin Tarantino, look at it more in terms of other exploitation films, such as women-in-prison films and the early bootlegging films of Burt Reynolds. What does the term blaxploitation mean to you?*

LARRY COHEN: *Every* movie is an exploitation movie. Every movie tries to get you to part with your eight dollars. Our job is to get you to spend your money, and come into the theater, not unlike a barker at a carnival sideshow trying to entice you to come and see the fat lady or the dwarf. That's what the whole business is about. You do whatever you have to to sell tickets. Every picture is exploiting something and some audience. So what if you're making films for a black audience? Why shouldn't they have their cinema, anyway? There was a long period when there were no black pictures. So, as soon as they started making pictures for a black audience, somebody went around yelling, "Blaxploitation!" It's rather foolish, obviously. I think it tainted the product, and people didn't look at the pictures more clearly until later on. I guess Quentin Tarantino had something to do with the reemergence of black film, because he said a few nice things about the pictures and people started seeing them again.

Black Caesar is really not any different from those Warner Bros. films, like *Little Caesar* and *The Public Enemy* (1931). It really is the same kind of a story about the rise and fall of an American gangster. It's not really your typical black exploitation film, where the black hero wins every fight, wins the woman, and gets everything. In *Black Caesar*, he loses everything and ends up in the gutter. He loses the woman who betrayed him, and he loses his entire empire. So, in that respect, it's really more like *Public Enemy* or *Little Caesar*.

AR: *How did* Black Caesar *come about?*

LC: Sammy Davis Jr. was looking for a picture in which he could play the lead, rather than playing a stooge for Dean Martin and Frank Sinatra. He felt he was ready for a starring role of his own. So his manager, Sy Marsh, contacted me. He said they'd pay $10,000 for a treatment for a movie that Sammy could play in. I said, "How about doing a gangster movie?" Sammy was a little guy, but so was Edward G. Robinson and James

Cagney. They were great as gangsters, and I felt we could do a black gangster movie. The rise and fall of a Harlem gangster. Of course it took another 35 years for them to make *American Gangster* (2007) with Denzel Washington.

So anyway, I wrote the treatment, and when it came time to collect my $10,000, Sammy was not paying. His manager said he was having trouble with the Internal Revenue Service, he didn't have any money, and he couldn't pay. So I was stuck with the treatment *Black Caesar*.

And then I went in to see Sam Arkoff at American International, and they'd seen a previous movie I'd done called *Bone*. He was impressed with the movie, and with the performance of Yaphet Kotto, so he said, "We're looking for some black product like *Shaft* (1971) and *Superfly* (1972). Have you got anything?" I said, "You came to the right person." I ran downstairs and got it out of the trunk of my car and brought it up. And we had a deal right there. So we were already off and rolling immediately—all thanks to Sammy Davis Jr.

AR: *Was the original treatment that you wrote for Sammy Davis Jr. much different from the film you ultimately shot?*

LC: No. It was pretty much the same. Of course Fred Williamson brought something different to it; he brought glamour to it. Fred was a good-looking guy. You know, he wore the clothes beautifully. He was great. He looked very much like Denzel looked in the modern version of the picture. There are a lot of similarities there. The shots look almost identical in the ad campaign shots, with him dressed up in his nice snazzy suit.

AR: *Did the critics or the studios tend to treat the blaxploitation films differently than they treated other pictures?*

LC: Well, you know, the critics never tended to treat any of the American International Pictures favorably. These were all "B" movies, and they fulfilled a function of appealing to a certain specific kind of audience. I think sometimes they might have been better than the "A" pictures. But they were never expected to get any critical raves. They were just expected to make some money, to generate some activity at the box office. So I wasn't disappointed. To tell you the truth, the reviews for *Black Caesar* were actually pretty good. They were better than they were for most AIP movies, but this was a better movie. It was a better script. It was a "B" movie, but it had an "A" quality script.

AR: *I've always felt that* Black Caesar *holds up a lot better than some of the other blaxploitation pictures.*

LC: A lot of the other pictures are just a lot of brutality—a lot of going out and shooting people. You know, Pam Grier's gonna go out and blow people away and stab them in the groin. It was just monotonous and vulgar. Our picture had its share of violence, but it all had something to do with the integral storyline or integral racism of America. You know, the picture was about crooked New York cops, and, as it turns out, there really were crooked New York cops. It was about using teenage kids to run drugs and money in the underworld manipulated by the police department. And it turns out it was true. They were using black teenage kids to do that. All the stuff I made up turned out to be true. I just basically concocted what turned out to be the truth.

AR: *Most blaxploitation films written by white screenwriters tended to have a lot of "jive talk," which didn't ring true. It sounded forced. I notice there isn't much of that in* Black Caesar.

LC: As I said, this was a good quality script. Also, in working with the actors, I kind of let them get comfortable with the lines. If they wanted to change something or put it into their own words, we did that. I wanted it to feel natural rather than forced, as you say. And the actors felt comfortable with it, too. They had a good time, I had a good time.

We shot up in Harlem. This was a period when some of the Hollywood movie companies were going up there to film movies like *Across 110th Street* (1972), and they were shaken down by all the local black gangsters. "You can't shoot on this street unless you pay us. You can't shoot in this area unless you pay us." So when I got up there with my small crew, we were approached by these same hoods again. And I didn't have any money to pay them, so I said to them, "You guys are great. You ever think of doing any acting? You'd be great as Fred Williamson's guys." So we recruited all these fellas who were members of a gang and put them in the picture. I even had them put into the ad campaign, on the poster. After that, we owned Harlem. We never had any problem doing anything we wanted. Opening day at the Cinerama Theater, there were all these black gangsters standing around the theater, signing autographs. It was a very enjoyable shoot.

AR: *Did you sit in on any of the screenings?*

LC: The first big screening we had at the Pantages Theater was a disaster. Everybody loved the picture, but they hated the ending where Fred died. In the original version, he was killed by a gang of street kids who stole his wristwatch and everything. They didn't know he was the godfather of Harlem; they just thought he was some dressed-up guy staggering injured through the streets of Harlem. They descend upon him like a pack of wolves and they kill him. When that happened, a lot of people in the audience—the black audience in particular—got angry. One black woman was screaming at me in the lobby. "Black people wouldn't do this to their own kind!" That is, of course, an erroneous comment, since most killings of black people in the black community are committed by black gangs and other members of the black community. Black people are the most common victims of black crime. What she said certainly wasn't true, but I called up Arkoff and I said, "Sam, we're in terrible trouble. We're opening this picture in a couple of days and the audience just hates the ending." He says, "Well, I told you not to kill him at the end." So I said, "Sam, we've got to do something about this." He said, "Well, what do you want to do?" I said, "I've got to take out the ending. We'll just have to cut the ending off."

So, with his permission, I went to New York where we were going to open first. I went to the Cinerama Theater the morning the picture was gonna open. I went to the projectionist and identified myself. We went upstairs and we cut off the last scene of the picture. Then I went across town to another theater on 59th Street and introduced myself to the manager there. We then went up and cut off the last minute of the picture. We then went up to 86th Street and did the same thing. And the picture opened to be a huge success. Really big. I mean, they started putting in 3 a.m. shows. The theater was closed for maybe three hours a day. They were running the picture continuously all day long. They raised the ticket prices by a dollar after the first couple of days. There was a line around the block. It was February, freezing cold, and the lines were up around the block. The police had those wooden horses put up, and people were waiting for an hour, hour and a half to see the picture. I thought, Wow, this is great. Every movie is gonna be like this! Of course I was wrong, but . . . Cutting off the ending really just took a disaster and turned it into a success.

Then videos and DVDs were made years later, and they went back to the original negative, which hadn't been cut. So now he dies at the end. The DVD and the VHS have the original ending. And in the foreign versions, which were again made from the original negative rather than the cut negative, he also dies at the end. So there are two versions of the movie—the home video version and the theatrical cut.

AR: *I'm going to name some of the people you worked with on* Black Caesar *and* Hell up in Harlem, *and I'd like you to comment on each of them.*

LC: Okay.

AR: *Fred Williamson.*

LC: I worked with Fred three times. The third film on which I worked with him was *Original Gangstas*, which he produced. And it was entirely different working with him as a producer than it was working with him as an actor. As a producer, he was now saddled with the financial responsibilities. And that made him extremely nervous and tense and concerned. So I didn't have the same devil-may-care relationship with him that I did on the first two pictures, where it was mainly just having fun. I'd say, "Look at that great big sign over Times Square. Let's climb up to the top of it and shoot a scene up there." He'd say, "Okay, Cohen, you do it first." And I'd have to climb up to the top of the sign and do it. And then naturally he wouldn't want to lose face in front of the crew, so if I would do it, he would do it. I said, "Okay, Fred, when the cab rounds the corner, I want you to jump out and roll on the sidewalk." And he said, "Yeah, sure, I'm gonna throw myself out on the sidewalk out of a taxi cab! You do it." So I would throw myself out of a taxi cab, jump up from the ground with a big smile on my face, and say, "Nothing to it." Then I'd go around the corner and scream in agony. So then he would do the same damn thing! He'd jump out of the cab, and he'd jump up and brush himself off, a big grin on his face. Then he'd go up the street and go into a doorway and scream in agony. Neither of us wanted to show the other one that we were in any way chicken. So we did all kinds of stuff like that. In one scene, I had myself picked up by some apparatus and then buried in a pile of coal. And he said, "I'm gonna get my legs chopped off if I try to do that!" I said, "No, you're too tall anyway, Fred! If I can do it, you can do it." We had a lot of fun doing those two pictures.

But later on, when he hired me to do the directing on *Original Gangstas*, it was a bit different because he was worried about getting his money. And his money was predicated on bringing the picture in under budget. And my interest was making the best picture possible. So we were a little bit at odds. Fred was really responsible for a lot of the success of that picture. He cast all the actors—not only the stars, but also the supporting players. He dug them all up, and they were all very good. And he found all the locations in Gary, Indiana, and arranged everything down there. Basically all I had to do was go in and direct the picture and make some sense out of the story. Sometimes it didn't make much sense in the script that he had, so I had to go in and rewrite it. It was a tough shoot because it was probably 106 degrees every day, and we had no air conditioning. Fred wouldn't spring for air conditioning. We had our problems there, but we made what I thought was a very good picture. And it actually got very good reviews when it came out. Of the three pictures, I think that was the best reviewed. I hope it's because I've gotten better as a director over the 20 years between them.

AR: *Gloria Hendry.*

LC: Well, Gloria worked on the two *Black Caesar* pictures. She was a very nice person. A very pretty, very athletic young girl. Never any problem. Always very eager to please. She's still a friend to this day. I see her sometimes at these retrospectives, and she's so happy to see me, and she has nothing but very pleasant memories of the pictures. And again, she was the type of person who would do anything you needed them to do. You know, run through the streets of New York, run through the theater district. I'd say, "Run into that empty theater, Gloria, and run down the aisle. We're gonna run into the theater after you." And this was without any permission or anything. And we did it. We shot scenes in all kinds of places we weren't supposed to be, but nobody stopped us. So she was game for anything. What can you say when you have somebody who'll try anything you ask them to do? You've got to like them, and I did like her. She was a swell girl.

AR: *D'Urville Martin.*

LC: D'Urville Martin was a friend of Fred Williamson's. He'd been in a couple of Fred Williamson pictures before ours. He was kind of a swinging kind of guy. You know, I never knew what was going on with people. I didn't know if they were smoking grass or taking dope or what. I never even thought about it. I just made my movie. So I don't know what the hell D'Urville was up to. But he always seemed to be happy. One day I did have some trouble with him. He got hostile one day. I don't know why. So I told him to lie down on the ground, I wanted to get a shot of him on the ground. He didn't know what the hell it was for. So he lay down on the ground and I shot a shot of him. Then after I got it, I told him, "Now you're dead. So if you give me any more trouble on this picture, I've already filmed your death." And I never had any trouble from him again. Not a peep.

AR: *Julius Harris.*

LC: Julius was in a lot of my pictures. I think Julius was a very, very gifted actor. He was wonderful as the father in *Black Caesar*. He brought a whole different dimension to the role. It was because of him that I wrote the part of the father into the sequel *Hell up in Harlem*, where I really elaborated on the father's character. There he evolved from a common everyman to Big Papa, the heir apparent to the underworld regime that Fred Williamson advocated. So I built up a big part for him in the second picture.

We had a lot of fun together. One time we took him to the Copa to see Sarah Vaughan in New York. We liked him. Anytime we ran into Julius, he was always very, very happy to see me. I must say that about most of the actors. I've very seldom had any actor who didn't seem delighted when I ran into them and want to reminisce about the experience.

AR: *Gloria Hendry told me you actually shot some of* Black Caesar *in your own home. Is that right?*

LC: Oh, yeah. The big mansion in California was actually shot at my house. Then we shot a scene in *Hell up in Harlem* where it was supposed to be a church—that was my house. For a scene that was supposed to be a nightclub, I turned my living room into a nightclub by putting up curtains and putting up tables. The scene where the district attorney gets hanged was shot out in my yard amongst the big trees. He's supposed to be out-side of a church, but really that was in front of my house. In *Black Caesar*, the scenes with Fred Williamson's office and with the lawyer's office were all shot in my basement. The scene with D'Urville Martin's dressing room in the church was actually shot in my basement.

I have a big house, and we had a lot of flats we could put up and make sets out of. So I preferred to shoot at home rather than to go rent studio space. I didn't have to go to work in the morning; I could just stay home. And they shot up the house pretty good in *Hell up in Harlem*, too. There was an attack on the house. They were firing machine guns off and all kinds of shit. At least we didn't do any damage.

I was making these pictures for a set price. And if I brought the picture in cheaper, I got to keep the money, so why not put the money into your pocket rather than give it to some studio?

AR: *You worked with James Brown on the soundtrack to* Black Caesar. *What was that experience like?*

LC: That was kind of a comical experience. James was wonderful, but he'd never written the music for a movie before. So we gave him a print of the picture and gave him the timings of the scenes. He went off and made the music and recorded it, sang it with his backup singers and everything. His manager, Charles Bobbitt, came to me with all the tapes. We transferred them to film and played them with all the scenes. Unfortunately, if the scene was five minutes long, James wrote seven minutes' worth of music. If the scene was six minutes long, James wrote nine minutes' worth of music. If it was a one-minute scene, he wrote two or three minutes. So I called up Bobbitt and I said, "This is what he did: if the scene was two minutes, he gave me five minutes' worth of music." Bobbitt says, "Well, then you have more than you need." I said, "It doesn't work that way, Charles. The music is supposed to fit the scene." So finally I had to go and get a music editor, and I sat there myself and cut and edited all the music cues down so they fit the sequences. I never told American International what happened. I just fixed it myself and gave them the finished picture. They were very happy. They were so happy, in fact, that they hired James to make music for *Slaughter's Big Rip-Off* (1973) with Jim Brown. And he did the same thing to them again! But this time they found out about it, and they didn't have me to fix it. So they went out of their minds about it. They were gonna sue him. It was a terrible mess.

So when time came to do *Hell up in Harlem*, I wanted to use James Brown again. And they said, "Absolutely under no circumstances will we ever work with James Brown again." I said, "He did the music for *Black Caesar*, it's great music." But they said, "No, we will not hire James Brown again! The only way we would do it is if James Brown wrote the whole thing on spec. If we like it, we'll use it." So I went back to Bobbitt and said, "That's the only way they'll do it." So the next day, I get a call from Bobbitt and he says, "The man accepts the challenge. He will write the entire score for the picture, record it and give it to you, and if you like it you can use it. If you don't like it, you don't have to use it." That was the most amazing offer I'd ever heard from a big-name artist like James Brown. He did just that. He wrote the music for the film, which was going to be titled *Black Caesar's Revenge*. And American International heard it and they said, "Ah, it's the same old James Brown stuff again. We've got a deal cooking with Motown, and we don't want the James Brown music." I tried to convince them but they wouldn't listen. So I called up Bobbitt. He said, "It's okay. We'll just take the music back and we'll use it somewhere else." And sure enough he did. James Brown put out an album called *Payback*, which became his most successful album. And not only was it a big successful album, but years later it was used as the musical score for a film called *Lock, Stock, and Two Smoking Barrels* (1998). So all the music that was written for me, with all the lyrics that applied to *Black Caesar's* sequel, all ended up in their film. We lost out on getting the most successful album James ever had, and we ended up with a second-rate Motown score. It wasn't bad, but we'd have been much better off with the James Brown score.

But what can you do? You know, you can't fight city hall. And that was the only time I had any interference from American International on either picture. They were just adamant about not giving any more business to James Brown.

AR: *I've heard there were a lot of scheduling conflicts when you shot* Hell up in Harlem, *so you had to shoot primarily on the weekends. Is that right?*

LC: Well, Fred was not available because he was doing *That Man Bolt* (1973) for Universal. He was going to be on that picture for a number of months, and Arkoff wanted to get a sequel and get it out there so he could capitalize. So I said, "The only way we can do it is to shoot it on the weekends. I'm shooting a picture for Warner Bros. called *It's Alive!* (1974), and I'm shooting five days a week. I could shoot Saturday and Sunday on *Hell up in Harlem*. So that's what we did. We ended up shooting seven days a week. I used mostly the same crew as well as the sound editor on *It's Alive!* and *Hell up in Harlem*. It was a madhouse. The poor editor didn't know from one day to the next what picture he was cutting. He wasn't sure what he was doing, but I was standing there next to him, so he got through it. We shot the picture mainly on weekends, and then when we went to New York without Fred, we used a double. Then we shot all of the reverse shots of Fred out in California. You have to know exactly what you're doing when you make a picture like that. You have to know exactly what every shot is going to look like, and what every cut is gonna look like. I carried the whole picture in my head so I could do it. I don't think I would recommend this to other people. But I did it, and I made it work.

AR: *I was amazed when I learned that you used a body double to such great lengths. You can't tell at all.*

LC: Fred didn't like the double. He thought the double's ass was too fat. He was pissed off. He said, "Where'd you get the fat ass on that guy?" I said, "Look, Fred, no one knows it's not you. Just cool it. Nobody will ever know."

We actually got Fred back to New York a few days here and there, even though he was still under contract to Universal. One day we were shooting in the American Airlines terminal in New York City, and right in the middle of shooting Lew Wasserman—the president of MCA/Universal—walks up to me! "Hi, boys," said Lew Wasserman. "What are you shooting?" I'm thinking to myself, I wonder if he's gonna realize that this actor is under contract to him. We were in conflict here. So I just said to Mr. Wasserman, "You wanna be in the picture?" I tried to talk him into being one of the gangsters. He was so busy getting out of that one that he never really found out what picture we were making.

CHAPTER 8

Don Pedro Colley

Don Pedro Colley grew up in the small northwestern town of Klamath Falls, Oregon. As a young man, he excelled in several sports, but he preferred track and field, and he received an offer to try out for pro football. Colley studied architecture at the University of Oregon and prepared for the 1960 Olympic Team as a discus thrower. However, a sixth-place finish in the Olympic trials derailed his plans. He dropped out of college and moved to San Francisco to "experience the sixties." Quickly running through his savings, he found himself homeless.

It was during this period that Colley discovered acting and joined a satirical comedy troupe known as "The Firing Squad." He soon began acting on stage in such productions as Shakespeare's *The Merchant of Venice* and Ibsen's *A Doll's House*. A role in a reprise of *Heaven Can Wait* opposite Jack Palance led to an agent and numerous guest spots on television series such as *The Virginian* and *Daniel Boone*.

Colley then started working in film, appearing in *Beneath the Planet of the Apes* (1970) and George Lucas's *THX 1138* (1971). Key among Colley's film projects of the 1970s are the blaxploitation classics *The Legend of Nigger Charley* (1972), *Black Caesar* (1973), and *Sugar Hill* (1974).

While occasionally popping up in films like Roger Corman's *Piranha* (1995), Colley has worked extensively in television throughout the past 30 years. These television appearances include recurring roles on *The Magical World of Disney* and *The Dukes of Hazzard*.

ANDREW RAUSCH: *You had a background in theater. I think there's a misconception that the blaxploitation films only used amateur actors. You had former football players like Jim Brown and Fred Williamson. And Pam Grier, as legend goes, was promoted from a secretary to an actress. But there were guys like yourself and Ron O'Neal and Glynn Turman who had extensive theatrical training.*

DON PEDRO COLLEY: Well, it gives you a bearing of how to prepare for a character, or the person that you're essaying. With today's film, it seems, they're more interested in the personality of the performer than the depth of characterization that is important in carrying a storyline. The emphasis is put on "You stand there, we'll shoot you and then piece the pieces together, and somehow or another we'll have a story." A theatrically trained performer brings that whole character to the storyline from his point of conception as a child up to that moment where you're saying that line in person, and it works its way through the facets of society. What is the religion of the time? What are the politics of the time? What is your financial situation? What type of job do you have? Did you have a dominant mother and a passive father? Did you have a dominant father and a passive mother? All of these things are important in putting together a *real* character. Then when the director says "Action," you bring him into your world. And that world is the audience inside this world struggling with you to try and get through to the next element that the character has to survive. And that's the excitement. Now it's just pretty kids and lots of titty.

It's a craft, and it takes energy to study it, and if you want to be one of the best, you study how the best did it. It's writing and painting and reading and sculpture and music. You can't limit yourself in terms of creative intake.

AR: *The title of your film* The Legend of Nigger Charley *was quite controversial. I was wondering, what are your thoughts on that?*

DPC: It's a fact of life. Cannot be denied. You can't cover up what did happen, or the way it was at the time. And the concept we went into in making the film wasn't something to stir the tribes up. It was more or less like a black Indiana Jones. You know, *The Legend of Nigger Charley*! [Laughs.] And how these three guys made it. The press kind of made them into something bigger, but these were just three guys trying to survive in the Old West.

That sequence where we're trying to learn to shoot guns . . . we didn't know what we were doing. We were just out there. There was an awful lot of that film that we tried to get on celluloid, but due to certain types of time constraints, I wanted more scenes that explained how we got from point A to point C. But these were all pretty amateur filmmakers, except myself. [Laughs again.] Many of the head honchos were playing Cecil B. DeMille. "I'm a producer and I have girls hanging over me all day long."

AR: *Were you at all apprehensive about making a film called* Nigger Charley *with a white director?*

DPC: Well, you see, I have to give you a little background. I was born and raised here in Klamath Falls, Oregon, and we were about the only prominent black family here. We acted and did and went and said just like we were white folks. None of the bowing your head and acquiescing to someone else's imaginings. So when I was approached with this storyline—and I had heard about the real exploits of this cowboy—I liked it. If Charley did something that impressed some person enough that his legend is passed on in tale and song and/or written page or whatever, it's important to bring that to the screen. So if you can get everybody on the same page, then you have something going on.

Marty Goldman wrote the script and directed the film, although he had never done a feature before. And most of the rest of the crew was in the same boat. Most of the actors and others hadn't done a feature film. A feature is a whole different rhythm when you're painting your picture than it is on television or on a sitcom. Sitcom is a whole lot closer to improvisation and *Saturday Night Live,* and even that's scripted anymore. So we were painting a picture as a major motion picture with Paramount behind it, and in those days there was still a little bit of a sense of style between studios. Each studio had a style in preparing and presenting pictures. Paramount pictures, this was big time.

So there we were on a five-generation plantation sitting right on the apex of the James and Appomattox rivers. Right there the two sensational features of Civil War times were at the front door of this plantation where we're working at. And not 50 yards down the river to the east was this monstrous weeping willow tree that had one arm that swung out over the river, and you could still see the old rope burns on the limb. How exciting is that? This was a three-story brick house. It's a huge compound, man. It's wonderful. I go upstairs to the third floor—nobody ever goes up there—and there's dust a quarter of an inch thick everywhere. I open up a door in a little side room, and in the vestibule of the window are stacks and stacks of *Harper's* magazines dated 1859. I pick up one, and in it is a pen and ink sketch of how they used to hold cock fights. And we're filming a cock fight that day! We'd snuck eight pairs of cocks onto the plantation because they were highly illegal . . . to fight real cocks. So I ran down to the director and the art director and I said, "Look what I found in this magazine. Isn't this something?" Everyone read it, and it brought us even closer up to date of the period we were shooting, which was before the slaves were emancipated.

So you see, I'm involved in history. All that other social bullshit and media politics and suppositions . . . What a waste of time and energy.

AR: *When people say that blaxploitation films had no redeeming value, do you believe that? What is your take on that?*

DPC: They got made. And no one else was doing this. Earlier in the history of film, guys like Archibald and Oscar Micheaux made films for a primarily black audience. The films were a bit amateurish, though. [Laughs.] I was embarrassed to be on the set, I swear to God. But there we were, and they paid me my little $700. We were becoming a kind of black Hollywood ensemble.

AR: *You worked with Fred Williamson and D'Urville Martin again right after that on* Black Caesar, *right?*

DPC: Right. You know, I had my nose in the air in those days, thinking my shit didn't stink because I was theatrically trained. [Laughs.] And this was all so one-dimensional shock value only. It's like the time I met Norman Lear when they had me in to audition for a part in *All in the Family.* All the people from his office were there, and his question was, what is my belief in what he's trying to do with his show. I said, "You know, it makes me uncomfortable personally because we're all human beings. We're all striving for a level where everybody communicates to each other on a human level, not on a black level, or white level, or Chinese, or whatever level. And yeah, it's good to draw the square heads out and make them see an example of themselves, but for me personally, it makes me uncomfortable." Well, consequently, I didn't get the job.

I just came from a generation here in Oregon where I got knocked out of the industry because they said, "Gee, Don, you talk too good." And I said, "Well, damn, I'm a character actor. I can do ebonics." I just wasn't raised in the dumb ghetto like down here in California. I didn't really have a ghetto. I learned from all people, all things, all places, all times; even little old ladies and bag persons. You know, there's something to be learned from everybody. So why limit one's self?

AR: *You worked with Fred and D'Urville on a couple of movies. What were those guys like to work with?*

DPC: D'Urville had done some work on Broadway, so he had some theater training and so forth. And Fred was a pretty boy. And I was trying to not be pushy-shovey but keep everybody together and working in the same direction. And it was very hard because D'Urville was having a grand time playing movie star. And Fred was, too. And so was Larry Spangler. Fred always had five women with him at all times. And Spangler was walking around in a tank top that looked like it was cut out of an American flag, with a Jewish Afro, dark sunglasses, and a drink in his hand. And he had his women following him around, and secretaries, and they're having a grand time, you know?

From day one, I was the bad guy. I mean, way back, after it was all agreed that we'd go to work, it started with contracts. This was before we ever left Los Angeles. They were hoping for a Woody Strode type: tall, muscular body, blah, blah. And I'm just a big guy. I lost a lot of weight, but still a little fatty. But I'm an actor. We make up for it in different ways. So they come to me at my house and give me a contract. I say, "Okay, I like it, but my agents have to read it first." "Oh no, they don't," they say. "I'm here now, and . . ." And I said, "No, I can't do that. Did you hear me? I can't do that." And they said, "You mean to tell me you don't trust us?" I said, "That has nothing to do with nothing, man. The way the rules of the game play out is, you present me with a contract. Then my agency, who are also my attorneys, sit down and look it over. Then, if it's all up to snuff, we'll go with it. Okay?" The guy growled going out of the house. He was pissed. So my agents look at it and say, "This is an up and up contract, but there are some things here. This isn't going to be the final draft."

So I'm packed and off on my way to New York City, where they're going to finish casting the movie. We are then to go from there to Richmond, Virginia, and then from there down to our location on the plantation. I'm scheduled for the first 30 days there. So I'm trying to assess the situation, because nobody's communicating with me. I'm already the bad guy and we haven't even begun shooting. And it's like they're waiting for me to make one more move so I can fall down completely. They think I'm a dummy and I don't know nothing, while they're all partying. So Fred and I get together and I ask him, "How are you gonna approach this thing? This is a piece of real American history, man. We got a chance to lay down something really fine here if we approach it honestly. You can't just go out there and say, 'I'm Fred Williamson, football player, and I'm pretty.' I don't think you want to represent yourself that way. Do you, man?" I'm in his ear, see.

AR: *Was he receptive to that advice?*

DPC: You can bring the horse to water, but you can't make him drink. That's the philosophy you have to take. And I had already learned that working with 20th Century Fox when I was in *Beneath the Planet of the Apes.* I could read and see what the processes were to make this thing work—to make this monstrous piece of art come together. And if you have one or two slackers somewhere, it can hurt you. If you don't get rid of the slackers or find a way to make that a positive, you know, you've got no chance. It'll pull the whole production apart.

So we get to New York and I meet Martin Goldman, who wrote the script, and Spangler. And Spangler looks at me and turns up his nose because he had something different in mind. Then there was a lot of whispering and a lot of bullshit going on. But I'm in New York already. And I still haven't seen a script reading. And I said, "Wait a minute. We still don't have a contract here, guys. There's no guarantee on anything here. No contract." And they said, "You go to this attorney's office in Times Square and he'll give you a contract." So Fred, D'Urville, and myself all go. We take a cab to the office. We get the contract, and those guys didn't care. They just grab a contract and sign it. I said, "You know, I can't do that. My agent told me—and he's the one who's kept me going the past eight years—to let him read over it. I'm not going to turn my back on him now. I will have to send them my contract. If they approve it, they'll send it back and I'll sign it and give it to the PA on the job." "No, no, no." Goddammit, they want to play games.

So on the train to Richmond, Fred and I have a suite. D'Urville took a plane. I requested the train because I wanted a chance to get out of the city and go back in history and time. And the train tracks south into Richmond do all of that for you—the foliage, the scenery, the feeling, the emotion that starts to build, knowing that you're going back into slavery days. That was what I was trying to get Fred to do: disconnect from Hollywood, from New York, from big money, partying, and so forth. So when we get down there, he's not so much a fish out of water as he would have been had we not had the chance to sit down and talk. Otherwise, it would have been a horrible disaster.

So here we are, we've got the first week's film in the can, and suddenly I'm getting noises from the production office because they don't have a contract on me. And I told them the situation—that the people in New York were supposed to send the copies to my agents in Hollywood. They would approve them, I would sign them, and then you can deal with them from that point on. "But we can't go on filming without those." I said, "Man, I'm just an actor. I don't know anything about that. You guys take care of that." That was the process right there. Next thing I know, I hear Larry Spangler in the background, pitching a bitch. He comes storming up to my hotel room. *Bam, bam, bam!* "Open this door!" I'm supposed to be scared. I get up and open the door and he says, "How dare you! What are you trying to do? Stop us from making this movie and shut us down before we've even started? How dare you! I'll send you back to Hollywood. Get your shit packed." I said, "Wait a minute. Listen, buddy. [Laughs.] You've got 14 hours of film in the can already. I'm quite sure the people at Paramount Pictures would like to hear how you're wasting their product over some frivolous bullshit. I don't know anything. I'm just an actor. You talk to my agent. They told me not to sign the contracts because they're not union qualified, and I don't know anything from there."

Next thing I know, I get a call from a representative at Paramount Pictures. They say, "Don, listen. We've been getting other reports about how these people are trying to do business. Would you mind being our scout on location?" I said, "Yes, I would love to, because I don't want to turn out a piece of bullshit product here. I want this to be the right thing." So now I'm the inside agent for Paramount Pictures, and I'm not gonna tell anybody.

There was so much in-fighting, and by this time nobody else on the set would talk to me. I was the bad guy because I didn't want to party and have fun like the rest of them, and I keep telling people, "This is the way we have to do this if we want to get this on film." And Marty, who's supposedly the director, has had his whole territory invaded by the assistant director! So the assistant director is saying, "Okay, guys, let's go shoot this." And then Marty would say, "Action," and the assistant director would jump up and say, "No, no, cut! Go back. What are you people doing?" And Marty's just sitting there, looking all kinds of befuddled. This keeps going and going, and I say, "We can't have that." So finally Paramount Pictures sends out an agent. By this time we're in Santa Fe, New Mexico. However, they covered up pretty good there in Santa Fe. So they didn't see that Marty Goldman's assistant director was pulling things apart. He wanted to be a director so bad, and he was so not qualified it was ridiculous. That was the problem. So many of the people thought this was all just a big amateur blowout, "let's go and have fun."

One day they wanted us to mount on the horses to do a shot. And this assistant director started hollering at me about getting on this horse. I got up on the horse and I said, "Listen, first of all"—and this was loud, in front of the whole company—"what you're doing is fucking up this film. You are an assistant director. You are not the director. Stop your bullshit. You're pulling people apart, and you're ruining a good project." And the guy looks at me like he can't believe I challenged him. I didn't challenge you, I shut your ass down! So one day I took Marty Goldman aside and I said, "Come here, come here." He said, "What, Don? What's up?" I said, "Come on, let's walk here." We walked about 250 yards. There's no one but Marty Goldman, myself, and the coyotes out there. I said, "Listen, man, you wrote this script. This is your project. You know what's happening. Do you want your name associated with this piece of shit? You may never work again after this. I'm an actor, and I expect certain things on a job. You're the director. I have to hear your command that you're in charge. When you say 'Action,' we're all acting at this point. When you've got someone else calling the shots, there's no rhythm. This is your job. Do your damn job and make that fool go sit down somewhere." "Yeah, Don, you're right. He's really been pissing me off." So we walked back to the set, and the assistant director runs up and says, "Where have you guys been?" And I looked at Marty, and he pinned the guy right there really good. After that, we got down to business. Even Fred got back to business.

There was one funny moment, though. In one scene when we interact with the Indians, I said to Fred, "Here we are. Our characters have been on the road for months. We're now hundreds of miles away from civilization. We should look like we've ridden the distance, so there's a transition in this movie from point A to point B. Our clothes should be dirty." I'm putting dirt on my beard, and I started to put some dirt on Fred. And he says, "Don't you put none of that shit on me! I'm pretty, man. And comb my hair. Dammit, Don, I'm pretty. I don't wear none of that shit."

Goddamn amateurs, I swear to God.

AR: *I wanted to ask you about one of your films,* Sugar Hill. *That has a fantastical plot, to say the least. What were your initial thoughts when you read that script?*

DPC: "I got a job!" [Laughs.]

AR: *What was that film like to work on?*

DPC: I immediately go to the library and start research work on voodoo concepts: how does it work, why does it work, what is its origin. And I had three or four different books on it. The character that was sketched out in the script gave me the form in which to build my house, and I went from there. I had to go in and audition for the director and producer and some others in this office. And I guess those who had been there before me brought their little Hollywood television performances of this character. So here we are in this little pocket-sized office, and I create Baron Zombie full, as if I'm standing in a canyon so my voice echoes from the mountainsides. And the laughter and sheer terror of this guy, who's come back from the dead—these poor guys in this office, their eyes were about as big as saucers. These guys just sat there with their mouths hanging open. I only had a week or so to put something together, so these were just thumbnail sketches.

Don Pedro Colley as the evil Baron Samedi in 1974's *Sugar Hill*.

So they liked my interpretation of the character, and they sent us off to Houston, Texas. And we found this old mansion that had been abandoned for a decade or so. They didn't even have to spray cobwebs or anything; there were natural cobwebs everywhere. It was great.

But here we are, once again, working with a company that thinks of this new film genre—black exploitation—as just that. It's just a bunch of fun and games, and cheapness, and let's throw this thing together. Nobody follows the rules, and everybody cuts corners. You hired me to do this thing, man. I can't cut these corners. I can't do anything, because they're not following the rules. I can't go against the rules, because once you guys are swept out of the way, I still have to go to work somewhere else. "How dare you!" So once again, I'm the bad guy. Because I wanted to follow the rules that are set up specifically in the contract by the Screen Actors Guild and all producers, I was the bad guy. These guys wanted to play these slipshod games.

They did that for all these black exploitation movies. They were playing fun and games. Instead of giving us our just dues, they wanted to cut corners and keep it cheap and also as cheap looking as they possibly could.

So we get off to Houston, Texas, and I'm prepared to work. Work is important to me, first, over everything else. Everything else. I don't care what it is, the work is what's important. So we get down there and I ask where my dressing room is. It's about 95 degrees and 98 percent humidity down there. "Where do you want me to change my clothes?" They say, "Well, we had a problem getting dressing rooms. You can change behind that flag pole over there." [Laughs.] I said, "Wait a minute. What? I can't do that." They said, "That's all right. We don't mind." I said, "I mind. Union contracts say you have to provide us with class A dressing rooms." So I went out and rented a 40-foot motor home and drove it to the set on my own. The assistant director came screaming up to me: "You cannot have that here on the set!" Why? "Because we have to put a union driver on it, and a union driver costs so much a week." I said, "Wait a minute. He makes more a week driving my motor home than you're paying me to act in this fucking movie of yours?" So I said, "Tell you what: I'm going to have my agents call your people. Here's what's going to happen: the whole production's going to be shut down until you get some dressing rooms here." They said, "You can't do that." "Just watch me. It's my right to do it. In fact, if I don't do it, I'm going against jurisdiction."

I call my agent. Sure enough, they shut down the production. [Laughs again.] So they went out and found a dressing room—a thing with four wheels—that looked like it had been rolled. And it had no air conditioning in it, and they would set up air conditioning with an outside power unit that was so loud that you couldn't film when the air conditioning was on.

AR: *Sounds like a pretty classy production.*

DPC: Oh, man, they're playing games and playing games. I'm doing my best to do my best and get the hell out of there. Then it comes up to a point where my character has to sing a line or two from Walt Disney's *Song of the South* (1946). "Camptown races all day long, doo-dah, doo-dah . . . " So I asked the assistant director, who's supposed to know all this stuff, "Did you get clearance to use this song? Did you buy or rent the rights from Walt Disney to do this song?" "Well, that's none of your damned business." I said, "Wait a minute. I don't think your own company's gonna like that when Walt Disney sues your ass for infringement." He says, "That's none of your business. We'll send you home." Yeah, right. We're eight weeks into filming this thing and now he's gonna send me home? "Okay," I said. "I'll sing the song. But you wait and see what happens." So I went ahead and shot the thing.

So we get back to Hollywood, and a few weeks later I get a call from the director. "We gotta have you come back and do another song," he says. "We were unable to get the rights." And I didn't want to say I told you so, but I told you so. "What we want you to do, Don, is to go out and find something else that has no restrictions to it. Then you come back and we'll substitute that. And you do it for free." I said, "No. First of all, for me to find something that's public domain, that takes research time. And then the time for me to relearn the process and the song, that's gonna take a minimum of a week. Research and rehearsals . . . then to come in and redo it . . . You're trying to tell me you can't pay me? You're still under contract. You owe me." And now I'm thinking if I make the wrong move at this point, they can get me blacklisted or a rep will go out so bad on me that I'll probably never work again.

So the decision was, instead of flat refusing to show up for the recording session, I showed up. That took the wind out of their sails, because they'd already decided that this was the direction they were gonna go. But they couldn't when I showed up. "Well, are you ready to go to work?" I said, "Well, I'm here." They said, "Well, then let's get ready." I said, "But I'm not gonna do it. I can't unless you guys have found a song. You gotta present it to me. You got a piano player here to help me get into this thing?

I told you I couldn't go any different than that. These are the rules." So they said, "Get out! Get out, and don't ever come back!" I said, "Thank you. You've just given me my release papers. Now there's no obligation on either side. I'm out of this, and there's nothing you can say about it."

So what they did, they found a young man with approximately the same timber and dubbed in something over that particular line. That was in those days when you weren't supposed to know anything, and everybody was giving you something out of the goodness of their own hearts. This was right after the Watts riots. "Why, those negroes are erupting! And if we don't start treating them right, they might get us!" [Chuckles.] It was a combination of those things. Black people's attitude was, you owe me. Now that you recognize that, I'm gonna be super good and super pretty. God, it was so ugly.

So by the 1990s, they said: "You know, Don, we can't hire you. You talk too good." I said, "First of all, sir, don't you mean that I speak too well?" "Yes, yes, but you know how you people talk." And I said, "No, I don't. I'm from Oregon. I don't know about any dumb shit from the ghetto." And he was like, "You know how you people act." So I said, "I know what you want." So I grabbed my nuts and went, "Booga-booga-booga!"

AR: *Were you surprised by the resurgence in popularity of the blaxploitation films?*

DPC: Maybe more embarrassed than surprised. [Laughs.] The production values could have been class A, but the approach toward making the product was, you know, this is just fun and games and it'll only last for a minute. And sure enough, some jerk off came along and said, "These are exploitation! You are exploiting those poor people!" And that was it.

CHAPTER 9

Jamaa Fanaka

A photograph of filmmaker Jamaa Fanaka circa 1975.

As is the case with all types of exploitation films, the blaxploitation cycle saw its share of strange and bizarre entries. However, the strangest (and most outrageously original) of all films in the cycle is, without a doubt, Jamaa Fanaka's 1975 film *Welcome Home, Brother Charles* (also known as *Soul Vengeance*). In this one-of-a-kind oddity, Charles, a black man, is sentenced to jail, where crooked cops beat him and castrate him. Once Charles is freed, he goes after vengeance—using his large castrated penis as a means by which to exact his revenge through strangulation.

The filmmaker responsible for this outrageous film, Jamaa Fanaka, was born in Jackson, Mississippi, in 1942. He began crafting Super-8 films as a child. Fanaka later attended UCLA Film School and completed this most notorious of films while still a student there. He followed up *Welcome Home, Brother Charles* with another blaxploitation film, *Emma Mae* (1976; also known as *Black Sister's Revenge*).

Fanaka has subsequently written, produced, and directed the *Penitentiary* trilogy, as well as the film *Street Wars* (1992). At the time of this writing, Fanaka was working on a documentary entitled *Hip-Hop Hope*.

ANDREW RAUSCH: *When did you know you wanted to be a filmmaker?*

JAMAA FANAKA: When I was 12 years old, my parents gave me a Super-8 camera. So I would shoot and record the rites and passages of the family, like graduations and Christmases. Anytime there was an occasion for the family to get together—Easter or a trip to Disneyland—I'd shoot it. And it intrigued me. But I had never thought of myself as a director. As a matter of fact, I didn't even know what a director was. Then I guess around high school, I started looking at directors and looking up what they do. The first one I read up on was William Wyler, who's still my favorite director today. I loved Wyler because he could make any kind of movie, from *Ben Hur* (1959) to *Friendly Persuasion* (1956). Wyler was very, very versatile, and that impressed me. In fact, it still impresses me. But that was where I got the notion of being a filmmaker.

AR: *I find it fascinating that you made your first three features while you were still a student at UCLA. How did you do that, and what was it like to make those films within that system?*

JF: I kind of refer to those as the horse and buggy days of filmmaking; before the digital revolution. The biggest impediment to making a film back in the 1970s was having access to the means of production. Making a feature film was just so expensive. I mean, if you wanted to be a writer, all you really have to do is find a piece of paper and a pen, and you can write. If you want to be a painter, you can put together some colors and you can paint. But if you want to be a filmmaker, you've got to have some money, and plenty of it. Even if you have acquired the equipment, you have to buy the film and you have to pay to have it developed. It's very expensive.

But when I got to UCLA, I was provided with the access to the means of production. They had Eclair cameras, and they had another camera—a sturdy camera called the Filmmo—that you could throw out of a doggone plane if you wanted to and just pick it up off the ground and continue filming. [Laughs.]

My UCLA education happened during the 1970s, back in the covered wagon days when affirmative action wasn't considered by many to be a bad word. The Board of Education, Topeka, Kansas, Supreme Court decision had come about, and subsequently another decision had come about, both of which said that black people deserved equal protection under the law. Affirmative action just said, hey, you blacks have been kept down for so long, and now we're gonna try to use some type of formula in order to give you a chance to catch up. And that was how I got into UCLA—through an affirmative action UCLA outreach. So, by going to UCLA, I had cameras and sound stages and a music studio, but most importantly, we black filmmakers had each other. For instance, acclaimed filmmaker Charles Burnett was my cameraperson on my very first feature, *Welcome Home, Brother Charles*, that I made as a UCLA undergraduate. In Los Angeles, darn near every third person is an aspiring actor. So you just put an ad in *Daily Variety* announcing the roles. And I was literally overwhelmed with applicants.

Of course, I was an excellent student. Affirmative action was good because it said we'll open up the door and give you some remedial training through the junior college system so that you can catch up and compete. Nobody other than the rich and connected goes to UCLA or any other university unless they are qualified to be there. So UCLA set up a system where the chances of minority success were multiplied, because you were given access to a lot of remedial training. Affirmative action got me into the UCLA Film School, but *I* graduated *summa cum laude*, which is the highest academic honor with which you can graduate from a university. And I was an excellent student, so I would apply for competitive academic grants. I got a $10,000 grant from the American Film Institute. I got Rockefeller and Ford Foundation grants, the UCLA Chancellors Grant, and the UCLA Black Studies Center Grant. I got a whole bunch of grants with which to make my films. And the grandest foundation of all was my parents. [Laughs.] They cheerfully put their life savings into my movies. That was how I made *Welcome Home, Brother Charles* and *Emma Mae*, which was my master's thesis.

After making *Emma Mae*, I really was supposed to go on and graduate with my master's degree. But to me, graduation meant nothing, because I had nothing to graduate to. Nobody in Hollywood would return my calls. And once I had graduated, I would no longer have access to the equipment and academic grants and the mutual help of my fellow students. So I held off registering my master's thesis, *Emma Mae*, in order to keep my university status. And when you look at *Penitentiary*, which was my third film made as part of my academic curricula at UCLA, take a good look at that scene in the prison yard, and you'll see that that was shot at UCLA Film School.

AR: *Really?*

JF: Yeah. [Laughs.] The prison yard was the quadrangle between the Drama Department and UCLA Film School. I used to walk through there all the time and see those high walls and think, yeah, I could make this my yard in *Penitentiary*. And then the center control of the prison is really the director's booth on one of the soundstages at the television department. Most of *Penitentiary* was shot in a really old jail that had been shut down for years. The City of Los Angeles has kept a couple of floors open for filming. As a matter of fact, most movies or television shows you see with prison scenes are shot there at that old jail. The directors just have the set designers redesign the cell and corridors and use different camera angles and it looks like Folsom or San Quentin—wherever the storyline says you are.

So that's how I made cinema history by making those three feature films as part of my academic curricula at the university. Because of that historical feat, many of my fellow filmmakers had started calling me the "poster boy for affirmative action." But Hollywood, needless to say, had no such affirmative action. As a matter of fact, there was no action for women, black, and other minority filmmakers in Hollywood, affirmative or otherwise. Hollywood has a reputation for being liberal, but it's really one of the most reactionary and racist institutions in America. I'll give you an example of how Hollywood works. During the time of the so-called "Hollywood Ten," the Hollywood unions turned against their own members. One of the founders of the Directors Guild was a man named Herbert Biberman. He was also one of the Hollywood Ten. After refusing to testify against his fellow union member before the House Un-American Activities Committee, the DGA turned on him and expelled him. They didn't just expel him, but they also removed his name as a founding member of the Directors Guild.

Something similar happened to me after I challenged the DGA's failure to enforce the affirmative action provision of the DGA's Collective Bargaining Agreement—Article 15-201. The DGA removed my name as founder of the DGA's African American Steering Committee and brought me up on the specious charge of acting in a way that was "prejudicial to the interests of the Guild." In my so-called disciplinary hearing, the DGA suborned perjury on the part of its black "Uncle Tom" DGA members. Since perjury in a union hearing is a federal felony, I took the matter to the FBI, but they refused to investigate because of what I understood to be matters of priority. Indeed, one of the district court judges in Los Angeles,

Judge Letts, stated to me in a hearing on the matter that the authorities have absolute discretion on who and who not to prosecute. As I understood it, if I had personally witnessed my mother being killed and went to the authorities, they have absolute discretion on whether to move against the killers. Sounds crazy. It is crazy. But look it up.

Anyway, I don't know how you could *unfound* something. Even if Albert Einstein had wound up being an axe murderer, you couldn't take his name off the theory of relativity. How can you unring a bell? But 50 years later, the union apologized for its betrayal of its membership, and their apology was a big event. And at this event, Herbert Biberman was reinstated as a member of the DGA and his name was put back on the founders plaque. But guess what? He'd been dead for over 20 years! So they may say their *mea culpas*, but whenever they do, it's self-serving. As a matter of fact, I really believe the Oscars are rigged. *I really believe that.* They always talk about Price-Waterhouse, or whatever accounting firm they use now, but sooner or later they have to hand the information over to the Motion Picture Academy. It was obvious to me that everybody knew Martin Scorsese was going to win the year that he finally won the Oscar for best director. That's not to say that Scorsese didn't deserve to win, but the fact is the Academy knew he was gonna win. They set it up so that three of the top directors from the 1970s just happened to be presenting the award? Hollywood is based on fakery, but it has allowed that fakery to permeate its own institutions.

But our salvation is the computerization of the world. As I have stated many times, I have never had a computer cheat or refuse to respond to my finger because it was not the right skin color. [Laughs again.] A lot of people are excluded from Hollywood. As aforestated, anyone who is not "connected" is excluded. But it's going to change. It's got to change. And the digitization of the world shall precipitate this change. Now with the Internet, people can get a digital camera, a computer, and some editing software and he/she is Warner sans the Brothers.

During the 1970s, I utilized the wherewithal of the university to such a capacity that John Young, who then was head of the film department, said he expected to come in one day and find the school changed to Jamaa Fanaka Productions, because I was determined to make movies and nothing was going to stop me.

AR: Welcome Home, Brother Charles *is definitely a unique film. Where did the idea for that come from?*

JF: What I wanted to do was take a ridiculous albeit widely accepted myth and blow it up in a serious manner. When the black man was brought here as a slave, the white slave owners would try to intimidate their women to stay away from the black men by saying that they had sexual equipment that dangles around their kneecaps. [Chuckles.] And that myth still kind of permeates society. So I wanted to take that myth and blow it up and make it extreme in a very, very shocking and surreal way. The myth was invented by the white slave owners, but like any lie, it sometimes comes back to haunt its source. So I took a negative image and made it into a positive image by showing the ridiculousness of it.

It's just like what we call chitlins—the intestines of a hog. It's the only parts of the hog that the slave owners would throw away. But somehow our ancestors were able to take those unwanted intestines and clean them for hours and hours. And then they would cook them for hours and hours. And now it's considered a delicacy! It almost costs as much as steak. So I applied that same resourcefulness to the making of films.

Remember, every race has had slavery. There have been white slaves, there have been Asian slaves, there have been Semitic slaves, and there have been black slaves. Slavery used to be looked upon as an inevitable part of society. Just like there is a middle class, there was a slave class. So basically, in *Welcome Home, Brother Charles*, I just wanted to show how ridiculous that myth was by poking fun at it in a very surreal and shocking manner. And it definitely [laughs] shocked people.

You see, the film as it was originally edited (before it was licensed for distribution) had a scene that showed that the knife that the cop used to try to castrate Brother Charles had been contaminated when the cop had disarmed a radioactive bomb. I first conceived it to be like the films of the 1950s, where everything was blamed on radiation, like giant ants or what have you. As it stands now, we don't know whether the penis strangulation is in the mind of Brother Charles or if in reality he's strangling his tormentors with his member, because this is the thing they tried to take away from him, for purposes of vengeance.

AR: *The title blaxploitation reaches over a lot of very diverse films. What do you think the legacy of those films are today?*

JF: The term blaxploitation, to a black filmmaker, was originally a very derogatory term, because it was used in a pejorative way. We felt that the term was invented to destroy black filmmaking. Today, however, the term

blaxploitation has lost that pejorative aspect and is used as another genre. Just as one might refer to a western or a thriller, you would refer to a blaxploitation film.

AR: *Yet another example of what you were talking about—turning around something negative and making it a positive.*

JF: Right. Exactly. When I went to UCLA, I think there were about 25 black film students there. And all of them were inspired by the hope that was engendered by films like *Cotton Comes to Harlem* (1970) or *Superfly* (1972), which both had black directors. *The Mack* (1973), which also inspired us, didn't have a black director, but it still had black writers and a black cast. The director apparently listened to them. So these films gave us the confidence that we could do it, too. No longer was filmmaking a field exclusive to white people. The blaxploitation era gave us something wonderful: it gave us hope.

CHAPTER 10

Antonio Fargas

Everybody knows Antonio Fargas. Not only is he hands down one of the most recognizable faces to come out of the blaxploitation era, but he's also one of the most recognizable character actors out there. Trained at New York's famed Negro Ensemble Company, Fargas started his career while a teenager when he appeared in the 1964 film *The Cool World*. Over the next decade, he became a character actor who could be spotted in the groundbreaking cult flick *Putney Swope* (1969) and in *Shaft* (1971), *Cleopatra Jones* (1973), *Car Wash* (1976), and *Foxy Brown* (1974).

However, Fargas is not as well known for his film appearances as he is for his recurring role as Huggy Bear on the television series *Starsky and Hutch*. Born directly out of the blaxploitation characters that were appearing on the big screen, Huggy Bear represents how mainstream the genre and those characters had become. Fargas spent four years on the show, playing the all-knowing street hustler who kept Starsky and Hutch supplied with the valuable information they needed to crack their cases.

After *Starsky and Hutch* was canceled, Fargas continued to work in both film and television. During the early 1980s, he had a recurring role on the soap opera *All My Children*, and in the late 1980s and 1990s, he made guest appearances on series like *Martin* and *Living Single*. In 1988, he appeared in Keenan Ivory Wayans's spoof of the blaxploitation genre, *I'm Gonna Git You Sucka*, and all but stole the show with his platform aquarium shoes.

DAVID WALKER: *Well, we'll start off with the most basic question I've asked everybody, which is the term blaxploitation itself, what blaxploitation really was, and what do you feel about that word?*

ANTONIO FARGAS: Number one, blaxploitation, in terms of actors who were around at the time, it meant work. It meant an opportunity of empowerment from the audience's point of view, as well as the actors'. Here we were dealing in black stories, no matter how exploitative they might have been from the outside. We were up there on the screen.

My first job was a film called *The Cool World*, and I was 14 at the time. The whole idea that I could go and sit in a movie theater and look up at the screen and see myself—where I saw John Wayne and other actors and just the fledglings of Sidney Poitier—that was an empowering thing. The whole idea of an audience being able to flock to the movie theater to see black actors up on the screen kicking whitey's ass sometimes, you know, pimpin', running drugs, or whatever, was a sense of empowerment. Empowerment that we as actors got a chance to work, and empowerment that we as a black American audience was able to go to a theater and see ourselves doing things that we had never seen before. And so if we were exploited, it also gave us a chance to be empowered, as actors from earning dollars working at our trade where we were denied access before, and also as an audience to be empowered.

DW: *There was a lot of political backlash from organizations like the NAACP, CORE, and PUSH. These groups attacked a lot of the people who were involved with the films of the 1970s, calling them "race traitors" and that sort of thing.*

AF: Well, that was done to the actors who played in *Amos and Andy*. It will always be done, because you got two things going. You got social conscience and you got the need for entertainment, and I think they could work hand in hand. Actually, they did work hand in hand. Because not only did it force us to end the "black exploitation period," but it also forced us to find *Sounder* (1972); it also empowered us to find *The Color Purple* (1985). It empowered us to move on. But at the same time, it served what I call the white power structure conspiracy, where they never sat down at a table—but that whole backlash by our social groups I think played into the hands to end that period. Because they said, "Well, if you don't want to be seen doing that, then you won't be seen doing anything."

But I think that the whole idea that there was so much money to be made by our images up on the screen that it forced them to come up with other situations to be able to use us, and it ended a period—a period that I think was sort of groundbreaking, that laid the groundwork for the artist, and the actors, and even the behind-the-scenes people to be more involved in this great, great money-making industry called the film and television industry.

DW: *You have the distinction of being one of the few actors from that era who went into television. Do you think that the blaxploitation genre had an impact on television?*

AF: Oh yeah. Timing is everything, and when I first started, it was just the beginning of the 1960s and of the civil rights movement, and that period reflected on what was going on off Broadway and New York. It reflected in the beginnings of the Negro Ensemble Company. It reflected in the beginnings of *Sweet Sweetback* (1971). It reflected in the beginnings of *Putney Swope* (1969). It had to move into television, and I just came along at a time when every series seemed to need one black actor—the ethnic spot on a TV series had to be filled by somebody. My particular four years that I spent doing *Starsky and Hutch*, it just happened to be that time.

DW: *Huggy Bear was always my favorite part of* Starsky and Hutch, *yet there are people who say the character was negative.*

AF: You had groups saying that the character I played, Huggy Bear, was an informer, so he was a negative to the black community. That was a difficult thing. But my obligation as an artist is to try to create a vivid portrait of a character—of a real character. My characters, I tried to base on what I've observed, what I've seen. My main emphasis was to give the character validity as well as to give him humanity that people could believe.

DW: *You were one of several people who came out of the Negro Ensemble. Seriously trained actors. Was there ever a feeling of frustration at the types of parts that kept coming up—the drug dealers and the pimps? And then a double frustration from the black community that was saying "don't do this"?*

AF: I think part of this business is frustration. You know, the best times I had in theater—some of the best times I had in the business—have been when I was in class, when I could do the classics. The times I spent with my peers in the Negro Ensemble Company, off Broadway in New York, those were very enriching times. We didn't get a chance to express ourselves across the board of how we integrated into all aspects of life in America. And so it was a sense of frustration. And I think the characters again, we kind of knew they were short-lived. We just couldn't go on this way, but there had to be hope for the future and getting through this, getting through it and surviving. Because one thing, you can't act at home. An actor only knows he's acting—or the artistry part of his vocation—when he is up there on the stage, on the screen, on the television. That is when an artist is. So no matter how much time we spend in class, no matter how much time we sit around calling ourselves artists and wishing for things to be better, it wasn't complete until we were up there, working on our craft. My feeling was that I had to work at my craft in order to put bread on the table, in order to keep a roof over my head, in order to call myself a working actor and not someone sitting home being a wannabe. So we had to take some risks, we had to take some heat, and I think it was all worth it.

DW: *At the time, did you realize you were part of something big, something that would become a part of history?*

AF: When you are living in the moment, you're not thinking about—at least some of us, the ones who just had a passion to act—we didn't think about producing. We didn't think about Nielsen ratings and all that. That sort of came later, through people such as Melvin Van Peebles, who got into owning something—owning his own film and seeing and looking at the gross receipts and all that. That is something that we got into later. Again, I just wanted to act, work at my craft, work at different characters. If I had known how popular Huggy Bear was to that series, I would have gone back to Aaron Spelling and Leonard Goldberg and said, "Let's renegotiate." But I was very happy making a nice salary. I was very happy to drive to the studio every day and work on something that was very popular. To be able to work with Tamara Dobson, and Pam Grier, and Max Julien—I mean even Max had a sense of ownership. When you write something, you have a royalty there that's going to last forever. When you act in something, you have a royalty. But the business side is something that I think the artist needs to evolve to if he wants to be a complete artist and a complete businessman within his art.

DW: *Going back to Huggy Bear and* Starsky and Hutch, *I know so many people that love that character. Maybe it's because we all saw him every week on television. Is that something you deal with often?*

AF: The rappers come up to me and say, "I really like what you did. I really appreciate it." And they give you props for the time that you put in. I mean, that's a reward in itself and it says we did a good job and we did the best we could with the circumstances we had. Now they have greater opportunity to do the best they can with the circumstances they're presented—and become more empowered and to give work to new writers and to people in wardrobe and to assistant directors. I just think it's a great, great time, and I'm just glad I'm young enough and got some legs enough to stick around a little bit to see it get better.

DW: *You've played some interesting characters over the years. Is there any one character or one film that stands out with a special fondness?*

AF: My greatest character that I've played—that I am playing—is Antonio Fargas. The only time I'm not lying is when I'm acting. In life, when I'm

Antonio Fargas as Doodlebug Simkins in *Cleopatra Jones.*

doing Antonio Fargas, that's the time that it's the most tough. So every film and every opportunity that I get a chance to act is the most special to me. It would be very difficult to break the illusion with people, to bring them to the set or let them see how it works. I just feel that all my characters are very, very special to me. I have a particular fondness for the opportunities that I've had to deal with gender and sex in films—where I've played a number of homosexual roles. They have been, in a sense, the most challenging because they were the most challenging to the people around me: the friends, family, peers.

To have dignity as a character actor. I always said—when people said, "Well, what did you feel about the challenges of playing the same kinds of roles or being a character actor who's only stuck in one or a couple of areas?"—I don't know if anybody said that to Jimmy Cagney or Clint Eastwood, when they had credit for doing different gangster roles or so forth. I feel the same way. I feel like if I can do something really well and if they call my name when they talk about people who took chances and were able to make characters live on the screen and on television, I feel real proud of that. And I just tell young artists and young people that they really should not be bound by mores—the social consciousness—when dealing with their art. One has to take chances, and it's nice to be able to take chances and get paid and to have a legacy of film that people can look at forever and say, "You know, that actor was consistent in his portrayals and in his heart."

CHAPTER 11

Sid Haig

Movie tough guy Sid Haig was born Sidney Eddie Mosesian in Fresno, California, on July 14, 1939. As a child, Haig grew so fast that he had no coordination whatsoever. So his parents decided to enroll him in dancing classes. At age seven, he was paid to dance in a Christmas show. This led to another show, which led to another, and so on. In high school, Haig discovered acting and spent much of his time on stage. After graduating from high school, he inked a recording contract as a drummer and appeared on the T-Birds' 1958 single "Full House." But acting was his first love, so Haig enrolled in the legendary Pasadena Playhouse—an acting school whose alums also include Robert Preston, Gene Hackman, and Dustin Hoffman. After studying there for two years, Haig packed his bags and headed for Hollywood (with friend and actor Stuart Margolin of *Rockford Files* fame).

Haig's first film appearance came in Jack Hill's UCLA student film *The Host*. This role led to a productive acting career that has spanned some 40 years, with appearances in more than 50 films and 350 television shows. Among these films are the blaxploitation classics *The Big Doll House* (1971), *Black Mama, White Mama* (1972), *The Big Bird Cage* (1972), *Coffy* (1973), *Foxy Brown* (1974), and *Savage Sisters* (1974). In addition to these films, the talented actor also turned up on the blaxploitation television series *Get Christie Love!* Other notable credits on Haig's filmography include George Lucas's *THX 1138* (1971), *Diamonds Are Forever* (1971), *Jackie Brown* (1997), *Kill Bill Vol. 2* (2004), and *The Devil's Rejects* (2005).

CHRIS WATSON: *You made eight films, including* Coffy *and* Foxy Brown, *with director Jack Hill. What was Hill like to work with?*

SID HAIG: I think he's a great director. First of all, he writes almost everything he directs. So it's his story from beginning to end, his vision. I think he has a very clear vision of what the final product should be and relays that to you, not only through the words in the script, but through verbalizing. Then he gets out of the way and lets you do your job.

CW: *You once said there are three directors who could hand you a script and you'd agree to do the film without looking at it. Tell me about that.*

SH: When you trust somebody and they hand you something, you know it's not a bomb that's going to go off in your face. And Jack Hill is one of those people. Quentin Tarantino is one of those people. And Rob Zombie is one of those people. Because in taking care of the project, they're also taking care of you. They will take you to some dark places, but it's okay. I know I'm safe with those guys.

CW: *Tell me about the first time you met Pam Grier.*

SH: We met in the lobby of this apartment/hotel we were staying in when we were doing *The Big Doll House.* We were in the lobby and this incredibly gorgeous woman was standing there, and I thought, Oh, my god. She was one of those alarmingly beautiful women—particularly back then. She hasn't slipped by any means, but when she was doing her early work with Jack, it was impossible to stop looking at her. She was just very compelling. And we got along great, instantly. There was some sort of kinship there. Those were great times.

And when I did *Jackie Brown,* Quentin didn't tell Pam that I was going to be playing the judge. So when I showed up on the set, she was totally shocked. We hadn't seen one another in 27 years. And it was as if we'd just had lunch together the day before. Our relationship picked right back up where it was back then.

CW: *Did you have any idea back in the beginning that Pam would become a kind of iconic cult figure?*

SH: I knew it instantly. I knew she still had to get her acting chops, because she was very raw, but she was also very determined to become successful. She put in the work. She took classes and she explored her own personal psyche, including both her wonderful points and her inner demons. And that's what you have to do to become an actor that's worth anything. You can't hide from yourself, because wherever you are, there you are. I knew she was gonna be big from the very first time we met.

CW: *You had a real scene-stealing role in* The Big Doll House. *You had all the funniest lines. Did you have any input regarding the dialogue?*

SH: Yeah, I guess I put a piece of myself in there. I came up in the midst of the cultural upheaval, if you will. So I knew how that whole process worked, how people worked within it and survived and moved on. So the dialogue, if I added any, came from that knowledge of getting by on the street.

CW: *I think you could teach an acting class by showing your performances from* The Big Doll House *and* Coffy, *and muting the sound. Just your body language. Your roles were quite different in those films. Do you get to choose your role when working with someone like Jack Hill, or were those roles written for you?*

SH: You know, I'm presented with a script. Jack would say, "I have this, and here's the part." I read it and 99.9 percent of the time it's right on with something I would want to do. I might have suggestions in developing the character, but the role is essentially what is on the page. And then it becomes reality.

CW: *How do you prepare for such differing roles? I would imagine that's an actor's dream.*

SH: I can tell you that the only roles I've played that have not been stereotypical have been in Jack Hill films, Quentin Tarantino films, and Rob Zombie films.

I'm gonna give you an acting lesson right here. There are certain questions that you ask yourself as an actor, overall, and within the body of each scene that you do. The question that is constant throughout is "Who am I?" And that starts with a complete analysis of building, if you will, the subconscious mind of this character, taking into account his total upbringing, his environment, all of his relationships, blah, blah, blah. "Who am I? Where am I?" You have to know that. You have to have that feeling of space. If I'm doing a scene in the middle of Alaska, and I'm shooting it out in the backlot of Universal where it's 110 degrees, I have to have that sense of it being extremely cold, so I can now tell you the audience where it is that I am. "Who am I? Where am I? Where did I just come from?" Because every time you find yourself somewhere, you bring with you whatever attitudes you came from. Okay, you came here off the freeway. That carries with it a certain attitude, and you bring that with you to this table when you come. Another one is "What am I doing? What is my objective? What do I want? How am I gonna get it?" That's usually provided to you within the body of the script, but the intensity that you put behind it is all yours. In a good script, there's always someone standing in the way of your objective. So the last thing is "How am I gonna get around them?" You find a way to win, even if you know in the script you're going to lose. The audience still has to know that you're trying to win.

So there you go! [Laughs.] That's what I do.

CW: *What, if any, was Roger Corman's direct involvement on films like* The Big Doll House *or* The Big Bird Cage?

SH: For me, virtually nothing. We were half a world away, in the jungles of Manila and its surroundings. So there wasn't a presence there, and to my knowledge there weren't copious notes being sent back and forth from Roger to Jack, mainly because the dailies would be shipped by air and would take three or four days to get to LA and then processed. So by the time Roger got a chance to look at what we'd done on Monday, we'd have completed Friday's work.

CW: *How long were the shoots on the Corman projects?*

SH: Five, sometimes six weeks. Mainly because we were covering a lot of territory on location. And the facilities weren't the greatest in the world, but they got better as time went on. I remember when we were doing *The Big Doll House*, Jack had the choice to make of whether he wanted a camera dolly or a set decorator. Couldn't have both. It was financially impossible. So there's an example of the facilities not being the greatest in the world, and having to work around things. By the way, Jack chose a set decorator over a dolly. I think we wound up making a dolly. But the shoots were very interesting. It was guerrilla filmmaking at its finest. Every day, you had to invent something just to get the day's work done.

CW: *Corman has said that when he first made* The Big Doll House, *he was told there was too much violence in it. So when* The Big Bird Cage *came around, he asked Jack to tone down the violence.* The Big Bird Cage *came out and wasn't nearly the success the first film had been. Do you think this can be attributed to the difference in tone?*

SH: I think *The Big Bird Cage* had a lot of really great elements in it, but there were just too many really beautiful women. Everything was a little too sanitized. It didn't have the grit of *Doll House*. It was kind of glitzy, you know? As a matter of fact, I introduced Teda Bracci to Jack for *The Big Bird Cage*, because there were so many beautiful women. And not that Teda is ugly. She's just a comedienne; she's funny; she's out there. And he kind of agreed, and that's how she got the role. So that kind of took away that "Which girl is more beautiful? This girl or that girl?" And it now became not a story about beautiful women, but a story about this prison, about this totally rotten place.

CW: *What was your reaction when you first learned that Pam Grier and yourself would be lovers in* The Big Bird Cage, *and what was the reaction of others to that?*

SH: I thought it was natural. That became a very hot topic, because we had that scene between the bars in *The Big Doll House* where we were feeling each other up, if you will. *The Big Bird Cage* took that to the next level, which was where it had to go. As a result, she and I became this sort of bizarre hot topic. I remember I was doing *Commando Squad* (1987) with Fred Olen Ray, and I was in the office, and he said, "You're really getting popular." And I said, "What are you talking about?" Well, he had called the *Hollywood Reporter* that day to give them the cast list for his new film, and the reporter said, "Sid Haig's name came up earlier today." And Fred said, "How?" This guy had started a survey of the top 10 most popular love duos, and Pam and I were number eight on the list. I said, "Okay. That's pretty bizarre, but okay."

CW: *Did being a white actor in blaxploitation films have any effect on either your career or your personal life?*

SH: Not really. As I said before, I was very streetwise as a kid. I was pretty much a chameleon. I traveled with a lot of different circles. So it was easy for me to not be a dope and fit in with my fellow actors, even though there were cultural differences. We were able to transcend any of that stuff and just do the work.

CW: *Some white actors have said that being in those films hurt their careers and that they were embarrassed by the films.*

SH: That's such bullshit. First of all, why'd you even take the job? If you were gonna do something you couldn't be proud of, why would you do it? I have a real problem with people like that. I know a woman who was an excellent actress, but she had a problem doing nude scenes. She called me one day and said, "I've been offered a role, but there's nudity involved." I said, "So what? Do you have to have sex on camera?" And she said, "No." So I said, "What's the problem?" And she said, "Well, it's a low-budget film. If this was a big-budget film, it would be different." So I said, "In other words, you're putting a price tag on your morality?" She hasn't spoken to me since, but I was right.

You don't do things for the monetary value. If you do art, you do art for art. And to take a job you know you aren't going to be proud of is cheating. It's totally cheating. And I know there are a lot of people who were involved with the blaxploitation era that were ashamed of what it was that they did. It's like the old line, if you can't do the time, don't do the crime. It's like, what's your problem? It was work, and it was good work. Jack Hill should be held on high for giving African American actors the opportunity to work when they were not working. When we did *Coffy*, there were virtually no African American stunt people. Bob Minor, who is a great guy, had to teach people how to do stunts. There was a hell of an opportunity for a lot of people there. And they took advantage of it, at the time. But to then turn your back on that after you become "successful" is like denying your parents. This was the stuff that breathed life into your career, and now you're turning your back on it. Not cool. I lose respect for people who do that. Sorry, that's just the way it is.

CW: *Were you at all surprised by the success of* Coffy?

SH: I wasn't surprised by the success of *Coffy* because the night we had the screening—and there were probably 900 people there—they just went nuts for it. They went crazy. And this was all industry people, who are extremely critical. Industry people will pan stuff even if they think it's good. Maybe because they're not involved with the film. Whatever. I don't know why people do that, but they do. But the film was totally accepted that night, so we knew that was gonna be a success.

The largest success internationally, I believe, was *The Big Doll House*. It played in the same theater in Tokyo for six months straight, with lines every night. I thought that was pretty wild.

CW: *How did you come to be involved with Eddie Romero's* Black Mama, White Mama?

SH: I was offered the job. [Laughs.] It was a deal where I had done three pictures back to back. And we were gonna do *Black Mama, White Mama*. And because I was already there on location, AIP said, "Just stay there and we'll get the cast there and start shooting this thing. We don't want to have to bring you home and then two weeks later send you back." Okay, fine. Well, then they say, "We're having trouble determining who we want in the cast." I said, "What are you talking about?" It was totally obvious who was gonna be in the cast. Anybody that didn't think Pam Grier was gonna be in that film wasn't watching what was happening with the market. So five weeks later, they finally decided to have Pam Grier do the film. Pam and Margaret Markov, which was great because I went to school with Margaret Markov. So that was a big-time reunion with the three of us.

But that's how that whole thing came about. I was scheduled to do it right after *The Woman Hunt* (1972). And they said, "Stay and we'll do this other film." So after five weeks of them playing with their toes or whatever, they finally decided to do what everybody knew they were going to do in the first place!

CW: *What was Eddie Romero like to work with?*

SH: Eddie Romero is a great guy. He was very meticulous. Everything was very well thought out. He was a gentleman and a very funny guy. He was very generous—to the point where my money was no good. We would go out to dinner, and he'd always grab the check.

One night he says, "Let's go to dinner." I said, "Okay, on one condition: I pick up the check this time." He says, "Okay." So we went to the Manila Press Club for dinner. We finished and were getting ready to go. I said, "Let's call for the check." And Eddie said, "There is no check. I'm a member of the Press Club, and they send the bill at the end of the month." [Laughs.] I said, "You bastard!" So he got me again!

CW: *You worked on the blaxploitation television series* Get Christie Love! *What was that experience like?*

SH: I've got to say, that was a shame. I don't get involved with people's religious endeavors, but the people who were watching after the leading lady, who were in this church movement, basically killed the show. Because every time she went to do something, they said, "Well, she can't do that." Her character—an undercover cop—goes into a bar and orders a drink. Well, she can't do that. She can't drink. And it was just one thing after another. That could have been a really great series, and she could have been a big star. But all of that was killed by religious zealots getting in the way of art. You can't do that.

I'm gonna do a little preaching here, so sorry. I get people on this all the time. If someone believes in God as these religious people say they do, and

Sid Haig as Malavael in the 1974 Eddie Romero film *Savage Sisters.*

they believe God created man in his own image, then they have to take into account that God created man as a creator. And to get in the way of the creative process through your own religious beliefs is basically going against the tenets of God. So how religious are you really? Now all the religions in the world can now hate Sid Haig. But that's the way it is, folks.

CW: *In closing, what are your thoughts on the blaxploitation cycle as a whole?*

SH: The whole blaxploitation thing was kind of a double-edged sword for me. I don't like the idea of anyone getting exploited, but at the same time, through that exploitation, some people got recognition and an opportunity to move forward. So from that aspect of it, it was cool. Maybe it's just the term blaxploitation that I have mixed feelings about. But it was certainly a great time, and I did a lot of those films. It was a phenomenon that happened, that just kind of grew out of the necessity to achieve some kind of parity among the black community of actors. Now they had an opportunity, even though they were playing these stereotypical characters, to work, which is what they wanted to do. That's why I feel that it's kind of silly to put down the work that you did early on, because those films broke careers. Antonio Fargas became a regular on *Starsky and Hutch* because of what he did in *Foxy Brown*. So it was a good thing for a lot of actors.

CHAPTER 12

Gloria Hendry

Gloria Hendry was born in Winter Haven, Florida, and raised in Newark, New Jersey. She trained for a career as a legal secretary, and her first job was assistant to the legal secretary at the New York City office of the National Association for the Advancement of Colored People (NAACP). She then went to work as a model and later found work at the Playboy Club as a Playboy Bunny.

This led to her being cast as a cocktail waitress in the 1968 Sidney Poitier starrer *For Love of Ivy*. Her small role would serve as the springboard to a prolific acting career. Hendry appeared in Hal Ashby's 1970 film *The Landlord*. In 1972, she appeared in *Across 110th Street* with Yaphet Kotto, Anthony Quinn, and Antonio Fargas. This was her first foray into the blaxploitation cycle, and she would ultimately become a staple. She had turns in the genre classics *Black Caesar* (1973), *Hell up in Harlem* (1973), *Slaughter's Big Rip-Off* (1973), *Black Belt Jones* (1974), *Savage Sisters* (1974), and *Bare Knuckles* (1977).

Aside from her work in the blaxploitation cycle, Hendry is also recognized for her appearance as Bond girl Rosie Carver in the James Bond adventure *Live and Let Die* (1973). This is significant because it marked Bond's first intimate scenes with an African American woman, further demonstrating the impact that the blaxploitation films of the time were having on mainstream cinema.

ANDREW RAUSCH: *Was being an actress something you aspired to?*

GLORIA HENDRY: No. I wanted to be an attorney.

AR: *Tell me how you were discovered.*

GH: I wanted to be an activist. There was a lot of turmoil going on at that time. Lynchings. Medgar Evers was killed. A number of other people were killed. This was in the 1960s, when the riots were going on. I was working at the NAACP as a secretary to Roy Wilkins. I was living in Newark, New Jersey. And I worked there for about four years after high school. It was an office of maybe five people on 46th Street, I believe. We used to get a lot of bomb scares. It seemed like we were always getting bomb scares. It was very distressing. I would come to work with knots in my belly. We would get phone calls with insults and racial slurs. It was all very painful. And I couldn't take it anymore—especially after Martin Luther King was killed. That was *my* president. And when John F. Kennedy was killed, Robert Kennedy was killed, Malcolm X . . . it was just horrendous.

So I became a Bunny. I finally just left the NAACP and went almost directly to the Playboy Club to work. And that was a big, big, big jump, because my family is very religious. And scanty outfits were definitely a no-no. As a matter of fact, I never dressed like that, even when the miniskirts were out. I was also doing some modeling. I also entered some beauty contests, and I became Miss Essex County. Then I entered the Miss Rhinegold contest—and Rhinegold was a beer—and I think I came in second place. And Barbara McNair was one of the hostesses of the contest, and I remember talking to her about the industry.

I had always been fascinated by film. My stars were Joan Crawford, Bette Davis, and Loretta Young. I mean, you hardly ever saw *us* onscreen, right? Lena Horne, and she didn't even do that many films, you know. Dorothy Dandridge during that period of time.

So anyway, to make a long story short, as I was working at the Playboy Club, one day Daniel Mann and a casting director sat at my station. And they asked me how I would like to be in a movie, and I said, "Yeah, right." [Laughs.] So I said they had to talk to our Bunny Mother, and they said they would. Prior to that, I had been doing a number of shows at the Bunny Club. Variety shows would come, and they would say, "Can we have Gloria for our show?" So I was getting my feet wet with people coming and taking me from being a Bunny to appearing in these shows.

So when this came along, believe it or not, it was *For Love of Ivy*. That was my first union movie. Not long before that, I was still doing illustrative modeling for jewelry, perfume, underwear. There weren't many of us working at the time, but there were a few of us. There were a number of people who were ahead of me. I was the young one out there. Richard Roundtree and I modeled together a lot at that time. We were always paired up. We broke a lot of color lines modeling for things like After Dark Tuxedo. He was in my portfolio, and I was in his. And that was around the time he got *Shaft*. And he told me about it, and I thought I was gonna be his girlfriend in that movie. I was so hurt. But, of course, later I got the opportunity to be in movies at the Playboy Club. And in *For Love of Ivy*, with Sidney Poitier and Abbey Lincoln.

AR: *You were a James Bond girl in* Live and Let Die. *Was there any negative reaction from the black community regarding the interracial relationship that took place in that film?*

GH: Yes, there was. As a matter of fact, you can back that up a little bit. The friction between black actors coming from theater to features began before that. The kinds of films they were making at the time—they called them blaxploitation. Most of the artists who really believed in their art refused to do those kinds of movies. They refused to do any action movies because they had no substance, as far as they were concerned, and they had no artistry, etc. They were exploitation movies, whereas theater was respected. I didn't come from theater, so I held none of those pretensions. I came straight from home to features. [Laughs.] I went straight from commercials, which was also seen as a no-no at the time. You didn't do commercials. This was when commercials really started to boom in the late 1960s and early 1970s, and it was really a no-no for a star to do commercials.

So to then switch it up and have this racial situation, especially with James Bond, was a definite no-no. Even more so that the role of Rosie Carver was white initially, and the role of Solitaire was black initially. If you read Ian Fleming's novel, that was the way it was written. I was hired at the last minute, and so was Jane Seymour. They were in production. And if you know the Bond girls, they are normally up and running with the entire cast. But they, at the last minute, while they were shooting— something happened—and they chose me. I was very shocked that I got the part. Very shocked because I didn't meet any of the criteria: tall, voluptuous, and white. And I was totally ethnic and not very tall at all. And wore an afro! So I was shocked, to say the least. [Chuckles.]

When the film came out, at a number of different theaters in the South and other places where there was a lot of racial discrimination, they blacked my part out. And with my own family, going from a Bunny and then to being a Bond girl, it wasn't very well taken. Bond movies were not accepted. They were exploitation; they were adventure; they had no substance, as far as they were concerned.

AR: *You hit all the bases there.*

GH: Yeah, at the time. It's a wonder what time does. As time goes by, things become legendary and classic. Isn't that something? Fascinating.

AR: *We always hear about the production values of the black films of the 1970s being quite low compared to their white counterparts. Obviously the Bond films were quite lush. You made* Black Caesar *within a year of making* Live and Let Die. *How different were those two productions?*

GH: Like night and day. The studios used to have a chokehold on production. It took individuals like Ron O'Neal and Melvin Van Peebles to

An iconic photograph of Gloria Hendry
as Rosie Carver from *Live and Let Die*.

change that. We kicked off independent filmmaking. We made that a reality. And then everybody else jumped onboard, because they were able to go the studios with *Superfly* (1972) or *Sweet Sweetback* (1971) under their arm and sell their film. And the studio had to do nothing but distribute it. So independent filmmaking, I would say, was a glorious and exciting time. We would sleep on the floor, or in the grass, or in the car, in a chair. What chair? [Laughs.] You stood where you had to stand when they were lighting the sets. Everybody was one take, and that was it. They shot one from this point of view, and that point of view, and maybe this point of view, and they moved on.

Nothing was lavish. Everything was as is, and sometimes—a lot of times—the scripts were written right there on the sets! And they would give it to you, and you'd have 15 minutes to memorize your scene before you had to shoot it. And the stunts—I did all of my own stunts in those films—falling down, fighting. When my wig fell off in *Across 110th Street*, that was not something that was planned. It was off. And that fight scene was not really planned. Antonio Fargas was terrific. He just threw me. I threw him. That's how it was. Most of the time it was right there. There were no stunts.

In *Black Belt Jones*, there were no stunt people. I did my own stunts. That was when things were becoming more sophisticated, because Warner Bros. made that one. They distributed it and they produced it. So that had more high style, but it was still low budget. But not as low as Larry Cohen with *Black Caesar*. That was so low budget that we shot it in Larry Cohen's home. He had a mansion in Coldwater Canyon. We shot that in his home, and he wrote scenes as we went. He'd say, "Okay, you've got 15 minutes." [Laughs.] And this was one take. "Whatever we get, we get." And we would sleep on the sofas. This was a very exciting time. And I got hurt a couple of times. Believe me, it was very exciting.

But on the other hand, *Live and Let Die* was a $10 million film. And at that time, that was huge. It's like a $50 million movie today. At that time, that budget was just incredible to think about. We wined and dined in gowns. We stayed at the best of hotels with maids. I had chauffeurs. They made my garments. They had a chair for me everywhere I went on set. I was taken to the set in a limousine with a driver. I was absolutely pampered and spoiled rotten when I did *Live and Let Die*. It was just wonderful. Everything was high style. There was nothing low about it. They took care of you very well.

AR: *In* Black Caesar, *you have that famous scene where you fight him off. That's sort of become known as the rape scene. What was the reaction of female viewers at the time that film was released?*

GH: Shocking. I don't think a rape scene had been the thing to do at that time, except between a husband and wife. Not that kind of rape. This had never been addressed. This was something different. I don't remember another movie where they addressed a rape scene between a husband and wife prior to that. I think this was one of a kind. And even today, the kids grab that. I have the understanding that a number of young people see that scene and just . . . The film has become a classic today.

AR: Black Caesar *and* Hell up in Harlem *were both released in 1973. Did you shoot those simultaneously, or just close together?*

GH: Well, we shot *Black Caesar* in 1972, and it was released in 1973. I then did *Live and Let Die* not long after, and then I did *Black Belt Jones*. I think that's when they said, "We've got to do *Hell up in Harlem*." He said, "You're a star now, so I'm going to use it." And we did the sequel, and they came out pretty close to one another.

You know, there was only a three- or four-year period before everything shut down on these movies. All of the stars were scrambling, trying to figure out what happened. By the time 1975 hit, those films were almost extinct. And before the 1980s hit, black filmmaking was extinct.

AR: *Today there are many black actors and directors working. But had those films been allowed to continue and progress, do you think things would be even better today?*

GH: There was a political arena out there, and it was very huge. There was a religious arena going on out there; politics; communities rising up about the bad images, the prostitutes, the drugs, the cursing, the sex. They had the teachers, the mothers, the fathers—the communities rose up and they really picketed. Groups like CORE and the NAACP picketed. It was so bad. And all us actors said, "We have to crawl before we can walk. Please don't shut us down. We need time to develop our stars so we can have the money to move on and make our own productions," because this was also the beginning of independent filmmaking.

So we knew we were on a hell of a journey. We would look at the scripts and say, "This piece of crap. Let's see if we can make this work." And the audience was just starving to see *us*. All over the world, they were starving

to see us onscreen. It was just different. And the studios were in trouble. If you look back at the time, and you look at the financial pages, all the studios were in trouble. That's the reason they took these independent films and said, "Hey, we'll gamble." And when the films started making money, they said, "We don't have to spend our money anymore?" Because they still had stables of actors that they made into stars. But once independent film-making came along, they began to release them. They didn't have to spend as much money.

So yeah, I agree. I said to myself, what if the Tamara Dobsons, the Vonetta McGees, Max Juliens, Judy Pace, Gloria Hendry, Robert Hooks, Marky Bei—there were so many of us out there—if they were given the chance to continue their careers, the films would have gotten better because the audience would have demanded it. Why cut it down? It's gonna graduate. It has to. People want more. People grow up and they become more sophisticated. So don't shut it down, because eventually it will hit its apex and move on to something else.

AR: *In the past, you've stated that you have a problem with the term blax-ploitation. Instead you've referred to this era as the Black Renaissance period, which is as good a title as any. Do you want to talk about that?*

GH: Exploitation? Movies are exploitation. They are. But for some reason, they put the words black and exploitation together and brought those words to the film—to *our* film. They called the other action films with Humphrey Bogart and these other guys, they called those "B" movies. And they called us blaxploitation. It just seemed to have a bad connotation. What's up with that? When that word was first put out there, it was done without love around it. It was thrown out into the consciousness with a negative feeling by whoever initiated it. And then it continued to move on. So by the time everybody gets it, they're getting it with a negative feeling behind the phrase black exploitation. But I will not say black exploitation. This, to me, was the Black Renaissance. That, to me, takes on a much larger picture. So I believe this was the Black Renaissance. And when Spike Lee kicked it off again, that was the second renaissance. But we started it.

CHAPTER 13

Jack Hill

Jack Hill was born in Los Angeles in 1933, the son of an art director for Disney and Warner Bros. Hill studied film at UCLA, where he was classmates with Francis Ford Coppola. While at UCLA, Hill directed his first short film, *The Host*, which featured a young Sid Haig. He was given his big break in the film industry when he and Coppola were selected for internships with Roger Corman on the 1963 thriller *The Terror*, starring Boris Karloff. Corman immediately recognized potential in Hill, and as a result, the would-be director was promoted to screenwriter. Hill then wrote additional scenes for and served as second unit director on Coppola's debut film *Dementia 13* (1963).

Hill, who would ultimately be recognized as one of the greatest exploitation filmmakers of all time, soon began writing and directing his own projects for Corman. He would ultimately direct nearly 20 feature films. Among them are the blaxploitation classics *The Big Doll House* (1971), *The Big Bird Cage* (1972), *Coffy* (1973), and *Foxy Brown* (1974). These films are significant because they established Pam Grier as a true star and also because they are generally regarded as some of the best films of the blaxploitation cycle.

CHRIS WATSON: *You've said there was a lot of racism in the film industry at the time these films were being made. What was the attitude of the studios toward these films?*

JACK HILL: I can only speak for the studio I was working for, which was AIP. Well, I got a taste of it from some other people, too. The people in production at the studios had contempt for all of these movies they were making—not just for blaxploitation.

Here's a good example. After *Coffy* came out, I was talking to other companies and producers about doing films. Here I had just made a movie that was like the number 12 grosser of the year on an extremely low budget, but all people would say was, "Aw, that was a black film. That doesn't count." And I talked to a producer who was interested in making a black film, and it was kind of a mystery to him as far as what worked in black films. He said, "I know they like to laugh, and I know the picture shouldn't be too good." I did not have further conversation with him on the subject.

CW: *Did critics treat the blaxploitation films differently?*

JH: Yeah. You have to read some of the reviews of the time. One described Pam Grier as "an unsympathetic black chick." One of them said "black tart." They used that kind of language that you would never use if they were, say, Jewish. "Jewish tart." You would never say that. Not if you knew what was good for you. And the reviewers treated them as junk films.

And now those films are all analyzed by sociologists and treated by critics as classics. People are finding all kinds of messages there. I was recently interviewed by a girl who was a college professor in Birmingham in England. She teaches *Coffy* in her course on black American culture. Writing a book on the subject—that would have been absolutely unthinkable back in the 1970s.

CW: *You made several films with Roger Corman. What was Corman like as a producer?*

JH: Well, it was like a split thing. On the one hand, he would give you lots of freedom once he'd approved what you were doing. He could do this because he knew as a director himself that the way to get the best results from you was to just leave you alone. He would not interfere unless you were going completely off the rails, and then he knew he could take over himself if he needed to. So he could take chances on people. Because he knew if something went wrong, he could just step in and fix it himself. Most of the people you would work for wouldn't have that capability or that confidence. So that was what was great about it.

The bad thing about it was that he would have mood swings. Sometimes he would come in in the mornings and there was like a black cloud over his head. He would turn purple and kind of give you all kinds of wacky orders that people would just ignore. And of course, he was just terribly cheap with money. He would sign contracts that he had no intention of keeping.

But you got to make movies.

CW: *So what were some of the budgets and shooting schedules like?*

JH: Quite often Roger wouldn't even bother to have a budget. He just tried to do it as cheaply as he could. He really wasn't that interested in taking the time to make budgets. He left that to you. Basically he just wanted to make everything as cheap as possible.

CW: *Sometimes budgetary restrictions force you to make artistic choices that actually benefit the film. Did you find instances of that?*

JH: Quite often. When you don't have money to do things, you have to come up with other ideas. And sometimes you are forced to come up with ideas that are very, very good. And the good thing about Roger Corman was that he wasn't like a lot of these people who would read the script and then you'd have to have two lawyers to sign off on it if you wanted to change a single line. And that does happen. Roger quite often wouldn't even read the script. He would read the first draft and tell you to change this or that, and then he would just assume that you would do it. And then you go out and shoot. If you wanted to make up something on the spot, that would be fine with him. That's kind of rare. [Laughs.] But it certainly is a great way to work. Unfortunately you can get into the habit of working that way and then you go to work for people who don't do that. It can be very tough and make you feel very restrained.

Roger was all for getting a maximum effect with a minimum of means. So working with him was excellent training.

CW: *Were there ever any extra challenges being a white director making what is considered a black film?*

JH: No. That never occurred to me at the time at all. The unfortunate thing in regards to racism . . . at the time I started doing those pictures for AIP, the studio was very, very conscious of criticism in the media about not having black people behind the camera. But when we made *Coffy*, we searched everywhere, and there simply were no qualified black technicians available. For one thing, it was a union film. And to get into the union . . . it was very difficult to get into the union and you had to have years and years of experience. And often you had to be the son of somebody who was already in—forget the daughter; women working in the industry were almost as rare as black people. But I hope that the success of those films—with a general audience, not solely a black audience—contributed to the acceptance by audiences of black characters and black lifestyles in films. And it gradually brought black characters and black lifestyles into mainstream films. And now you rarely see a film without black or Hispanic actors in prominent roles. So if I made any contribution in making that happen, I am very pleased about it.

CW: *Pam Grier's character in* The Big Doll House *was originally written for a white woman. Is that right?*

JH: Well, it didn't specify, and if it didn't specify, then you assume that it is, so yeah. I interviewed all kinds of actresses, just people who were strong. I didn't restrict it to white or anything else. I interviewed Pam. She just came in in kind of a cattle call. I was looking for an ensemble, so I would have groups of girls come in and read in groups so I could see how they played off of each other. And the first time I saw Pam, I was really struck by the presence and authority she had, even though she hardly had any experience at all. I don't know if she'd had any training. I didn't even ask. She just struck me right off as being such a powerful personality that I felt she'd be right for the movie. And she was.

CW: *What was she like to work with from a director's standpoint?*

JH: She was great. She was thoroughly professional. She prepared very thoroughly. She was just totally professional in every way, and she learned very rapidly. Sid Haig helped her a lot as an actress. They had quite a few scenes together. So all I can say is that it was a very happy relationship all the way around.

CW: *What inspired you to cast Sid and Pam as lovers in* The Big Bird Cage?

JH: I cast them because I thought they had worked so well together in *The Big Doll House*, and basically almost stole the show. Sid, of course, was someone I had worked with almost from the very beginning. I liked to write roles for him. I just felt they were a good couple. You know, chemistry. They have chemistry.

CW: *Your films often feature women in positions of power. Is that a theme that interests you personally, or was this just by chance?*

JH: Both. It just kind of happened that way because that was the assignment. And once you get a reputation for something, that's what everyone wants you to do. But also, I enjoyed it. I was looking for something a little bit different to do. Also, I always felt that actresses loved to play those types of roles, so that kind of makes it fun for everybody involved. And as it turned out, audiences liked it also.

CW: *You once joked, "I plead guilty to racism," referring to* Coffy. *What did you mean by that?*

JH: I never said that. There's a lot of misquoting in this business. Unless it was reverse racism. A lot of people accused *Coffy* and *Foxy Brown* of being racism in reverse. I might have said something like that. [Laughs.] Because it was fun. I was never trying to send any kind of message, or make any kind of statement. Everything I did was just what I thought made a good yarn—good drama. It's been pointed out that not only are all the bad people [in these films] white, but they're also men. That's not entirely true, but people have said that. Maybe it just seems that way because the normal run of films before that were different.

The great thing about the blaxploitation movement, if I may use that term, is that . . . you see, the civil rights movement put a lot of black actors and actresses out of work. Because before that, they were playing mostly maids and servants, comic relief like Stepin Fetchit and things like that. So the studios didn't want to do that. They didn't want to put people in demeaning roles, but they didn't really know what else to do with them. So blaxploitation opened up a whole field for black actors to play in. So if someone was supposed to play a pimp, he didn't find that demeaning at all. "Can you play a pimp?" "Boy, can I play a pimp." That was the attitude. Whether they thought it was demeaning at that time, I don't know. But they certainly never indicated that to me. Maybe in hindsight they might look back and feel that way, but it was a way to get started. They were really happy to have those roles at the time. Especially Robert DoQui, who played King George in *Coffy*. He told me he was so happy. For years after that, he said people would come up to him on the street and say, "Hey, King George!" He was famous for playing a pimp, and he loved it. Because it was a good role. It had a lot of size to it.

CW: *You once observed that most black actors who were involved with these films look upon them with great fondness, yet many of the white actors now look upon them with disdain. What are your thoughts on this?*

JH: Who can figure actors? Actors were very, very happy to get the job at the time. Then suddenly they change their minds after a few years, especially if they got successful with something else. That was the reaction in those days. But after 30 years—now that the pictures are acclaimed as classics and people like you are interviewing people like us—they suddenly change their feelings about it. Like Peter Brown, who was very happy to get the job in *Foxy Brown* at the time. I saw him a couple years later, and he didn't remember who I was, and he referred to the film in some really, really demeaning way. And then 20 years after that, I ran into him at a convention where he was signing autographs on a picture of him and Pam Grier. And it turned out that that was what he was best known for. So he changed his feeling. Like I said, who can figure actors?

CW: Foxy Brown *was originally supposed to be a sequel to* Coffy, *and was even initially titled* Burn, Coffy, Burn. *What factors led to this being changed?*

JH: The studio sales department declared that they didn't want any more sequels, and somebody in that department came up with the title *Foxy Brown*. And a star was born! I think it was a mistake. I think we could have had a franchise. And the head of production, Larry Gordon, who was al-

ways very supportive of me, felt that way, too. But the sales department had the last word in cases like that. I think it was stupid. At least I thought it was stupid at the time. But as it turns out, *Foxy Brown*—maybe it's the title, which is so over the top—has become the more popular film. I suspect that's the reason for its popularity. [Laughs.]

CW: *Which of these films is your favorite?*

JH: I don't really have any favorites. I think that *Coffy* is, in many ways, just a really, really good piece of work. I'm really proud of it. Unfortunately, it had to be done on such a low budget. I think it could have been really good had we had more money to spend. It was a good script and a good story. We had a great cast, and it was just well done in spite of its handicaps and limitations. And that's the one that people who study these things tend to find the most interesting, as well. And I can tell you that the audience reaction to it was almost frightening. People would stand up and yell at the screen. It was quite thrilling. [Laughs.]

CW: *A projectionist told me that the theaters had to have security when they would show blaxploitation movies. He said that if the audience saw whites or Mexicans working in the theater, they would throw stuff at them.*

JH: I never heard that. I did hear one time that a lot of theaters stopped showing the films because there was too much damage to the theaters. [Chuckles.] I never saw any of that at any of the screenings I went to. That's catharsis, I think they call it. There was a real participation by the audience in the action on screen. They talked back to the actors and yelled at the characters on the screen.

I don't know how it got started, but it may have been a custom that began in the black churches, where they respond to the person who's giving the sermon. That could be where they got into that kind of habit. But I did see that with *The Big Doll House*, too, and that was not a primarily black audience. People talked back to the characters. That's a phenomenon. One critic mentioned in his review when *Coffy* was playing in the drive-in theaters that people would honk their horns at various places in the film. I never saw that happen, but it makes sense.

CW: *You've said that you wrote some stuff in* Foxy Brown *simply to spite AIP. Is that right?*

JH: I would hate to use the word spite. Well, you could use that word. [Laughs.] I didn't like the way they were treating me. I did put some things in it because of the studio. I think maybe because *Coffy* was such a big hit, they were afraid I was gonna run wild or something. They really tightened up on things. So basically I got so disgusted with it that I threw things in with the idea that they would say no, that was going too far. [Chuckles.] But they bought it.

You know, it was only at the last minute that they invited me back to make a sequel. There were reasons they didn't want to work with me. Actually, what happened was that they had invited me to a screening of a movie they were very proud of. And I walked out of it, very foolishly. And they swore I would never work there again. But with *Coffy*, which was one of the biggest hits they ever had, I think Sam Arkoff overruled the other guys. But they invited me back to do the sequel at the very last minute, so to speak. So I didn't have the time to work out the sequel as well as I had with *Coffy*. I just tried to throw in everything over the top and have fun with it.

CW: *Are you ever surprised by the impact that these films have had on popular culture?*

JH: Yeah. At the time, most of the films I made were expected to play one summer—maybe two summers if they were a hit—and then be forgotten. It was only after the advent of home video and the revival of the films that the whole attitude towards them changed. Yeah, I was surprised. I mean, you never set out to make a cult movie. There was no such thing at that time. Basically I was given an assignment to do a certain type of movie, and I just did the best I could with it. I never treated any of my assignments lightly. I always tried to do something better than what anyone would expect. And most of the films were commercially successful at the time, and some of them were major hits. But the idea of them being studied by sociologists 20 years later was certainly never in anyone's mind. [Laughs.]

CW: *To what would you credit the resurgence of these films?*

JH: I think people today are able to find things in the films that they are missing in films today. Everything today is made from fear. Everything is just a clone of something else. At least until recently, when there's been a kind of revival in independent filmmaking, where people can go out with some videotape and make their own film. But the mainstream industry is just trying to play it safe. So these films have a certain kind of vigor and insolence, which is maybe a characteristic of my films. Impudence. People find them very refreshing and exciting.

CHAPTER 14

Jim Kelly

A still of Jim Kelly from the film *Golden Needles*.

In 1973, film audiences around the world were captivated by a chop socky picture called *Enter the Dragon*. Considered by many to be the quintessential film of the martial arts genre, *Enter the Dragon* helped to catapult its star, Bruce Lee, to international fame. The film also brought attention to Lee's costar, a relative newcomer to the world of film, Jim Kelly. Kelly, an international middleweight karate champion who sported a funky afro, captivated audiences with his cool and confident screen persona. He exuded an onscreen charisma that rivaled that of Lee himself. It was instantly apparent to everyone who saw the film that this cocksure young actor was destined to become a superstar. Following the untimely death of Bruce Lee, as producers scrambled to find the next king of martial arts, they didn't have to look far, since audiences had already fallen in love with Jim Kelly.

Kelly soon introduced the world to a new hybrid: martial arts–influenced blaxploitation films. Kelly's blaxploitation filmography includes *Black Belt Jones* (1974), *Three the Hard Way* (1974), *Golden Needles* (1974), *Take a Hard Ride* (1975), *Hot Potato* (1976), *Black Samurai* (1977), and *The Tattoo Connection* (1978).

DAVID WALKER: *To many, your meteoric rise to success seemed to happen overnight.*

JIM KELLY: I think some people might think that Jim Kelly just became a star overnight; he was just all of a sudden in the right place at the right time. Somewhat I was in the right place at the right time, but there's more background to it than that. First of all, the sacrifice. When you have a goal in life, usually you have to make an incredible sacrifice. I don't care if it's a football player, basketball player, or the corporate world. Whatever it may be, there's usually a lot of sacrifice. I refused to let people tell me I couldn't become an actor. And a lot of people tried to tell me that. I had a good job working in a shoe store here in Los Angeles. And they offered me a job in San Francisco to become a manager of one of their most elaborate stores. I told the guy, "Look, man, I can't do that." He said, "Are you crazy? You must be crazy. You mean to tell me that you're going to turn this job down in San Francisco because you want to pursue an acting career?" I said, "Yeah." So I didn't take the job, and I ended up quitting the shoe store job. I ended up going down to Manpower at 5:30 in the morning with all the hobos to get labor jobs. I would go out digging ditches somewhere just so I would have free time to pursue my karate, train, fight, and prepare for the world championship. I could have been in an air-conditioned shoe store selling shoes, but that's not what I wanted to do.

The main thing is to set your goal, and don't let anyone keep you from pursuing it. Lay out your game plan and go for it, no matter what anyone else says.

DW: *When I was a kid,* Enter the Dragon *was one of my favorite movies. My cousin Sean and I wanted to be Jim Kelly. Every kid I knew wanted to be you. Who did you want to be? Who were some of your heroes?*

JK: When I was growing up, in junior high school and elementary school, at the time, my hero was Willie Mays. He's actually my second cousin, but I didn't know it at the time. When I got into high school and started playing sports, Jim Brown was my hero. Jim Brown was, to me, like the man. He motivated me because I was heavy into football. After that, Muhammad Ali was my hero. He was very inspirational to me, in the ring and outside the ring. I still have people that I am inspired by even today.

DW: *You had a pretty promising career in football, but you dropped out of college and gave up on your dreams of a pro career. What happened?*

JK: After I graduated from high school, I had over 100 football scholarships. I chose the University of Louisville in Louisville, Kentucky. So I went there and played football. The reason I quit school there was a racial thing. Maybe that was a big mistake in my life, to quit because of that. One of my best buddies on the football team was a guy named Charlie Johnson, a black guy from Alabama. One afternoon in the practice session, the head coach called him a nigger. It kind of upset me, and I said, "Hey, why am I putting out my blood, sweat, and tears for this coach if he's going to go out and call a black guy a nigger?" So I left the school.

I started studying harder in martial arts, and I started setting goals. And then one day, it came to me that I really had to decide what I wanted to do in life. I decided that I wanted to become an actor, because I felt that for me to be happy and satisfied, since I wasn't going to play professional football, acting would make me happy. Acting would give me everything I needed out of life to be successful. And those things were to make a lot of money, become very popular, and be very influential and motivational to young black kids.

I went to the World Karate Championships in 1970 to watch. And I told my buddies, "Look, I'm going to come back here next year and I'm going to be the world middleweight karate champion." And they said, "No, Jim, you can't do that that fast." I said, "Yeah, I *am* going to do that." I went home that night and laid out my game plan. My goal was to become International Middleweight Karate Champion of 1971, and to use that goal to pyramid into becoming an actor.

DW: *Let's talk about the* Melinda *experience.*

JK: The producers talked to me and said, "We want you to teach the star [Calvin Lockhart] karate, but come back tomorrow. We want to talk to you again." So I went back the next day, and they told me they were going to give me a costarring role in the movie. I said, "Oh yeah, a costarring role in the movie? Okay." Remember now, I don't know one thing about the acting business at this point. I knew nothing. They said, "Don't worry. The director will talk you through it. You have the look, the look we're looking for."

I thought I was terrible. I thought I looked good on screen, I had the presence, but my acting skills were terrible.

DW: *So you did* Melinda. *Meanwhile you're now operating your own karate school and waiting for the next film. What happened next?*

JK: All of a sudden one day, my agent, Nora Sanders, called me at my karate studio at around five o'clock in the afternoon. She said, "Jim, they're casting a film out at Warner Bros., a fight film. Now you won't get the part, but I want you to go out there and meet the producers. They already have the guy they want, but they're having a little problem negotiating the contracts. They're looking at other people, but they'll take him eventually. This is just an opportunity for you to meet the producers."

I met with Fred Weintraub and Paul Heller, the producers of *Enter the Dragon*. They asked, "Do you know karate?" I said, "Yeah." They said, "Well show us a few moves." So I started jumping around, moving around, kicking all over the place. They said, "Take this script and look at the part of Williams, blah, blah, blah. Check it out, come back in five minutes, and let us know what you think." When I came back in, they asked me what I thought. I said, "Okay, it's pretty good. I like that part." They said, "Okay, you've got the part. When can you leave for Hong Kong?"

DW: *What was it like working on* Enter the Dragon*? What was it like working with Bruce Lee?*

JK: I was in Hong Kong for three months with *Enter the Dragon*. That was an experience. Not only was Hong Kong an experience, it was an incredible experience working with Bruce Lee. Now, in case all my fans out there don't know, I wasn't supposed to get killed in that movie. John Saxon was supposed to get killed. At that time, that was my second film, and John Saxon's agent said, "Look, if you want John for *Enter the Dragon*, Jim has to get killed. Not John." So, of course, I got killed. I only had two films to my credit.

When I look at *Enter the Dragon*, I see good parts and bad parts of it. The good part was that it gave me a lot of exposure. It opened up incredible doors as far as my next move in the film business. What I really didn't like about the film was that I didn't really get the chance to do my thing. It was Bruce Lee's film, and I love Bruce Lee. As far as I'm concerned, he's the greatest martial artist that ever lived. But I didn't get a chance to show all those people who saw that film my true talent.

DW: *You said you thought Bruce was the greatest martial artist who ever lived, but man, he went through some shit to get there.*

JK: Bruce caught hell trying to get to the position he was at. They really didn't want Bruce to have that. Bruce should have been a superstar even before *Enter the Dragon*. But he wasn't because he was Chinese. The TV series *Kung Fu* was originally written for Bruce Lee. That was written for him. The guy wrote the screenplay for him. The studio said no, because we can't have a Chinese guy as an action hero in America. So Bruce was down and out. He went to Hong Kong to start making movies over there, because he couldn't get work here. So he left, and the rest is history. He faced an incredible amount of racism in this country.

DW: *Do you have any theories about what happened to him?*

JK: I don't know what happened to Bruce Lee. I've heard so many stories. I really don't know. But I know one thing: before whatever happened happened, I was supposed to do another film with him. Before I left Hong Kong, Bruce and I talked, and he said, "Look, Jim, we're going to do another film. Will you come back to Hong Kong and star in my next film with me?" That's the way we left it. The next thing I knew, well, you know what happened. That could have been one hell of an experience, to do a film with Bruce and be one of the stars in the film with him. At least I had the chance to work with him, meet him, and learn a lot from him.

DW: *Once you were done filming* Enter the Dragon, *things just sort of exploded for you.*

JK: When I finally got back to Los Angeles, my agent called. She said, "Jim, we've got to go to Warner Bros." The deal was that Warner Bros. wanted to talk to me about a three-picture deal, to star in three pictures for them, plus an option for a television series. *Black Belt Jones* was the first one; *Golden Needles* was the second one; *Hot Potato* the third one.

Black Belt Jones was an incredible experience. It was my first film where I was the star. I'm the man. Gloria Hendry was in that, a very beautiful lady. I enjoyed working with her. But it was me; I was the thing that had to make that thing work. And that film made a lot of money; it made close to $20 million. *Black Belt Jones*—made for maybe $400,000—made over $20 million at the box office. I've never made a film that didn't make money, or very good money. I made a film for like $100,000. A $100,000 budget, and that film, *Black Samurai*, made something like $15 million. I always thought that if your films made money, that's what it's all about.

Then I did *Golden Needles* with Joe Don Baker, Elizabeth Ashley, and Burgess Meredith. That was a successful film, too. Then I did *Hot Potato*, by myself again. Oscar Williams wrote and directed that. We shot that in

Thailand. A movie shot for $300,000 maybe. It made something like $2.5 million in New York in one week. Over $2 million. So now here's a film that's made for $300,000 . . . $2 million in New York alone. Like I said before, I made a lot of money for these people. And at this time, I wasn't getting any kind of percentages.

DW: *After you finished up with your three-picture deal, you moved on to some independent films.* Three the Hard Way *teamed you up with two of the leading actors of that time, Fred Williamson and Jim Brown, who was one of your heroes. What was it like working with Jim Brown?*

JK: It was an incredible experience working with Jim. At that time, when I worked with him in *Three the Hard Way*, he had already done so many action films. I guess you might say Jim was the first real black action hero, from the films he had done before I worked with him. I can't think of anybody in those type of action films before Jim. Sidney [Poitier], of course, has always been a great dramatic actor, but when you come to the hardcore black action film, Jim was the man.

It was like working with Bruce. I learned so much from working with Bruce Lee. When I worked with Jim Brown, I learned different things from him. As a matter of fact, we were in the Canary Islands—me, Fred, and Jim—and Jim and I were talking one day on the set, and he said something interesting that has still stuck with me today. He said, "In life, and in this business especially, never let them kill your spirit. They might take your money, they might take your car, they might take your house, but never let them kill your spirit." And I remember that, and that's very true. I tell people that myself today. People might take your money, your car, they might take your wife, your girlfriend, they might do a lot of things. But never let anyone take your spirit. Once that happens, everything's over with.

DW: *The films that you, Fred, and Jim were in were all part of what has become known as blaxploitation. What are your feelings about that word?*

JK: Black exploitation to me, I don't really know how to define that. What about white exploitation? I don't even deal with it.

DW: *There definitely is a double standard in the industry. What do you think fuels all the inequities that are so prevalent in the film business?*

JK: Racism. Power. Money. Images. And when I say images, I mean that in the industry, there's a fear of projecting black males in the real strong,

ENTER
JIM
"DRAGON"
KELLY

HE CLOBBERS THE MOB AS

BLACK BELT
JONES

A WEINTRAUB-HELLER Production
"BLACK BELT JONES" starring JIM KELLY · GLORIA HENDRY · Screenplay by OSCAR WILLIAMS · Produced by FRED WEINTRAUB and
PAUL HELLER · Directed by ROBERT CLOUSE

R **RESTRICTED** From Warner Bros. ⓦ A Warner Communications Company

positive image. The action hero. There's a fear to project black males in those positions. It's amazing to me.

The controlling people in Hollywood—the power people—fear black males making too much money or becoming too strong and too powerful. You can say the bottom line is money, but it's not true. You tell people that, and they say you're crazy; all that matters is if your film makes money. No, the image is very important—what image you put out there, what image you project. Sometimes in Hollywood, they would prefer to not make money than to project a certain image. That's just the way it is. It's amazing. I know that's hard for some people to believe, but I know it's true.

I don't know what myself, as a black man, and all the other black men in this society have done throughout history to justify that fear. The fear doesn't matter if it's in the film industry or the corporate world. It's just the way it is in this country—in America.

We have incredible athletes: basketball players, football players, boxing champions. Why is it, in an industry like Hollywood, we can't even have an action hero? It's like when they made the movie *Rocky* (1976). To me, Rocky was like the great white hope. In the boxing world, there hasn't been a white champion since Rocky Marciano; but in Hollywood, they created *Rocky*, and all of a sudden he's bigger than Muhammad Ali. You ask a little kid, "Who's the greatest boxer in the world?" And they say, "Rocky." *Rocky*? Hollywood made *Rocky*. They couldn't get that image in the real ring, they don't even have a great white hope, so they created it in Hollywood.

DW: *That's very true. I'd never really thought of it like that. I know I always found it amusing how Stallone was able to go back and win the Vietnam War in the Rambo films. I guess it's sort of the same thing.*

Let's change the subject and talk about some of the political backlash that black action films of the 1970s faced.

JK: Sometimes we're our own worst enemies. Our biggest problem in society is racism, but after that it's us. It's blacks against blacks, our jealousy of each other. We're fighting each other all the time. We hate to see one of us get ahead, and that's one of our biggest problems. I don't know for a fact that such organizations as the NAACP went to the studios and caused a lot of problems, as far as black action films are concerned—that they were too violent. I don't know if it's true or not. I heard that, and I wouldn't doubt it.

DW: *All that protesting helped in some ways to end that whole era of films.*

JK: Jim Brown, Fred Williamson, and myself, we were the last of the black action heroes in Hollywood. And that's sad to say. Even the guys today that are doing action films—I don't consider them to be action heroes. There are some incredible dramatic actors. Denzel Washington, Wesley Snipes, very good actors, but they aren't action heroes. Like I said, Jim, Fred, and I were the last, and the reason again: the fear of projecting a black male in those positions. Let's just take, for example, some white action heroes. Let's take this guy by the name of Chuck Norris. My personal opinion, and I know Chuck, I remember when he was fighting in karate tournaments, he was a karate champion. But to me, he was never able to transmute that onto the screen. You take Chuck Norris, and just change the color of his skin, he'd be lucky to get a job in Hollywood as an extra. I'm serious. Just change the color of his skin to black, and I guarantee he'd have trouble getting a job as an extra. But his skin is not black; it's white. And they pushed and pushed and made him a star. I'm just using him as an example. I could go on. At least Van Damme, now he has some screen presence, some charisma. Chuck Norris doesn't even have that.

DW: *It's been over 20 years since you did your thing on film. Have you seen any significant changes over the years?*

JK: It's like the gap never closes. It never closes. We see certain types of actors working, but it really hasn't changed much. We have what Hollywood is safe with. They're safe with comedy. Hey, I love Eddie Murphy. He's an incredible comedian, and he should make millions and millions of dollars off what he does well. But we do more than that. We have other actors, we have other people that can do other things besides comedy and things that are safe in Hollywood. You're okay as long as you project a certain image on the screen, but after you go past a certain level, "Hey, wait a minute. We can't do that." And it doesn't matter who you are. I don't care if you're Sidney Poitier. I don't care if you're Spike Lee. Spike Lee can only do certain things. That's it. They're going to control the situation.

DW: *Despite the fact that you haven't done a film since the early 1980s, you still have a fan base.*

JK: I have worldwide fans. I have fans of all nationalities, all colors: black, white, yellow. I think that's incredible. Even with all the racism in the world today, I still have fans of all nationalities and races. I get fan mail from all over—Europe, Asia. As a matter of fact, I got mail from white, blue-eyed, blonde South African females. I was in England a few years ago, doing a personal appearance in London, and people stood in line outside in the rain for over two hours just to get an autograph from me. I thought that was amazing. And in that line, maybe there was one or two blacks. It was all white. My market is incredible as far as crossover is concerned. My fans draw from all nationalities, but I can't get any quality scripts.

DW: *I've heard that you've turned down roles in films like* I'm Gonna Git You Sucka *(1988) and* The Last Dragon *(1985). Do you get offered a lot of work?*

JK: I turn down three films a year. I turn down a million dollars a year. Because I refuse to do what they offer me, even though they're starring roles. They're leads. But the scripts are so bad, or the image they want me to project as a black male I won't do. It bothers me a little bit, but I'm comfortable with myself. I'm happy with what I've done so far, with the people that I've touched and motivated in the world. I've had star athletes come up to me and say, "Jim, when I was a kid, you were my hero. You motivated me." That really makes me feel good. When you have a guy like Marcus Allen, or Lee Haney, the greatest bodybuilder in the world, tell you that when they were growing up you were the man, that feels good. I still have parents that say, "Jim, you know, you've got to do more movies. You've motivated my kids so much to be successful in life." When I see that, I'm happy. That's more important to me than having a million dollars in my pocket (although I'd like to have a million dollars in my pocket, too). I've experienced a lot of things. I've met a lot of great people. I'm pretty happy with myself.

CHAPTER 15

William Marshall

Like many actors with exceptional talents and abilities, William Marshall is seldom remembered for his vast contributions to the world of live theater; rather, he is remembered for one role in particular. Trained as a classical Shakespearian actor, Marshall is best remembered for his role as the supernatural soul brother Blacula. Far from the crowning achievement in a film career that included *Othello* (1981), the films *Blacula* (1972) and *Scream, Blacula, Scream* (1973) would nonetheless serve to secure a space for Marshall in the chapters of American pop history.

After a stint in the military in World War II, Marshall discovered acting. His film career began in the 1950s with such films as *Demetrius and the Gladiators* (1954) and *Lydia Bailey* (1952). Unlike Woody Strode, whose acting range was limited, Marshall found himself in some ways to be the heir apparent to Paul Robeson. His dignified speaking voice and regal manner made him a welcome addition to any of the many films and television series in which he appeared. One of his more significant television roles was his guest appearance on *Star Trek* as Dr. Richard Daystrum. (As any true *Trek* fan knows, Daystrum was the inventor of the original computers used on all Star Fleet ships, and after whom the Daystrum Institute is named.)

Although the *Blacula* films were among the few films that featured Marshall in the lead, he continued to work in the medium through the 1990s. He also managed to capture the hearts of a whole new generation as the Cartoon King on the Saturday morning show *Pee Wee's Playhouse*. Sadly, William Marshall passed away on June 11, 2003, due to complications from Alzheimer's.

DAVID WALKER: *What got you out of your hometown of Gary, Indiana, and into acting?*

WILLIAM MARSHALL: My mother felt that certainly Gary was not the place for me. It had infinitely marvelous groupings of those who were enjoying working in the steel mills, which she felt I didn't seem to enjoy very much. Then Ira, her sister, said, "Get him out of Gary. He's done with the war. Let him be done with the steel mills of Gary." That's how I happened to arrive, on one of those big Greyhounds, here in California.

DW: *You were part of a very interesting time in the history of American film. It was a time that has come to be known as blaxploitation. Do you have any feelings about that term, or what it may mean?*

WM: I'm not really sure what it meant beyond there being an incredibly large audience that has come into existence, because they are seeing aspects of themselves that are anything but demeaning. Quite the contrary. They're seeing aspects of themselves that made them proud. Prince Blacula.

DW: *You've had an impressive career that includes live theater, film, and television. But of all the characters and projects you've done, it seems* Blacula *is the most well known.*

WM: *Blacula* was a very enjoyable experience as an actor, and as an African American actor in particular. There seemed to have been a tremendous amount of interest. Not seemed; there was. Particularly where black youth were concerned. They had something to identify with. It probably wasn't the most exciting or the best thing. I don't know. It's difficult to be objective about it.

DW: *Was it a fun project to be involved with?*

WM: I did enjoy doing the film, because I was able to make certain contributions that they hadn't considered in terms of the storyline—aspects that would be more interesting to audiences than what they, the producers, had conceived.

DW: *I've heard rumors over the years about certain contributions you made to the film. What were they?*

WM: The character I portrayed had an African background. That was what I came up with. The producers were not particularly interested in any concept of African people at that time, or with that aura surrounding the figure. I rather insisted. I felt that this would be the selling point, particularly for young African American men and women.

DW: *So it was your idea to make Blacula an African prince. Did you bring any other creative ideas to the film?*

WM: He wanted to appeal to monied people, to putting an end to the further enslavement of African people. This was my concept. And the producers fought that of course, because it was a little too political for them, and not the way they wanted to go. But I kept pushing the issue. I said, "There's no other way to go. We've been going down all the while. Now we're trying to raise up and demonstrate the measure of self-respect we have as a people, and that's growing, and there are certain things that can encourage this kind of thing. That's primarily why I'm interested in the film. They wanted me to do a film that when I talked with them about it, and heard what they were saying, had nothing that was meaningful to me and mine.

DW: *So you feel that part of the reason* Blacula *and so many of the other films of that era were so popular was because we were starved for images of ourselves on screen?*

WM: I was one of them. What I suggested to the producers, after having met them, was that it's important that these people in particular have a right to see a demonstration of themselves in a very positive way. We've had a tutored experience in that area, our young people in particular. Again, that's what they, the producers, were afraid of. Don't be afraid of it. It's the thing that's going to make the film. It's really going to make the film. They weren't sure. How could I know? After all, I'm only a negro.

William Marshall as the vampire Prince Mamuwalde in *Blacula.*

DW: *Obviously, though, you were right. I always loved the fact that Blacula, or Mamuwalde, was an African prince. And I think you're right: that's what appealed to the audiences at the time.*

WM: I think it proved itself to be just what I thought it would be. Something they enjoyed, to the extent that they wouldn't leave the theater. I would hear the candy vendors complaining about the fact that that's all they did, was buy candy and ice cream, of course, and sit in the theaters all day long. I thought that was something very positive, but the businessman behind the candy counter didn't think it was very good, because he wasn't making enough money that way.

DW: *The producers were worried that people wouldn't want to see the movie because of what you wanted to put up on the screen, but it was the reason people kept watching the movie over and over again.*

WM: They saw something they were responding to. They saw something. They saw a man walking straight, who happened to be a black man. And he was called a prince and all that. And we've never been that fortunate to have ourselves or our people being thought of in this light. And this again is why they stayed in the theaters all day long. A brand new, rich, wonderful, American experience.

DW: *Looking back, did you think that* Blacula *and other films of that era would have the impact that they had?*

WM: Yes, I did think that it would have a long-lasting appeal. That is what stimulated me to a great extent in terms of our black youth, in particular, responding to black actors and actresses in this film and the others who were walking a dignified walk, talking an interesting talk and point of view about where we were at that time as a people—what we were thought of as being.

DW: *It isn't the easiest thing in the world to help change the way blacks are viewed by themselves and by others.*

WM: I love and respect humankind. I love and respect in particular black humankind. I know our history. And I know how damnable it appears to be, this history that we have. We've been damned by those who have kidnapped our bodies from Africa and dragged them here. It's called slavery.

DW: *You've said that you felt there was a need for more positive images of African Americans. Is there a responsibility to create those images?*

WM: There has to be. And that has to be the case for all of us. For those who didn't get the opportunity to somehow find a limb to pull themselves up. We have to show who we are and what we are about as a people. We have to let black folks out there know that we have pride. We have dignity. We are humans; very special humans. We haven't kidnapped anybody.

DW: *Any parting words of wisdom to share or inspire?*

WM: We have to activate our dreams. And if we don't, it's not a dream and not a promise of anything but a repetition that we've experienced over the years of disdain.

CHAPTER 16

Rudy Ray Moore

Rudy Ray Moore is a legend. He began working as a stand-up comedian in the 1950s after he was drafted into the army. After leaving the service, Moore began performing on the "chitlin' circuit"—second-rate clubs that catered to black audiences. Moore, along with fellow comic Redd Foxx, quickly earned a reputation and helped to usher in the age of the "adults only" comedy that was pioneered by Lenny Bruce in the 1960s.

But Rudy Ray Moore is known for more than just his foul-mouthed sex jokes; he is also known as the Godfather of Rap. Delivering many of his comedy routines in rhyme, Moore is considered by many to be one of the first rappers. His early comedic raps influenced an entire generation of future rappers like Ice-T and the late Eazy E, who would refer to him on their albums and occasionally even sample parts of his records. During the 1970s, Moore formed his own label, Comedian International Enterprises, and released the first of nearly 20 albums. His discography includes the classics *This Pussy Belongs to Me* and *Dolemite for President*. During this period, Moore was inspired by the tall tales told to him by a wino named Rico; these tales would serve as the basis for his character Dolemite.

In 1975, Moore used his own money to produce his first film, *Dolemite*, which was directed by D'Urville Martin. The outrageous, crude, amateurish, and just plain bad film became a cult hit. It also earned enough at the box office to warrant three more films: *The Human Tornado* (1976), *Petey Wheatstraw: The Devil's Son-in-Law* (1977), and *Disco Godfather* (1980). Moore's guerrilla style of filmmaking and marketing, as well as his success with the urban market, made him the 1970s equivalent to black film pioneers Oscar Micheaux and Spenser Williams.

Although he was often dismissed by highbrow film critics, Moore's contributions to the history of black cinema are undeniable. After an impressive career spanning some six decades, Moore passed away on October 19, 2008, at the age of 81.

DAVID WALKER: *Just in case there is someone out there who doesn't know who you are—someone who's been living under a rock—tell me a little bit about yourself and how you got started.*

RUDY RAY MOORE: I was doing stand-up comedy, and I made records. And I made a record called *Dolemite*. I decided to make it a screenplay and put it on the screen. And as a result, when the movie came out, people said, "Is Dolemite as bad on the screen as he is on the album? If he is, we gotta go and see it." People came out in droves. That's how it all started, after I made the record. People made so much fun of me for doing that. And when I made the record, I carried it to the distributor. And they asked me, "Rudy, what do you expect us to do with this piece of shit?" I said, "Sell it." And they said, "Man, we can't do nothing with this. You've gone mad." Two days later, he called me back and said, "Rudy, bring me a thousand of those albums. I'm so sorry. I didn't know what you had. I wish you the very best." I said, "The very best I don't need. All I need is the money. Just give me the money for the record."

That's how it all started, and my career has blossomed because there's a new generation that's come along that's into me as much as they were 20-odd years ago. Big Daddy Kane, the late great Eazy E, Eric B and Rakim, Dr. Dre, Snoop Doggy Dogg—all of those people idolize me—and they sample my records and use them in their records, and it's given me a big name today. I go in person and draw lines of people—auditoriums and nightclubs full of people. I take my hat off to the young rappers today, because they are responsible for the Godfather's new life in show business.

DW: *Did you ever think you would become the legend that you are? This great influence on generations of people?*

RRM: No. Honest to God, I didn't. I really did not think the stuff I did 25 years ago would be living on the market today and doing as great as it is doing.

DW: *How did you get into the film business?*

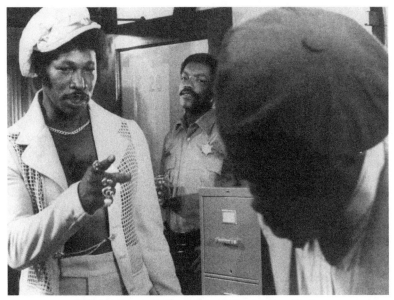

Rudy Ray Moore laying it down in *The Monkey Hustle*.

RRM: I was making party records and I created this character named Dolemite. Naturally I felt that if I could turn Dolemite into a screenplay, I could get a piece of the rock. When I say the rock, I mean a piece of the industry which we've been denied so much of. So I put my little money together and made this film. And do you know, I was made fun of? People said, "Oh, this fool is over there spending his little money he made off that record to shoot a movie that will never get shown in a theater." And today, 26 years later, this picture is still on the market and renting very well in video stores all over the country.

DW: *You took a very do-it-yourself approach to filmmaking.*

RRM: You got out and got some money together yourself and made the film, because there were no companies that were going to finance you. Oh, there were a couple of companies that rode the bandwagon, because they knew this type of thing was selling. So they would get the black actors and actresses and put them in movies. I think MGM did some, and American International did some. But the filmmakers that were like myself, that had no backing—the young man Jamaa Fanaka that did *Penitentiary* (1980), *Welcome Home Brother Charles* (1975), and *Emma Mae* (1976), and Melvin

Van Peebles who did *Sweetback* (1971)—we did all of this ourselves with the little crumbs that we could rake together. We got our movies out. These are the things that made us (black filmmakers) what we are today, and we wish that people would recognize our contributions to the film industry.

DW: *Some people get upset with me, but I've always looked at your career like Oscar Micheaux or Spenser Williams. These guys went out and raised the money they needed to make the films they wanted, which they then marketed directly to the black audiences. And this is what you did.*

RRM: I pay homage to the pioneers that came along before the filmmakers of my period came along. If they hadn't done what they did, we wouldn't have had the inspiration to do our thing. But I have to say this to the younger filmmakers of today: they fail to recognize the way that we did things and give us no credit at all. I won't call any names of the young filmmakers of today, but they're extremely crude to us for not giving credit for the things we've done.

DW: *I'll name names. Spike Lee doesn't acknowledge anybody from the 1970s. He acts like he invented black cinema.*

RRM: I consider Spike Lee a great filmmaker. I don't like to down brothers, but I would like to say that brothers who have done so much in the film industry should recognize where they come from and give a little bit of credit back where it is due.

DW: *You've done a lot for black people in film. People think that the black films of the 1970s were made by white people, but your films were mostly crewed by blacks. Your writers were black. Your producers and directors were black. You made important black films. D'Urville Martin directed* Dolemite.

RRM: D'Urville Martin was my first director. I came along at a time when makeup artists, directors, screenplay writers didn't have all the great opportunities they do now. Myself personally, I gave Jerry Jones, my writer, his first break. Marie Carter, who is now a big makeup artist in Hollywood? My film *Dolemite* was the very first film she did makeup on. Cliff Roquemore, my later director, his first film was *The Human Tornado*. I had a lot of firsts that I brought along and helped in the film industry. That's one thing I'd like to make mention of so the general public will know that I wasn't just out there for myself. I was out there with a self-help program for others—to get other people jobs as actors. Ernie Hudson—we know him, a great actor today—my film *The Human Tornado* was his first screen acting role. I gave him that break.

And speaking of the late great D'Urville Martin, he was the one person that gave me a lot of incentive in the film industry. He taught me how to take direction on the screen. When I first started working, and he first started directing me, I didn't know direction. But by the time he got through with me, I knew screen direction.

DW: *What's your opinion of the word blaxploitation?*

RRM: Blaxploitation, in my opinion, is just about zero. It is so crude for the system—when I say the system, I mean the people who made motion pictures long before we had a chance to get in it and do our thing—they termed it blaxploitation. When we came out and did pictures where we had the dominant roles in the film—we weren't getting kicked in the ass and beat upside the head—then they termed it as blaxploitation. I think it is extremely crude to us as a people. It is as crude and insulting to black people as the word nigger would be. You call the nigger this, nigger that. Well, blaxploitation is just as crude. I think the people that created this term don't realize that.

DW: *I think the films of that time were important. For one thing, they gave us heroes.*

RRM: When you say heroes, what do you mean? The actors of that period?

DW: *Exactly. There really hadn't been any black action heroes before the 1970s. I think it was an important thing for black people to have heroes they could identify with.*

RRM: You had the one and only Dolemite. That was me, and I considered myself as being great for that period. When I say I was great, I was great. I wasn't conceited; I was merely convinced. And we had the great Fred Williamson, known as the Hammer. Jim Brown made a great impact on the screen. Jim Kelly, the karate fighter. Not only was Bruce Lee out there doing it, but we had another man of our own, Jim Kelly, who did a great job as one of our heroes. And Isaac Hayes—singer, musician—came along and did the same thing on the screen.

DW: *Some people feel those films were too violent.*

RRM: We're not the only ones that dwelled on violence in movies. I'll tell you, when I was going to the movies, sitting in all-white pictures, I watched pictures like *Scarface* (1932). And I watched James Cagney in the most violent pictures that have ever been made—shootouts, car blowups, and all of that. *The Godfather* (1972) was one that came along later, and they never called that Italian exploitation. The pictures that we made with the violence in them were not any more violent than the pictures that were made by the system in the days when black people weren't in films. It's crude just to be down on us and make ours blaxploitation, because theirs was never referred to as whitesploitation—or white exploitation—whatever you want to call it.

DW: *After a while, the films of the 1970s became the center of a lot of controversy.*

RRM: There were organizations that were very critical of our involvement in the movies in those days. Personally, I think for our own black people to do that against people trying to make it in the film industry by whatever means necessary was wrong. Some of the groups that talked about the type of films we were doing never did put any money together and say, "Instead of you all making the kinds of films you all are making, let us put together some more positive messages and we'll finance them." That never did come about. Yet and still, they criticized the types of films that we were doing. If I would have made the kinds of films that these groups wanted us to make in those days—like a message film—it would have died at the box office the first day. Due to the fact that I made films that were controversial and hard hitting, they stood up in box office lines from coast to coast. Thus made it possible for me to stay in the film industry and be an example for young filmmakers today. Should I have done what those groups wanted me to do, I wouldn't have been able to do that, because that movie would not have made it. You know, like a preachy type of thing trying to convert people. People go to the movies to be entertained, not to go to church. So, in other words, when I did my movies, they were made to entertain. People came in there and left fulfilled. That was our mission back in the days that we did the movies that they called blaxploitation.

DW: *You made one of those message films.* Disco Godfather *was pretty clearly an anti-drug movie.*

RRM: It was an anti-drug movie, and it was a mistake that I made. What I did in my day, I was trying to make movies that would be hard hitting, that I could get a piece of the action with. My first movies were a little more violent, like *Dolemite*, *The Human Tornado*, and *Petey Wheatstraw*. But I had done quite a bit of that, and I was going to try to clean up my image and do something that had a message in it. So I did *Disco Godfather*, which is about the psychedelic drug angel dust, and it was a mistake. The picture did not do well, like the other more violent, hard-hitting pictures.

Me trying to clean up my image and trying to do something our groups might like pretty near destroyed my film career. I haven't had a film since that time to star in of my own.

DW: *What do you think was the cause of the black films of the 1970s dying off the way they did?*

RRM: It was caused by the complaints of our groups, the complaints of our leaders. They complained to the big film companies that they were using and exploiting us, and making these violent pictures that were not good for the image of young people coming up in a new generation. This is why the film companies stopped doing those films. I was doing it on my own, but when I tried to change my image, it destroyed my box office appeal, thus ending my film career. All of that had something to do with trying to please these groups by making pictures that would appeal to the so-called highbrow organizations.

DW: *I was thinking about this the other day. Twenty years ago, it was the blaxploitation films that were under fire for being negative. Now it's the rappers. What do you think about that?*

RRM: I'd like to say people, like this lady called Miss C. Delores Tucker, who are trying to stop the rappers from doing what they are doing, I think it's better off that [rappers] do what they are doing instead of being out in the streets robbing and stealing. At least they're setting themselves up in business. I do not endorse all the stuff in their material, but I do endorse their effort. When people start getting down on rappers like Dr. Dre, Ice Cube, Ice T, and the many rappers out there that have done so well in show business, they're getting down on me. I am the Godfather of Rap, and all of the rappers are my children. Get up off the backs of my children.

There's a lady, she's got all this Psychic Friends stuff—Dionne, I think her name is—she is trying to tell the rappers what they should or shouldn't do and how they should do it. I think this lady is out here trying to make some money. And she's making it with this thing called the Psychic Friends, which you know and I know is completely phony; there's nothing to it. I take my hat off to her for making money like that. But if you run around here and talk about others that should get their acts together, I think this lady should get her act together. Because that is a phony world she's trying to shoot at a lot of black people across the country. "All you need is a telephone and an open mind"? Well, I say this brothers and sisters: all you need is a telephone, an open mind, and a pocketbook full of money to pay that phony organization you're calling to ask what they can do for you, which is absolutely nothing! I say to Dionne, "Honey, I like to see people make money. You're making a lot of money down there. But for you to tell these people all these lies, I should get me a two-by-four and beat you all the way down Central Avenue. Get up off my brothers and sisters of the rap generation. These are my children. Leave them alone!"

DW: *Getting back to film, have there been great changes in the industry since your day in the sun?*

RRM: The change has been a chip off the old block. We are the block, and the new filmmakers are the chips. The chips are films like *New Jack City* (1991), and the karate picture that was produced by Motown, *The Last Dragon* (1985). They came along in the same violent vein that we did.

DW: *What do you think about some of the current things going on in Hollywood? Jesse Jackson and others are now talking about launching a boycott because of a lack of black presence. These are the same people that helped to shut down the films that were being made 20 years ago.*

RRM: I take my hat off to Jesse. He is a tremendous leader. But I think Mr. Jackson has a lot of influence with a lot of people, and I truly do believe that if he got out there and tried to raise money with different groups and business firms, I believe he could get that going for us instead of criticizing. I think we should do some things for ourselves, and we've got enough black people and enough money to do that ourselves.

DW: *So you don't think black filmmakers and black audiences should be dependent on white Hollywood for our entertainment? You think we should do it ourselves?*

RRM: Of course. There are so many black people with money. I mean billions of dollars. I'm pretty sure with Mr. Jackson having so much influence, he could ask them to donate money to a company to create the great image black films—even hard-hitting black films. What we are out there to do in the film industry is to make money. We're not out there to try to convert people. We want to entertain them. I don't think it would be wise to have black people put their money together and make some films that aren't going to go anywhere. The bottom line is to create film companies that will produce pictures that will be highly entertaining. Mr. Jackson should try, since he has so much influence—much more influence than I do—to get people with money to pull it together and let us do our own thing.

CHAPTER 17

Ron O'Neal

A publicity photograph of Youngblood Priest (Ron O'Neal) in *Superfly*.

Ron O'Neal grew up in Cleveland, Ohio, the son of a struggling jazz musician who was forced to take a job working in a factory to support his family. O'Neal's grades in school were good enough to lift him out of the ghetto and into Ohio State University, where he was bitten by the acting bug. He then joined a Cleveland acting troupe known as Karamu House, where he trained from 1957 to 1966. The following year, at the age of 30, O'Neal relocated to New York City, where he began teaching acting classes to support himself. During this period, O'Neal appeared in numerous summer stock and off-Broadway productions.

His big break came with a role in a Broadway production of *Ceremonies of Dark Old Men*. He then appeared in Charles Gordone's Pulitzer Prize–winning play *No Place to Be Somebody*. For his virtuoso performance, O'Neal got glowing reviews and received an Obie Award, the Drama Desk Award, the Clarence Derwent Award, and the National Theater Award. O'Neal then went to work in Hollywood, landing bit parts in *Move* (1970) and *The Organization* (1971).

In 1972, O'Neal appeared as anti-hero drug dealer Youngblood Priest—the role for which he would forever be identified—in Gordon Parks Jr.'s *Superfly*. The film became a tremendous hit. Made for a meager $149,000, the film raked in more than $18 million at the box office, making it one of the most successful films of the blaxploitation era. O'Neal received praise for his performance, and there was even talk of an Academy Award nomination. He then directed and appeared in the film's sequel, *Superfly T.N.T.* (1973). O'Neal's subsequent films include *When a Stranger Calls* (1979), *Red Dawn* (1984), and the blaxploitation reunion picture *Original Gangstas* (1996). On January 14, 2004, O'Neal succumbed to pancreatic cancer, dying one day after *Superfly* was released on DVD.

DAVID WALKER: *Let's start out by talking about blaxploitation—what that word means, and what it means to you.*

RON O'NEAL: I think possibly the term blaxploitation, that has come to be the term to describe black films, or African American films of the 1970s, was really coined for me personally—or *Superfly*, the film—for reasons which I will explain.

Let me tell you something about the climate. It's difficult to know what the climate was like back then. *Superfly* came out in 1972. The first really black film, and probably one of the best of them, was *Sweet Sweetback* (1971) by Melvin Van Peebles. Marvelous film. Much misunderstood film. This was some time in 1970, 1971. In 1964, they were still shooting us with water hoses and dogs. You couldn't ride in the front of the bus in parts of this country. We're talking seven years after the assassination of President Kennedy, and Malcolm, and King. And we're talking about the dream is still sort of alive then—the King dream was still there. And there was a promise, a hope, for the future of race relations that I frankly don't see now. Nor do I have it myself, frankly. In that climate, maybe it was about time for the industry to change, to try and catch up with some of the last moving events that had taken place.

What do I mean by that? Well, traditionally we had one black movie star. At the time, it was Sidney Poitier. Before that, it was James Edwards, an actor that many people don't know. But he was *the* black movie star. He had an unfortunate social occurrence here in Hollywood, and they blacklisted him. He didn't work for 15 years. Let's say this happened on a Friday. On Tuesday they came up with Sidney Poitier. I think you get my point.

Well, along came Melvin with *Sweet Sweetback*. And then MGM came out with *Shaft* (1971) and *Cotton Comes to Harlem* (1970). Then came *Superfly*. All in the span of 18 months or so. We were trying to emulate and achieve what we saw white films achieving—what white movie stars we admired were doing. Charles Bronson, Clint Eastwood, Burt Reynolds. Not John Wayne. Although I happen to like John Wayne, we weren't trying to do John Wayne's thing. You know, the action heroes of the time. We were beginners in the craft, most of us. We hadn't worked a lot as actors—on film anyway. What we were trying to do was a very different thing than what is happening now, in modern African American films, which tend to be mostly about kids, gangs on the block and so forth. We didn't make movies like that. We were trying to show a mature, intelligent black man, operating with all the panache and verve of James Bond. That's what we were trying to do. We were trying to prove that we are as good looking and have as much panache, as much ego, as any white actor. We were trying to be part of the system.

When *Superfly* opened, it opened to incredible reviews—for the most part. There were some that really hated the film. The *New York Times* said they thought *Superfly* was the best gangster movie they had seen since James Cagney in *The Public Enemy* in 1933. There was no comment on the film then. *Superfly* played for about six weeks to absolutely packed houses. We broke every box office record. And the audiences were not black. There were more blacks than normal, but it's a very New Yorky film—those who know New York will know what I'm talking about. New Yorkers loved that movie. All kinds of New Yorkers. You couldn't get a seat. We broke every existing box office record. The music was fabulous.

Now, the term blaxploitation. One of the problems with black people, the cry has been, that whenever blacks try to do anything, other blacks have a tendency to pull them down. The crabs in the barrel syndrome. Well, this is exactly what happened with black films. Every black person with an axe to grind, with a point of view, with a platform—and we all know that opinions and platforms are like we-know-what, everyone's got one! Everyone with a point of view jumped on the bandwagon of criticizing *Superfly*, in order to get the press they could not otherwise get. By this I mean CORE, the NAACP, all of them. Roy Innis actually told me this. He said, "Ron, I liked the film. I took my daughter to see *Superfly*. We understood what the film was about. But I'm going to take you on on the *Today Show*, and I'm going to cut your mouth out." We were having breakfast, okay? He was buying me breakfast. And I was unbelieving. I was so naive. I was just a stage actor. I did poetry concerts and things. I was raised to a level of power, or involvement in circles of power happening around me, that I was not used to, or prepared for.

Superfly was released by Warner Bros. The term blaxploitation was not an accident, and it was not a term created by white people. Blaxploitation was a term created by a black person. A black press agent named Junius Griffin, who was at the time the head of the Beverly Hills NAACP. At the time it sounded like an oxymoron to me. He had tried everything in his power to get the Warner Bros. account to handle the PR for *Superfly*, and he didn't get it. There was a big brouhaha, and he was either fired or he quit. I'm not certain which. So he formed his press agency, and guess what his very first film was. His first account was *Sounder* (1972), starring Cicely Tyson. A lovely family film, admittedly made for the mental age between eight and 13. It was from a children's book, about a dog, barking all the time. It was a very nice Walt Disney kind of film. It was a very mild version of slavery—of what the South was like. And there were no heavies. It was an interesting film, because no one was at fault in *Sounder*. Life is just terrible for some people sometimes.

Sounder died in New York when it opened. I know because I went to the opening. Keep in mind, up to this point, there was very little criticism of *Superfly*. *Sounder* opened—we did more in a day than they did all week, in two theaters. All of a sudden, out came, in the *New York Times*, a vicious attack on *Superfly*, by Cicely Tyson, the star of *Sounder*. She then admitted that she had not seen *Superfly*, but she knew it was a piece of junk. And then, on the heels of that, from the pen of Junius Griffin, came the term blaxploitation. He was very tight with Johnson Publications, and that's where the term was popularized, through *Ebony* and *Jet Magazine*. Blaxploitation. Johnson Publications publicized Junius Griffin's little jingle word—blaxploitation. To the utter damnation of all black films, and black artists, and hopefully to himself, as far as I'm concerned. If that's personal, I'm sorry. But that's the way I feel. Because this has changed not only my life, it has changed a lot of people's lives, and unfairly so.

DW: *That all seems so unbelievable. So unfair.*

RO: I'm not ashamed of anything that I did in *Superfly*. I've done a lot of things that I'm very proud of. From Shakespeare to poetry concerts to everything else. And I've turned down roles that I thought were not what black actors should be doing, and other black actors jump up and do them. And I turned them down because I didn't think they were appropriate. Well, you find out that all it does is cost you money. No one cares. Anyway, I care, so I guess that's enough.

DW: *Well, I care, so I guess you're not alone. It almost seems like history is trying to sweep all that happened to you guys, and everything about your films, under the rug. I'm amazed at some of the things I've turned up. I read a quote by Tony Brown of* Tony Brown's *Journal that said that all those involved in those films were race traitors—guilty of treason.*

RO: Since this is for the archives of history, and for the truth—you see, what it has taken me a life to learn, and it's heartbreaking—and not to pick on Tony Brown, he's no better or worse than anyone else out there—but I went on the *Tony Brown Show,* and Tony Brown, as one can describe, knocked all black films, *Superfly* in particular. Then, after the program, he took me out for dinner and apologized and said, "Ron, I'm sorry, but I have to do this because they're trying to cancel my show. And you're the hottest thing going now. This controversy that has risen about *Superfly* and black films is very hot, and everyone's on top of it."

You need to understand: this was all very new. We never had black people on the screen like this. You've got to understand this: *you could not see black people on the screen!* They were nonexistent before these films. We'd all rush to see some guy playing fourth or fifth role—so-and-so, there's a black guy driving a truck in this movie. It was like that! That was the climate. And then we'd all rush out.

So Tony Brown's just taken me over the coals on his program, taken me out to dinner, and apologized. Explaining that it was nothing personal, it was business. As a matter of fact, he "would be delighted to produce my next film." Could we talk about it?

That sort of hypocrisy; that sort of dualism; that sort of backstabbing—I've never learned to deal with that. But it's a reality of this business. Black or white. But it hurts more when it comes from your own people. From people that you would think would have some sympathy, or some empathy, for your cause. That they would try to help you. Because you're not just helping me, you're helping your people. But I've found it doesn't work like that. It's more like, "I've upped my income—up yours."

DW: *Let's step away from the 1970s for a while and give me time to calm down. I'm starting to get pissed off. You know? Let's talk about the films now. This so-called new wave of black films.*

RO: When you talk about the films of the 1990s, black films, or they're now called African American films, before that it was negro, or colored—I don't know, they change the name, but we still come out the same. In any event, when you talk about the modern African American films, I can only speak of them as part of the audience, as an onlooker, because I've never worked on any of these films. They don't use us in any of these films, who were in the 1970s era, for one reason or another. The plot doesn't demand it or whatever. I don't know.

And they say there's a new wave in all this. It may be a new wave, but you know it's an interesting thing: these films are not producing stars, for the most part. There's Denzel and a couple of other guys. The producer is the star of these films. The director is the star of these films. And they take unknowns, and rappers, and it's about homies on the block. Maybe I'm getting old, I don't know, there's a place for that. Maybe they're wise. Maybe they're going in the only direction that's possible to go.

DW: *Yeah, but they're going backwards from where you guys were going.*

RO: I mean, where's the black Charles Bronson? No one is trying to do that. Where's the black Clint Eastwood? Where's the black Sean Connery? Something I was often accused of was being the black Sean Connery. Then I was told, in a friendly way, by a well-meaning white producer, "Ron, you can do everything that Sean Connery can do. Except who needs a black Sean Connery?" I said, "You've made it not such a bad day for me, because at least I know I'm not crazy."

DW: *So why is there no black Eastwood? Or better yet, no black equivalent to the Schwarzeneggers or the Van Dammes, or whoever the hot shit, white boy action heroes are?*

RO: Now, when you talk about the black actor, the trouble with being a black actor is we need stories. And if you try to write it—and I've tried my hand at writing, I've tried to get one over—forget about it. They've got 10,000 reasons what's wrong with it. All the reasons it can't be done—x, y, z. Okay fine.

They just don't write for us. Black people are not seen in that way. And I'm getting into areas of definition, if you think I have a tendency to go on and on, I'll really go on and on about this sort of thing. It's sort of war. It's sort of an ideological war—an image war. To me, the media is the most powerful force in the United States. I mean, the media can even make General Motors back up. Okay? They can create and make or break presidents. One of the last golden circles—sacred circles of white endurance—in this country is the motion picture industry. It's like John Wayne. For years John Wayne was the American male, archetype male. These are the guys that we all want to be. The Marlboro Man, and this and that. Well, they have trouble looking at a black person with the same sort of adoration that they look at John Wayne or Clint Eastwood. They have trouble giving that up. I'm talking about less the population of the United States, because I happen to think that the population of the United States is a much less racist, and more fair community, given a chance, than are the organizations—the organisms—that supply our entertainment. In other words, I think the entertainment business is about 20 years behind the kids, the people in the streets. They always have been. And they're very, very cautious. But that's the last place—where the dreams are made. What do we want our girls dreaming about in Kansas when they go to sleep? Do we want white girls in Kansas going to sleep with pictures of Ron O'Neal over their bed?

Now Michael Jackson got over. When you become Michael Jackson, you can make $100 million a year. Something not threatening about Michael Jackson. Nonthreatening blacks do very well. Me, as you can tell, I got a big mouth. I ain't never been ugly; I'm approaching my older years, and I still don't look too bad. [Dennis] Rodman has the same complaint. Whereas [Michael] Jordan is America's dream child. He does everything correctly. Of course, any of us would know, no one is perfect. Michael's an image. I know this. I'm probably wasting my time saying this. It's all about this image thing. They'll take a few blacks and carefully cultivate them to reach a certain position, that satisfies the need—the public relations need—to appear to have a racially open policy. And if it means they have to give you $7 to 10 million a year, now, to do that—rather than $70,000 or $700,000, which is what it was back in the 1970s—they're more than happy to do that.

DW: *Before we started, you had mentioned your experience with Al Pacino. Can you tell that story again?*

RO: Marvelous actor, Al Pacino. He and I started out together on the New York stage. We shared some acting awards together. The only time I ever met Al Pacino was at an audition for the New York Shakespeare Festival, downtown on 8th Street, for *Richard III*. We both auditioned for it. I had just won the Obie Award, the Drama Desk Award, the Clarence Derwin Award, and the Theater World Award for *No Place to Be Somebody*. The play won the Pulitzer Prize for drama. Al had won the Tony Award for being on Broadway in *Does a Tiger Wear a Necktie?* I saw him in the play; he was absolutely electric on stage.

Well, anyone who knows anything about show business knows that when you go to an audition, you often run into these little sandbox situations, where a director already has someone he wants for the part, or they have this little clique. Well, they declined both Al Pacino and Ron O'Neal and cast someone else. If I told you the man's name, you would have never heard of him—a friend of the director, I do believe. They told Al Pacino he was too short and Italian, and told me I was too black. I said, "I'm too what?" and burst out in laughter. Because one of my problems as an actor was being so light-skinned and having straight hair that I could never get a job in these black plays. I'm the only actor in the world that was never in Jean Genet's *The Blacks*, or *Roots* (1977). I was literally *No Place to Be Somebody*.

So we, Pacino and I, walked all the way from Greenwich Village up into the high 70s and 80s, and just talked about it. We were both not really happy about it. And we both said, "Well, you know, this is show biz. The way it happens. You gotta keep going."

Within a year, he was playing Michael Corleone in *The Godfather* (1972). And shortly after that, I was doing *Superfly*. I made more money in *Superfly* than he made in *The Godfather*, [but ultimately] he made as much money in *The Godfather* as I made the whole rest of my life as an actor.

DW: *Maybe we should talk about some of the other films you've done. The world knows you mostly for* Superfly, *but there were other films*—The Hitter *(1979)*, Sophisticated Gents *(1981)*, Brothers *(1977)*.

RO: One of my favorite performances, speaking of other films that I've done along the way—none of which were as famous as *Superfly*, or infamous, if you will—one of them was *Brothers*. Produced by a marvelous gentleman named Ed Lewis, starred Bernie Casey and Vonetta McGee, based loosely on George Jackson and Angela Davis. I was privileged to play Bernie Casey's cellmate. I thought it was probably the best performance I've ever given on the screen. One of the reasons was I wrote all my scenes.

Ron O'Neal as Otis in the 1979 blaxploitation film *The Hitter.*

I didn't have any scenes; I only had two lines. So Ed Lewis asked me to write some stuff, and I did. So all my dialogue and Bernie's dialogue I wrote. It turned out very well.

The only other film that I thought was representative of my work was *Red Dawn*, which I did in Russian and Spanish. There were some good moments in that. Frankly, I've not been pleased with most of what I've had to do. I have what you call charisma. The camera likes me, so I just had to go in front of the camera, say my lines, and not bump into the furniture for the most part. It's not satisfying. I wanted to do *Kramer vs. Kramer* (1979), for instance. You know, roles with heart, with substance, where the plots have a density, and there's something happening. Instead, I was either playing some cop chained to a desk, or I was Tonto, playing second banana to a wonderful actor, Edward Woodward, on *The Equalizer*. But I was very unhappy on the show, because I did what they asked me to, but they didn't ask anything of me. It's like taking Michael Jordan and telling him, "Don't shoot." It's the only way I can describe the feeling. At the same time, to watch your career slowly going down, down, down . . . I haven't been on an audition in three, four years. A couple black people have called me up to do videos—to do this, to do that. My agents don't even know about that. They only find out when I get a check. They say, "What's this for?" And I see parts on television—judges, psychiatrists, Indian chiefs—with some marvelous actors playing them. And I'd like to do them. But I don't know what's happening.

DW: *To me it's a crime. Some of the most talented actors of all time came out of that era, and very few of them work with any regularity. When was the last time you saw Calvin Lockhart in anything of merit?*

RO: There's no appreciation for the black actors of the 1970s, because we were cut off at the knees. We became persona non grata. People were afraid it was catching. It was like we had leprosy. Has-beens. Well, it's better than being a never-was. You become not en vogue. And people want something new. They don't want to deal with that. It's a curious thing. Don't misunderstand me. No one is staying up nights, to generate any of this that I'm talking about. It's just the way it is. It's like flipping a coin that keeps coming up tails. How can you keep flipping the penny, and it keeps coming up tails? Somehow the penny keeps coming up tails—but no one is doing it.

Let me make the point in a more graphic way of explaining. The peculiar thing about being a black actor . . . It's difficult enough for anybody who's considering to be an artist of any sort—a writer, musician, actor, singer. It's very difficult—it's very rewarding, very challenging. But let's take the popular black singer and the black actor. The difference between the two: black singers can be millionaires by the time they're 25 years old because they don't have white people looking over their shoulder, telling them what to do, how to write the song. They sing a song they like. They sing it for their people—they don't make the song for white people. They make the songs for black people. And black people go out and buy them by the millions. Keep in mind that black people are 30 percent—fully 30 percent of the motion picture audience, the American moviegoing audience, is black. Thirty percent! That means that 30 percent of the actors should be black, 30 percent of the movies should be black, 30 percent of the movie stars should be black, all things being equal. Not so! In music, you can do that, because you can go into some studio, cut some master tape, they print out some records, and it goes to the record store, and they hype it on the black radio station, and somebody becomes a millionaire. And they deserve it.

Well, that's all I ever wanted to do as a black actor. I never wanted to try and please white people in Kansas. I'd like to be everyman. I would like to think that my artistry, my education—I have a fairly decent education in Western literature—I'd like to think that my talents are universal and apply to everyone. But I didn't create this scenario. My desire was to function within the system as it exists—not as it ought to be. And the way it is, is a racist system. So I said, okay, how about separate but slightly unequal? You be Clark Gable in *Gone with the Wind*, and I'll be Dark Gable in *Coolin' in the Breeze.* I have no problem with that. They have a problem with that. You want to know why? Because movies require theaters to exhibit them, and there's a limited number of theaters, and their schedules are limited. If these theaters are tied up with black films that will never, ever make as much money as a white film does, they lose money.

They control theaters. It's sort of like blackmail. The major studios can tell the theater chains, "I want you to take this dog of a picture, so I can bail out, and get my money out of it. If you want the next *Star Wars*, or the next *Twister*, or whatever, you've got to show this dog." That's the working relationship—a vicious working relationship—between the exhibitor and the studios. It's a power trip. There's little room for the black producer and the black film in that. What we need are places to exhibit our films. We need to find a way to be able to take our 30 percent away from them. Black people are hungry for entertainment.

I'm getting to the point of it, I guess, that it's so clear. Black people are 30 percent of the audience, but white people pick the plots, the stories, and heroes they want. And they fit black people, if they can, carefully and comfortably into their sense of reality—into their sense of what is real. So that the black person you see on the screen is a black person as seen by them— be he hero or villain, be he deserving of either a pat on the head or the utter damnation of law and order.

The trouble they've had with Ali, the trouble they have with Rodman, the trouble they've had with black athletes, they've demanded the same things everyone else was getting. They've had trouble dealing with black athletes with their egos and their business sense, and their refusal to knuckle under—to be good ol' boys. And I ain't never been good at bein' a good ol' boy. Unfortunately, they will always find someone who is good at playing the good ol' boy role. And then guys like you and me, we're standing around going, "Well, what the fuck is this?"

I'll give you an example. True story. I did a thing called *Freedom Road* (1979)—starred Muhammad Ali. This is a classic example of what I've been talking about. A scenario about show business in general, politics, racism—all tied together. Produced by Zev Braum, a good guy. Written by Howard Fast. It was probably the greatest role I've ever read for a black actor. It was based on Frederick Douglass, and it starts off in the slave days, and he's a "dey's" and "dem" and "do's" and "yassa" guy—completely illiterate, never been more than 10 feet from his plantation. It ends up, many years later, he's Frederick Douglas, a U.S. senator, debating, and he sounds like William F. Buckley.

So, the actor had to have all this range. And he had to be young enough to play a guy in his 20s, and then in his 60s. The range was from here to there. It was a terrifying role, something like playing Cyrano de Bergerac. I was so excited when I read it, and I was asked to play a high yellow politician, a well-educated black of the day. I come to find out they elected to star Muhammad Ali in the project. Well, when I went to meet with the producer, I asked him, because I really wanted to know, and I said, "Tell me something. This role, being as difficult and wonderful as it is, why on earth would you ever cast, as great a heavyweight fighter as he is, why would you ever cast Muhammad Ali in this part? This is a role that would tax the ability of any highly trained and experienced actor. It's a wonderful, marvelous role. Why would you cast Muhammad Ali?" He says to me, "Well, Ron, you don't understand. There's business reasons for that." I said, "Oh, I understand business. I've directed two pictures. I've produced two pictures. I know about foreign markets and all that stuff. I'm no expert, but I can carry on a reasonable conversation about it. I understand." He said, "Well, we need a name. We need Muhammad Ali's name because this movie was presold to a European market. We don't even care what the Americans think about it."

I said, "That's very interesting. But I have to say this: I'm a little outraged. Not only that, I'm outraged. Do you have any idea how important and wonderful this story is to me and to all black people, and hopefully even all Americans? This is the kind of story that is never told about black people. To see the rise of this man, and the eloquence he has at the end. And this is not fiction, this was a real person. And for you to cast a prizefighter who can barely speak? And I say this with humility, but when you talk about acting, Muhammad Ali can barely speak. Why would you do that?"

He said, "I told you; it's for business reasons." I said, "Really? Then let me ask you this then, Zev. You're Jewish, right?" He said, "Right." So I said, "Why is it when you do your stories, your stories get one standard. Our stories, there's always a reason for them being a bunch of crap." Keep in mind, I haven't got the job yet.

He said, "What do you mean?" I said, "When you tell your story, *Holocaust* (1978), I've seen it several times, and it's one of the finest mini-series I've ever seen and it's won all kinds of awards. It's generated all kinds of income. Runs. Reruns. Re-reruns. Now, answer me quick, Zev—now, you're Jewish, and it's *Holocaust*, and it's about your story, and your plight with the Nazis in Germany and Poland. Who was the star of *Holocaust*? Name me one actor who was in *Holocaust*." And he couldn't.

I said, "I can name one: Michael Moriarty. Most famous person in that, and at the time, I don't think anyone in Kansas knew who Michael Moriarty was. Following your logic, why didn't y'all cast the second most famous person at that time—Joe Namath? Why didn't they cast Joe Namath in *Holocaust*? He was the great quarterback. He predicted the Jets would win their first Super Bowl. If it's box office, how come you all didn't get Joe Namath?"

You know what the guy looked at me and said? He said, "Ron, you want this job or not? It pays $2,500 a week. You want it? Take it or leave it."

I said, "I'll take it, suh. Thank you, suh." And what happened was, of course, along the way, it was fine [for Ali] when it came to doing the field hand part. But then regrettably—box office and all that is fine—but once he was elected to office, he had all these long speeches, and Muhammad Ali could not learn them. Not only could he not learn them, he could not say them, regrettably. I have great respect for Ali as a person, but he was out of his field. I just might as well have gotten into the ring with Muhammad Ali myself. And he probably would have said, "Ron is a pretty good athlete, but he don't wanna be in the ring with me."

So how it ended up was that every morning, when I came to the set, they had yellow pages of his dialogue that had been rewritten for me. They kept trying to get Ali to learn his lines, and Ali would say, "Man, I can't learn that stuff. Give it to Ron O'Neal. Let him say it." I got $2,500 a week. The show went down the tubes. I stayed up to see it one night. They showed it the first time in L.A. at three in the morning.

DW: *You're up on a lot of others. Even I haven't seen* Freedom Road, *and I've seen everything.*

RO: In a word, this is where my career, this is where the careers of black actors have gone. As long as they are deciding our fate and destiny, and I don't mean this in a militant way—I'm for blacks, I'm not against whites, I'm for blacks. They can't write for me. They can't sing for me. They can't dance for me. They can't do nothing for me. Nor do they want me doing their thing. And until that happens, they're going to decide which ones of us are cute, which ones are funny, which ones of us can dance, and which ones of us are acceptable as leading men actors.

If I sound a little jaded, I'm sorry. But what can I tell you? I've given my whole life to this business. And as someone once said, "Well, Ron, when the question was asked, 'Who wants to be an actor?' you raised your hand." And I did. Okay.

DW: *Is there anything you wish you would've done differently? Any regrets?*

RO: I wish I could have been a boxer, often. A prizefighter. There's something that's very clear about being a prizefighter. That's why Ali could do all the things he did. The thing about being a fighter is that at a certain point, they have to let you in the ring. And if you're as good as you say you are—if they like you or don't—you can leave your opponent lying face down in the center of the ring. You can walk out of the ring and say whatever you want. They can't take that victory away from you.

CHAPTER 18

Larry Spangler

Larry Spangler was born and raised in Lancaster, Pennsylvania. He attended Valley Forge Military Academy in Wayne, Pennsylvania, and Franklin and Marshall College. He then went to work in advertising at the *News Journal* in Wilmington, Delaware. Within one year, Spangler was promoted to assistant national advertising manager, which gave him the opportunity to travel around the country at a young age.

Once he was on his feet, Spangler relocated to New York City and landed a gig as national sales manager for *Sponsor* magazine. Within six months, he was named head of the magazine's Chicago office. There he made friends with physical fitness guru Ed Allen. Having always dreamed of working in film and television, Spangler saw an opportunity in Allen. The two became partners and produced a syndicated physical fitness television show. Spangler then went to work at Westinghouse Broadcasting, where his job was to retool Regis Philbin's show so that it could be syndicated. The success he found there enabled him to establish his own company, where he signed football legend Joe Namath. He then produced the syndicated television program *The Joe Namath Show*.

This led to Spangler's producing the feature film *The Last Rebel* (1971), which, of course, starred Namath. While working on the film, Spangler became friends with legendary actor Woody Strode. One day in conversation, Strode mentioned that his mentor John Ford had spent many years trying to make a film about the legendary black cowboy known as Nigger Charley. However, Ford had been unable to secure financing for the project. Spangler was interested in the historical aspects of such a project and immediately saw box office potential. He secured the rights to the material and cowrote a screenplay with Martin Goldman. This eventually resulted in the blaxploitation classic *The Legend of Nigger Charley* (1972), produced by Spangler and starring Fred Williamson, D'Urville Martin, and Don Pedro Colley. The film went on to become one of Paramount Pictures' highest grossing films of 1972.

The following year, Spangler wrote, produced, and directed a sequel, *The Soul of Nigger Charley* (1973). He also wrote and directed a third black western with Fred Williamson, *Joshua* (1976).

ANDREW RAUSCH: *There was some controversy when* The Legend of Nigger Charley *was released regarding its title. Would you like to talk about that?*

LARRY SPANGLER: Actually, in the beginning, there really wasn't a lot of controversy. The truth of the matter is that we got the film made as an independent and then opened it up for bidding once it was finished. That's how we were able to shoot it for under a million dollars and have so much production value. But the whole time, Paramount was lying back there in the woods, waiting to get it. After the first week of dailies, everyone knew it was a hit. You could just sort of tell by looking at it, and this had hit written all over it. You know, we filmed it where we should; it was so authentic. And Fred was just so superb as Charley, and D'Urville was so funny as his sidekick. It just all worked. There was no question that it was going to be a hit.

Then the underground of the black community was quite supportive. Back in those days, you didn't really need to have a lot of advertising. They knew all about the film from coast to coast! The way I found this out was that my children's nanny, who was black, knew as much about the picture as I did, and I was making it. You follow me? They had their own chain. You didn't have to run any advertising. They knew it was coming. So Paramount wasn't afraid of the title at all.

We were then banned in St. Louis, I think, and we were banned in some southern city. But then a Paramount salesman went down there and ironed it all out. So then it ran there also. But not a lot of white people saw the movie. And it's too bad, because it was a very good western. There was a lot of controversy then, but not really. [Laughs.]

AR: *Once the controversy did get started up regarding the title—*

LS: That was later. You see, this was prior to *Roots*, where they used the word nigger all over television. So we were ahead of *Roots*, and then as the civil rights movement grew and whatnot, I guess people decided, well, you can't use that word. But then the sequel was called *The Soul of Nigger Charley*, and that didn't seem to bother anybody. And then all of a sudden, everybody got proper. You know, blacks called each other that for years, so it was no big deal. Then after that, Paramount just got cold feet. So by the time DVD and all that came along, they were afraid to put the movie out. By that time, the industry had changed a lot, so it just got lost in the shuffle. So that was pretty much that.

Fred Williamson in *The Soul of Nigger Charley*.

AR: *How much of the films was based on fact and how much was fiction?*

LS: Quite a bit was fact. We also retained a man named Dr. Eric Lincoln, who's since passed away. He was, at the time, the foremost professor of black history. He'd written many books, and he scrutinized the script. So even though it was commercial, in a sense, we still followed the John Ford model, which was probably more historically correct. But that would have been an epic like *Roots*, and we didn't have that kind of money. [Laughs.] We couldn't make it that way, so we had to make it the way we made it.

But there's no question that there were many, many black cowboys back then. There's no question that they were very, very skilled. There's no question that they intermixed with the Indians, and there's no question that blacks sold other blacks. That's how it was. Get over it. All of that was historically correct.

And then the fantasy part of it is Freddy escapes, which that was true. And then he works his way across the country and is befriended by the Indians. So that part is, basically, thin line correct. But if you were doing a real documentary on it, you would see all of that in its entirety and how it actually played out.

AR: *There were very few black westerns, and yet you've made three of them. What is it about that subgenre that appeals to you?*

LS: The thing that appealed to me about *The Legend of Nigger Charley* was Woody Strode. He was, I think, the first black decathlon athlete. I just loved him. While we were making *The Last Rebel*, we became very friendly. He told me those John Ford stories, and he said that John Ford couldn't get *Nigger Charley* made. But he said, "The way you attack things, you could probably get it done." And I'm sorry he said that, because it took me like four years to get it done. So that intrigued me. And of course you've never had so much fun making a movie because Freddy was so into the role. We had the greatest stunt crew—we had John Wayne's stunt crew and everything. And I was told that ours was the first film to use a New York crew out west. I didn't take the normal western crew; I brought mine with me. [Laughs.] And they did a great job. It was just really fun. There's no other way to say it. When you're an independent like me, you live your movies. You don't go to committee meetings. I wouldn't even let anyone see the dailies hardly. I just did it my way.

And of course they wanted a sequel. They keep making sequels even today. What do they do? They keep making them, right? So this was way ahead of the curve. So we did the sequel, and [Paramount president] Frank Yablans got in a big argument. We had a big opening plan, black tie and all that, and then Yablans pulled the plug on me. He really screwed me over, but that was okay. That hurt the release of the sequel. And then the word nigger was going out of fashion, and that hurt the film, too. So that's where that was at.

But Freddy and I made *Joshua* just because of the frustration of having *The Soul of Nigger Charley* not do as well as it could have. We didn't have much money, but we went out into the woods and did it. That one was actually fun to make, too, but I had to keep going back and threatening my backers because the checks kept bouncing. [Chuckles.] But that was a lot of fun, too.

But westerns get in your blood. I loved those good old authentic westerns. You know, all my guys got dirty. We didn't have any clean cowboys. We looked like we lived out there.

AR: *Obviously there were a lot of black cowboys. Why do you think there haven't been more black westerns made?*

LS: Well, they made *Buck and the Preacher* (1972) with Sidney Poitier and Harry Belafonte, and that was one approach. Then after that, I think what happened is that they don't really know how to do them. You sort of have to stay in the John Ford frame of mind. I did not like *Silverado* (1985), for example, because they looked like they just stepped out of Brooks Brothers. If you're gonna make movies like that, then that to me is not a western. Your cowboys have to look rugged. They've got to have dirt under their nails. I mean, it's the west. That's the way it was. When these people now say "black western," they want to purify it and glamorize it. You've seen some of them that they've tried. They have stupid bandanas around their necks and, you know . . . get a life! Even if they tried now to go do one, I think it would be difficult, because it would just be too pretty. And that's not what the old west was about. It was anything but pretty. It was rugged and it was dangerous. Robert Altman had it right in *McCabe and Mrs. Miller* (1971). Look how rugged that was. Even though it was telling the story of a prostitute, he got the point across: it was brutal. And, of course, Peckinpah with *The Wild Bunch* (1969). He might have exaggerated a bit, but look at his cowboys; they all looked like they were real. I mean, he really got into that. And that's the way they did them back then. They don't do that anymore. The whole system has changed.

AR: Unforgiven *(1992) was pretty gritty.*

LS: Well, that was Clint. Yeah, that was just amazing. That was just unbelievable what he did with that. But all of his westerns have a dirty, filthy quality to them. He learned that from Sergio Leone. And I learned it being in Italy and dealing with guys like Woody.

The thing about *The Legend of Nigger Charley* and *The Soul of Nigger Charley* and why I would like to see those come out in its DVD form is that I would like to see little black kids latch onto that. Then I could come back and make a movie with Freddy and his son. And Freddy's still up for that, which is interesting. And with the work that I'm doing now in high technology, and as I get richer and richer, I could probably fund it myself if I could convince Paramount to give me all the rights back. I'd have to do it my way. I couldn't follow all their goddamn rules. They wouldn't know what to do. They wouldn't put the picture out, anyway, because they'd be afraid of doing something politically incorrect. That would scare them. That'll probably never happen. But Freddy's still in great shape, so it could. He looks good for his age. He'd be up for it. I mean, he knows the story as well as I do. And I think that was his peak performance in that first movie.

AR: *From a director's standpoint, what was Fred Williamson like to work with?*

LS: Well, Fred, being an athlete, was such a professional guy. We really got along well. We partied together, and I liked him from the first time I met him at the candy store and picked him out. He was just a really great guy to work with. There's just no other way to describe him. So we hung out with everybody from Jim Brown to all of the black guys who call each other nigger. I wasn't allowed to say that. The only guy I could call nigger was Freddy. [Laughs.] And D'Urville.

I still see him occasionally. I play a little golf with him, but I don't get to see him that much because we live in different worlds. But, shit, you'd do a movie with him any day of the week. He's just too much fun. He's just a good guy.

And the first film was definitely a big hit and should go down in history as the masterpiece. If you look at it frame for frame, it's just a great picture. And I don't take credit for that. I think the director, Marty Goldman, deserves a lot of the credit for that. Of course it was my picture, though, because I funded it and I lived and breathed it. So if you did anything wrong,

I would rap you right over the head. You didn't have much chance to make the film fail, because I was so fired up that it just had to be a hit.

It's just a shame that *The Legend of Nigger Charley* isn't out there remastered on DVD.

AR: *As you know, Quentin Tarantino is a big fan of the* Nigger Charley *movies. He's been instrumental in making the public aware of those films.*

LS: My son was working with Michael Madsen on that film *Kill Bill* (2003). And then Quentin found out the last name, and what they finally said to him was, "Larry Spangler wouldn't be your father, would he?" And he said, "Yes, he is." And Tarantino went nuts. He started telling him all about the movie. Of course my son had been a little boy on the set. And then he told him, "I've got the Italian poster for *The Legend of Nigger Charley* over my fireplace." And he said he had to pay a fortune for it. So obviously he's a fan, and I guess he's told that to Freddy many times. And then he wanted to meet me, but I just wasn't able to get it into my schedule. But at some point, I'd love to sit and chat with him about it, and tell him all the interesting stories that took place. That was a wild time back then, and of course I was white and they were black. It was very interesting.

AR: *Was that ever awkward in any way?*

LS: Not at all. You see, from junior high on, I went to an integrated school and I played three sports. The black people . . . well, I didn't even know they were black. Color doesn't enter into it. Now, with my work, I deal a lot with the Chinese. I used to work a lot with the Japanese. I don't think in terms of color. If you have the talent, you're in. If you don't, pound it. I don't believe in all that crap our government sets up. You either have talent or you don't. So no, I had no problems. The blacks loved me. They were just amazing. By the way, all three of our crews were integrated and we had no problems whatsoever. In those days, it didn't seem to be an issue. It's more of an issue today, I think. We have a way of turning things into trouble.

AR: *Speaking of the way things change, were you at all surprised by the resurgence in popularity of blaxploitation films?*

LS: Not really. The black market just keeps growing in size. They can swing almost anything if they get behind it. Everybody wants that market.

It's still out there. You just have to go and remind it that it's there. I think Tarantino got a lot of blacks out to support *Kill Bill*. And again, if you make a good movie, it doesn't matter. If you can go out and actually make a good movie, people will rally around it and get excited about it. It's just that simple, but Hollywood keeps forgetting that.

CHAPTER 19

Glynn Turman

Glynn Turman's acting career began at the age of 13 when he originated the role of Travis Younger on Broadway in the groundbreaking play *A Raisin in the Sun* opposite Sidney Poitier, Ruby Dee, Claudia McNeil, and Diana Sands. He then attended the High School of Performing Arts in New York City. After graduation, he apprenticed in numerous repertory companies, including Tyrone Guthrie's Repertory Theatre.

Hollywood soon beckoned, and Turman landed a recurring role on television's *Peyton Place*. He made his feature debut in the 1970 telefilm *Carter's Army* (also known as *The Black Brigade*), alongside Richard Pryor and Billy Dee Williams. Turman ultimately became one of the stars of the blaxploitation cycle, and was one of the most talented actors to grace the genre, appearing in *Five on the Black Hand Side* (1973), *Thomasine and Bushrod* (1974), *Together Brothers* (1974), *Cooley High* (1975), *J.D.'s Revenge* (1976), and *A Hero Ain't Nuthin' But a Sandwich* (1978).

Turman has since appeared in many films, including *Gremlins* (1984), *Men of Honor* (2000), and *Sahara* (2005), and has had recurring roles on the television series *A Different World* and *The Wire*. In 2008, he won an Emmy for his guest appearance on the HBO series *In Treatment*.

It should be noted that this conversation is actually two separate interviews conducted by David Walker and Andrew Rausch.

DAVID WALKER: *You came along at a time when things were really starting to change in Hollywood. Back in the 1960s, we saw a lot of barriers being* *broken down, some quality roles for black actors, all culminating in the black films of the 1970s. What was it like back then?*

GLYNN TURMAN: Very exciting. Very exciting time to have been a young black actor in Hollywood. The atmosphere in this town—you know it was different. It was a different Hollywood than it had ever been before. There was a hotel, the Montecito Hotel, and such talent came through this hotel. I remember seeing James Edwards at this hotel, and Ivan Dixon, and many, many other brilliant artists. And of course we were like a new, young regime coming through, and they were passing on this knowledge and this struggle. It's interesting that the struggle that they were talking about at that time was not so different from what we talk about right now—than what we're talking about right now. The equations that are probably different are that what you see as black people having achieved across the board, in that, more now, we are the store owner—the small businessman or person. And without that equation before, we were limited. It's surprising how much more freedom that ownership equation gives you.

For instance, black exploitation would not have been called black exploitation, as it is not called black exploitation now. Well, the only thing different I see is that there's a wider spectrum of films, dealing with different subjects. Why is that? Now you have black directors. Now you have black producers and black authors. Then, just to be in front of the screen seemed to be enough. Or not enough, but just a barrier that you could not hardly get past. Many of us knew how essential it was to get past that barrier. But it was indeed just that—a barrier—for that very reason to keep us in the position of exploitation, to keep one viewpoint in the main focus of the American people and the world. Whether it was done deliberately or not can always be debated. But the fact that it made money—this one genre made money—there was no reason to explore any other genre. Why take the chance? Well, I remember having many heated arguments with many producers over the fact that there must be different sides of the story told, and that it would be profitable. "No, it won't be profitable." I've actually walked in offices and had discussions, and had people tell me, "Nobody really cares." Why not do a love story? "We don't want a love story. Who cares? We know you guys can . . . do it!" [Laughs.]

All right. Thanks. So who cares? Well, the truth of the matter is, I care. You care. You know? We care. That's why it's not called black exploitation now, when you can get a picture like *Waiting to Exhale*—it would never have been made in the 1970s.

DW: *But no matter how narrow the scope of vision was back in those days, the 1970s changed everything. Barriers were broken down. The way we were viewed in film was changed forever.*

GT: We're a resilient people. If it weren't for Stepin Fetchit, there would never have been Sidney Poitier. The crowd never seems to move fast enough for us. There are so many parts I wish I would have played when I was 27. But I'm definitely thankful for the parts that I was able to play. And I thank you for acknowledging, and taking the time with this particular piece you're doing, to acknowledge the struggles, and the progress, and the importance of those films that were made in the 1970s, because a lot of very fine talent was honed at that time, and brought a lot to the screen at a very crucial time in history. I don't think we'll ever see a time as crucial as the 1960s and 1970s in America—that's why there are always so many documentaries about it. I mean, you had King, and Kennedy, and Malcolm. So all the art that came out of that time was very, very profound—all the playwrights' themes were so profound. And so that any breakthroughs got through the cracks were part of the master plan, I presume.

DW: *A lot of people, myself included, feel the explosion of black films of the 1970s was on par with the Harlem Renaissance or the birth of hip-hop in the 1980s. Did you feel it would ever be so important?*

GT: Not at all. I'm still amazed. I'm really still surprised. I had no idea that *Cooley High* would become, quote, a classic, as I'm told it is now. I had no idea. We weren't aware that was what that time was. I was just looking for a job, man. [Laughs.] Just give me a gig.

DW: Cooley High *is one of the most amazing films of all time. I've always felt it was one of those films that was unfairly labeled blaxploitation. It addressed these issues that have long been relevant to the black community but didn't become known to the mainstream until films like* Boyz N the Hood *broke out over a decade later.*

GT: I watch it, and my kids watch it, and my grandkids watch it. And as I sneak a peek at it, I realize how important it was. And I asked myself, not too long ago, "What was the difference in this film? Why was this film such an important film, and why has this film lasted so long? And why do so many of the new films have at least one scene that's straight out of *Cooley High* in it? And what are the new films missing that was in *Cooley High*?"

Eric Monte, who wrote *Cooley High*, had a wonderful line, that the character I play actually spoke in the piece. Garrett Morris, who played the wonderful teacher, who was really hip and all the way for kids, asks Preach, "What do you want, man? Don't you want nothin'?" And Preach says, "I want to live forever." And that was the distinguishing thing between that film and the films of today—*Cooley High* glorified living, glorified life; the glory was not in the taking of life.

ANDREW RAUSCH: *Your films* Cooley High *and* Five on the Black Hand Side *are two of the more positive films from that period. Why do you think there weren't more films like those made?*

GT: Well, they fell into that genre that I spoke of, which was the money-making genre. First of all, you have to remember this was in the early 1970s, just out of the civil rights movement. Because of this, it was very popular at the time to see black men and black women in powerful roles kicking whitey's ass, so to speak. And when the studios found that there was a money-making upside to that image, then that was the image they chose to promote. So I think it was only by accident that movies like *Cooley High* and *Five on the Black Hand Side*, which was produced by a black producer named Brock Peters, were made. They dared to say, hey, we'll go see other things than just us ranting and raving about the man, and so on and so forth.

DW: *I'm sure people probably talk to you about* Cooley High *all the time, but it is such an amazing film. I think it's probably the most universally loved film of that era.*

GT: *Cooley High* was a wonderful experience all the way around. We had our 20th anniversary and went back to Chicago. Pooter, Corin Rogers, put together this wonderful celebration with Larry Jacobs and myself, and we all went back to Chicago. And to see everyone 20 years later was just fantastic.

You talk about some of the movies that are made today, and with some of the quote, gangbangers, or heavy rap artists . . . well, the guys who played Stone [Sherman Smith] and Robert [Morman Gibson] in *Cooley High* were actually part—the top part—of a group of youths called the Blackstone Rangers in Chicago at the time. I guess they could be equivalent to the Crips or the Bloods, or whatever we have today—whoever's in vogue. Michael Shultz and Steve Krantz saw these two guys walking down the street, and they didn't know this at the time, and they said, "You want to be in a movie?" And these guys said, "Yeah, but you know, we have other things to do." [Laughs.] When they found out who they were, they said they were gonna have to curtail those activities until the film was over.

Well, these guys turned out to be the greatest cats. They worked hard, but you know, they had business to take care of on the side. We were doing the car chase scene at one point, where we stole the car, and they were late. I mean *really* late. I mean three o'clock in the morning late. When they finally showed, Mike Shultz and Steven Krantz just went off. "Where have you been?" They were at the police station. "What were you doing at the police station?" They said, "Suspicion of murder." Shultz said, "Oh, excuse me. Makeup, could you touch them up?" [Laughs again.]

Well, they weren't involved. These guys, 20 years later, one of them was deceased. But the other one runs a very, very well-respected youth counseling organization in Chicago, and is doing very well. And it was *Cooley High* that turned his whole thing around.

DW: *It seems that some of the contemporary black filmmakers are slow to acknowledge the contributions of the people from the 1970s. Do you feel that you and your peers haven't been given the respect or credit you deserve?*

GT: I don't know. I've received a lot of respect from the young filmmakers and performers of this period. But you know, it's an inherent thing; you always have to move the old regime over. "Get out of the way and let me say this now." It's only fair, because we'll stay on the stump as long as someone will listen. But there is that desire to say, "Okay, I got you. Now let me add this to it." I think that's all that really is.

DW: *The films of the 1970s caused a big political backlash. A lot of people don't really understand how bad things got. As an artist, trying to make a living, did you ever feel a sense of pressure or responsibility?*

GT: It was a fine line to walk. Like I said, everyone had an opinion, and opinions were very vocal—very animatedly expressed at that time. The frustration I understood on many different levels. The frustration of those who considered themselves the keepers of the image of black Americans—the spokespersons for black Americans—I understood what they were saying, to a large degree, because they were looking at an overall picture. And like I said before, we were being fed a steady diet of mostly one particular type of image. Which, I maintain to this day, is like being fed too much candy. If you're hungry, candy will take the hunger away for a minute, but it's not going to nourish the body. I always just wanted the full meal—the full-course dinner. I love the Jim Brown and Fred Williamson movies; I love *Superfly* and *The Mack*. I just wanted to enjoy all these films without having to become a critic, without having to become anything other than just a moviegoer. I didn't want to watch it with my race. I wanted to watch it as a popcorn eater. And because it was so much of the one thing, I was never allowed to do that.

AR: *Did you personally find any of the films offensive?*

GT: Any of them?

AR: *Right. Any of them.*

GT: I would say that there were some I was glad it wasn't me that was in it, you know? But I always saw the value there. I always saw a value in their just being made. I always felt that if these films could just keep being made, and made long enough, then eventually the tide would have to change and the films would have to get better.

DW: *A lot of people I've talked to have expressed similar feelings. They were happy for the chances they had, but they wanted room to grow. It's like a Catch-22: you want to work but don't want to feed into a system that refuses to allow growth.*

GT: When you're fed that one diet, the burden it puts on you . . . for instance, I get more compliments on *J.D.'s Revenge* than for any of the other films I've ever done. I do not like *J.D.'s Revenge*. I got in a big argument and didn't want to do the publicity tour to promote the film, which got me out of favor with the studio—which at the time was really paying my bills. I'd just come out of *Cooley High* and went right into *J.D.'s Revenge*, but I felt when they put it together, they went for all the exploitive elements, when the script I read was clearly a Dr. Jekyll and Mr. Hyde story. The reason I protested so much was because of the message it would send. If there had been other films, I wouldn't have had to protest so loudly. Could've sat back, could've went on the tour, could've done the whole thing, and I would have been in the next AIP film. [Laughs.]

But you make these choices, either consciously or subconsciously, and play out that hand. And because the scale is tipped so much in one direction, it has a very powerful influence on what you as a performer—as an artist—are able to do or not do. Which is very unfair. You think, what is racism? That's a by-product of racism. That's a by-product of the exploited. That's how you become exploited, when you have to defend your work on those terms, because of what is lacking in society. It had many good things to offer, that period, but at the same time, all your decisions are very heavily weighed, or should have been very heavily weighed, or usually heavily weighed. Especially the people you've been talking to. They're very powerful people, very bright people. And I know these are the things that we all went through. And who the heck needs that? Who wants to go through all that? [Laughs again.] Give me the script, give me some money, and let me go to work. But that's what came with those times.

Glynn Turman in *J.D.'s Revenge.*

AR: *You said that* JD's Revenge *was not always intended to be an exploitation film. In what ways did the film change?*

GT: Well, I just think in terms of its exploitation of the gore and the guts and the eyes and the cow. All of that gore and blood stuff. I sort of saw it as more of a cerebral sort of picture, and they took it into a place where it was really more of a guts and gore kind of story. But I guess that worked for them, because it proved me wrong. [Laughs.] It turned out to be a very popular film.

AR: *Coming from a background in theater, did you approach a role like Ike in* JD's Revenge *the same way you would have any other role?*

GT: At that time, I was still very theater work conscious. I was still extremely technique motivated and conscious of the acting schools I had learned. So I was applying all my Method acting and theater training to my approach with that film [laughs] and that particular role, which was actually quite challenging. So yes, I applied my theater training and background to that film; very much so.

DW: *After about five years, the wave of black films seemed to come to a halt, just stopped. By 1977, excluding* Car Wash *(1976) and a few others, blaxploitation was dead. What brought about this death?*

GT: Economics. The thing that started the black pictures of the early 1970s was economic. It cost a dollar ninety-eight fifty to put together a black film, and the return on that dollar ninety-eight fifty was so great that it was able to pay the bills of the companies that indeed did make those films. They had not been making much money. If you look at the charts, at that time, Hollywood was in a slump you would not believe. And once again, we as a people came to the rescue. And they found, "Hey, these guys are going to keep the lights on. If we just keep doing this, we can pay the bills until we get out of this slump." Which is exactly what happened 10 years later. They got out of the slump; the pictures started hitting again. They were able to make the big picture again, and they said, "Thanks, boys and girls. See you later. Don't call us, we'll call you."

DW: *Everyone I talk to has a different opinion about the term blaxploitation. What are your feelings?*

GT: It's an unfair term that's blown out of proportion, in that the entire business is exploitive. That's the whole point. That's how they make pictures. That's why they make pictures—because they can exploit them. Black, white, female pictures, dog pictures, horse pictures—whatever—if they can't exploit it, they aren't going to make it. It has a negative connotation, but it's a reality. Again, the only thing that I was always upset with at the time was there was not enough diversity. And that was it. You're gonna have to exploit films—you want the films to make money. That is a very expensive business, and you have to make money to make the next picture. And that's all that's supposed to mean. The problem is, it became something else. It ended up meaning something else. It meant that you're only going to be able to say this—this is all we want to hear from you. Well, I actually have this aria I want to sing. "Shut up! We don't want to hear that. You will sing only this. You will say only this." Well, then that becomes propaganda.

DW: *What do we do to make things change?*

GT: It's land. It's property. All the wars are fought over land and property. The ideas come and go with the people, but it's the land. And I used to think at a time, well, if we were just the producers, or if we were just the directors, or the writers, had the money, we could do and say what we want. We can do that anyway. But then where do you say it? The truth is, if you don't own the theater, if you don't own the store, you can't sell the wares—you can't get your wares bought. Until we realize that across the board, we're losing a land, as black people, on a scale that is unprecedented. If you don't own the land, if you don't own the space, then no matter how profound your pieces are, you're always gonna have to ask someone, "Can I put this in your store?" And they always have the right to say, "No, I don't want to sell it. I don't care how good it is. I don't want to sell it in my store." You have to own your own store. You have to be the theater owner, the distributor.

AR: *In the past, you've said it was important for black people to "take control of their own propaganda." Is this what you meant by that?*

GT: Somebody said, "Quit bitchin' and start a revolution," you know? [Laughs.] It's along those same lines. If you don't like what's being said about you or you don't like the way you're being portrayed, then stop bitching about it and portray yourself. If you think you're being short-changed, do it yourself and put out what you feel is the truth. That's the American way. If you're going to be a true American, which I believe I am, then you have to have the balls to step up and do that. That's not the most humble approach towards civility. We're not the most humble people as Americans. We're a very aggressive people. So if you're gonna be an American, it's not enough to just rant and rave about wanting to be free. You have to pay the cost of what that means, and what that means is that you have to be very aggressive.

AR: *In terms of black cinema, do you feel that this has happened?*

GT: Absolutely. Yes, I'm very proud of these young people of color, both men and women, who have come up to the forefront. I respect them because they have indeed stepped up to the plate and made routes and inroads and taken their destinies into their own hands. And to me, that's the sign of a true American.

AR: *Now I'd like to switch gears a bit. You worked with many great actors in those films. I'd like to ask you about some of them. I'm going to name an actor and I'd like you to comment on them.*

GT: Okay.

AR: *We'll start with Max Julien.*

GT: Max was a very insightful man. Very business savvy and very courageous. He's a very, very courageous individual.

AR: *Richard Pryor.*

GT: [Laughs.] I loved Richard. That's all I can say. I just loved him. Richard was just remarkable all the way around. He went from the sublime to the ridiculous. He was just remarkable.

AR: *Garrett Morris.*

GT: Oh, Garrett. Garrett is a terrific character. A very talented, very energetic, very inspirational dude.

AR: *Vonetta McGee.*

GT: Oh, gee. I'm sorry Max saw her before I did! [Laughs again.] She's a buddy of mine. She's just a wonderful, warm human being. Very down to earth.

AR: *Robert Hooks.*

GT: That's my buddy there. Robert is probably one of the most underrated individuals as far as ingenuity and assertiveness. People still don't realize the contributions that Robert Hooks has made toward the business in regards to black performers. His contributions have been enormous.

AR: *Lou Gossett Jr.*

GT: Well, Lou is like my big brother from *Raisin in the Sun* to now. I owe a great deal to Lou. He got me my first agent in New York. He has always been there to look out for his little brother.

AR: *Juanita Moore.*

GT: Oh, she was a sweetheart. Juanita had such class and dignity. She was what you might call a gentle giant. That's what I would call her.

AR: *Moses Gunn.*

GT: Moses was, I think, another very underrated actor. He is a terrifically talented man, both on stage and in film. He honed his craft, and he owned it.

AR: *D'Urville Martin.*

GT: Ah, D'Urville. He left us too soon, but he sure left his mark. I've never seen anybody enjoy what they did as much as D'Urville Martin enjoyed acting.

AR: *What do you see as being the legacy of these films?*

GT: Well, I think, in a nutshell, that the legacy of the black films of the 1970s is that they did in fact prove that there was a black theatergoing audience who did want to see themselves represented on the silver screen. That's what we did. We showed people themselves up there on the screen, which had never really happened before. That was new. We gave them something to do on a Saturday night, instead of just going to see films by and about other people. And I think that was important.

CHAPTER 20

Melvin Van Peebles

A publicity photograph of writer, director, and composer Melvin Van Peebles.

You can't have a serious discussion about the blaxploitation cycle without mentioning Melvin Van Peebles. It would be like talking about the Bible and not mentioning Jesus. Van Peebles, who has been dubbed the Godfather of Black Cinema, made his earliest short films in 1957. Van Peebles then traveled to France, where he found success as a novelist. In 1968, he directed his first feature-length film, *The Story of a Three-Day Pass*. The film, which Van Peebles made in French, garnered him accolades and awards. He then followed this achievement with his first Hollywood production, the 1970 comedy *Watermelon Man*. The film, written by Herman Raucher, told the story of a moderately racist white man who wakes up one morning to find that he has somehow been transformed into a black man.

However, it would be Van Peebles's next film, *Sweet Sweetback's Baadasssss Song* (1971), for which he would be remembered. The now legendary independent film was written, directed, produced, composed by, and starred Van Peebles. The film, which Van Peebles boldly dedicated to "all the Brothers and Sisters who had enough of the Man," was a major indie success and is generally considered the first blaxploitation film.

Van Peebles has since helmed a number of films, including *Don't Play Us Cheap* (1973) and *Gang in Blue* (1996), which he codirected with his son Mario Van Peebles. In addition, he has found significant success as both an actor and a musician. Van Peebles is also the author of the book *Sweet Sweetback's Baadasssss Song: A Guerilla Filmmaking Manifesto*, and is the subject of the films *Baadasssss!* (2003) and *How to Eat Your Watermelon in White Company (and Enjoy It)* (2005).

ANDREW RAUSCH: *Tell me about your path to becoming a filmmaker.*

MELVIN VAN PEEBLES: I wrote a photo essay about my having worked as a grip man on a cable car in San Francisco. I'd wanted to be a writer, and I thought I had a unique perspective regarding this particular story. So one day, a guy gets on my cable car and he's asking me questions about the essay. My real name is Melvin Van Peebles, but I think he expected it to be something like Leroy Johnson. [Laughs.] So he didn't think I had written the essay. And so he said, "Well, who set up these angles in these photographs?" And I said, "I did." And he said, "Well, who wrote the text?" I said, "I did." "Well, who did the layout?" I said, "What's layout?" He said, "That's how you lay the page out." And I said, "I did." And he was dumbfounded. He said, "It just reads right along. It's like a movie." And I thought, shit, I should make a movie. And that's how I became a filmmaker.

I found a guy who had a camera, and he said I could use it if I took him and made him the director of photography, whatever the fuck that was. So I said, "Sure, okay." And I made my first film, and I projected it up on the wall. He said, "We haven't edited yet." I said, "What's that mean?" So someone gave me Eisenstein's *Film and Form*, and that book consisted of my film education. Period. That was all I ever had.

My first "feature" turned out to only be 11 minutes long, but what the hell? [Laughs again.]

AR: *You made your first full-length film,* The Story of a Three-Day Pass, *in France. How did that come about?*

MVP: Well, back before they had videocassettes and DVDs, they used to have film nights in gyms and auditoriums for film fanatics in the States. And there was this guy named Amos Vogel, who's still around, and he used to take films out and show them around the country. He was a film fanatic before it became *de rigueur* to be such. And the Cinemateque in France invited him to come and screen some of his films there. And I had leased my first few short films with him while I was on my way to Europe, where I was getting my PhD in astronomy. So Amos Vogel took these films there and screened them, and the French loved them. They then looked me up and sent me a letter in Holland. They said, "Wow, why aren't you making more films?" Well, I had gone down to Hollywood, but Hollywood was very lily white at the time. There was no chance of getting in. So I had gone back to my first love, which was celestial mechanics, which is a type of mathematics and astronomy.

So anyway, I go to France, and they were very nice to me. They screened my films, everybody kissed me, and then they drove off. And I'm standing there with two wet cheeks, three cans of film, not able to speak a single word of French, and not having a penny in my pocket. So I decided right then that I was either going to make it or die there in France. So, little by little, I learned French through immersion. Then I discovered that there was a French law that said a French writer could have a temporary director's card. So I wrote and published five novels in French and then asked for my director's card.

And there you are.

AR: *Could you tell me about the genesis of* Watermelon Man?

MVP: I was at Universal. My film *The Story of a Three-Day Pass* had won the Critic's Choice Award at the San Francisco Film Festival. I had returned to San Francisco as a French delegate. Nobody had known that I was American, let alone a black American. But I came back as a French delegate and won the festival! So from there, I was knocking around Hollywood, which was suddenly opening its doors to me. And my agent called me and said he had a script for me titled *The Night the Sun Came Out on Sleepy Hollow Lane.* He named several actors who were interested: Jack Lemmon, Alan Arkin. But none of the actors had seemed right yet. So he sent me the script so I could read it over the weekend. I called him on Monday and said, "I think you sent me the wrong script." And he asked why. "This character's black." And he said, "Yeah, but he's white for the first five minutes." And I said, "Well, why don't you get a black guy to play a white character in whiteface instead of a white guy to play a black character in blackface? Is that possible?" And that's how that project came about.

AR: *I understand the original ending of* Watermelon Man *was quite a bit different in the screenplay. Could you tell me about that?*

MVP: Well, he goes to take another shit and he wakes up and he's white again. It was all a bad dream.

AR: *You've scored all of your films yourself. Did you have any formal training prior to that, or did you just kind of teach yourself the way you did film-making?*

MVP: I still don't have any training. If it ain't broke, don't fix it! I numbered all the keys on the piano, all 86, because the piano was missing two keys. And I just started pecking away the melody I heard inside my head. And even today, I go into the studio and the guy says, "Oh, you wrote that in D minor? Blah, blah, blah." And I just say, "What the fuck do I know about any of that? Just play it."

AR: *Let's talk about* Sweet Sweetback's Baadasssss Song, *which you made yourself. What was the budget on that picture and how did you raise the money?*

MVP: I've never told anyone the budget. And the money was mine. I own everything, and I have no partners on that.

AR: *I remember reading that Bill Cosby had played some role in financing?*

MVP: Yes. He loaned me some money. Toward the end there, I needed some money. Bill stepped in and loaned me 50 grand, which I repaid to him rather than giving him a piece of the film.

AR: *Tell me about the distribution of* Sweet Sweetback's Baadasssss Song.

MVP: Everybody turned it down, so forth and so on. Then a company called Cinemation came along. They were in chapter 11 and they took it. Only two theaters in the entire United States would show it. Not even two cities, but two *theaters*! [Laughs.] And it broke box office records at both theaters immediately. After that, of course, everybody called me. And the company was not set up to hide the money, so I got the money. They couldn't afford any carpets to hide the money under at the time.

AR: *Different people call you a lot of different things: a rebel, a pioneer. Spike Lee has dubbed you the Godfather of Black Cinema. How do you see yourself?*

MVP: I'm not really much of a navel-looker. I have this method I live by. I have the newspaper delivered to me in the morning. I look in the obituary column each morning. If I'm not in there, then I get my ass up.

AR: *You made a documentary about the history of black cinema,* Classified X *(1998). How did that come about?*

MVP: A French company asked me if I wanted to make an anthology film about blacks in Hollywood. I said, "No, I'm not interested in that. But I will tell you the story I want to tell. You want that, fine, I'll make that. But I make it my way and I make the decisions. I'm the boss or I'm not making it."

So I made sure I was the boss. I'm also the producer and the narrator, and I also own 50 percent of the print. So I got to be the boss and do it the way I wanted to do it. People say, "Why don't you try to get American money?" I say, "Bullshit. I don't want American money. I'd rather be the boss and make what I want to make, the way I want to make it."

AR: *Your son, Mario Van Peebles, directed the feature* Baadasssss *about you. You've also been the focus of numerous books and documentaries. That must be quite surreal.*

MVP: When I first saw my son Mario's film, I said, "It's Seabiscuit on two legs." [Laughs.] I've become Seabiscuit!

AR: *You've become quite a cult figure.*

MVP: You know, I don't think it could happen to a nicer guy! [Laughs again.] People say, "You're so brave" or "You're so tough." I'm not. I'm not anything. It was like that movie *Network* (1976); I just wasn't going to take it anymore. People say, "How are you doing this?" or "It must be so difficult." Nope. It's not difficult at all. I just do it.

CHAPTER 21

Oscar Williams

Perhaps the most common myth of the blaxploitation era is that beyond Gordon Parks Sr. and Melvin Van Peebles, there were no black filmmakers behind the camera. The truth is that black writers, producers, and directors were not only hard at work, but they were responsible for some of the best films to come out of the 1970s. Such films as *Melinda* (1972), *Cooley High* (1975), *Trouble Man* (1972), *The Spook Who Sat by the Door* (1973), *Blacula* (1972), *Car Wash* (1976), and many others were among those that were either written, produced, or directed by black talent.

One of the most prolific black filmmakers to come along during the 1970s was Oscar Williams. Exploding on the scene in 1972 with *The Final Comedown*, which he wrote, produced, and directed, Williams displayed a genuine flair for powerful storytelling. Produced in conjunction with the American Film Institute and Roger Corman, *The Final Comedown* is a powerful film and stands as one of the finest of the blaxploitation era.

As a writer, Williams would go on to create some of the most memorable films to emerge from that period—*Black Belt Jones* (1974) and *Truck Turner* (1974)—both of which he also produced. His writing style was unique in that he infused comedy into both films without making them ridiculous. Williams, who now teaches intermediate film production at UCLA, also wrote and directed the disappointing Jim Kelly vehicle *Hot Potato* (1976) and directed the comedy classic *Five on the Black Hand Side* (1973).

Billy Dee Williams and Celia Kaye in a still from Oscar Williams's film *The Final Comedown.*

DAVID WALKER: *Talk about the neurosis of America and how it relates to film.*

OSCAR WILLIAMS: If you were to talk about the mass neurosis of the American audience, or America as a whole—it goes beyond film. The proof or the product of it is what we see in our society today. We have a society of people that really don't want to grow up and don't want to take responsibility. They say you should take responsibility for yourself and your actions. But at what point does that happen?

To look at the psychosis of America—you cannot deny it, because of the product of that psychosis. You've got kids wandering around the street with guns—shooting at one another—shooting at us. At one time, we were afraid of a group of people with guns; now everyone has guns. I think the fear now is that those guns are going to be turned on us, like we, as America, turned them on Indians, turned them on blacks. The great fear is that what we put on others is now coming back to us. And it is a logical fear.

But in that logical fear, we keep saying, "Take responsibility." No one takes responsibility, or no one wants to take responsibility, for correcting now, today, what we have done in the past. We tend to want to say, "Well, that happened in the past, so let's go on." How do you go on, as an individual, with something that has shaped your present? Something that is making you act this way now? You cannot go on. You've got to try and reach back and correct it. Because if you go on, you're going to go on crooked; you're not going to go on straight.

Everyone seems to throw the phrase out, "Well, people should take responsibility for themselves and their lives." What does that mean? At what point do we as a society—and a civilization—take responsibility for what we did to the American Indian? They are suffering today, for what was done to them. Now, should they take responsibility and clean their act up? We put this act on them. Just like a certain act was put on blacks when they were slaves. I often hear friends of mine say, "Why do blacks always bring up the slavery thing? Why not go on?" Well, why do we continually make cowboys and Indians in movies? Why do the Jews talk about Hitler and Germany? Because it was something that has helped shape the direction they have taken today.

It would be erroneous not to deal with the past that has had so much—and still has so much—to do with you as an individual and a person today. But try to put that in film, and you're not gonna get it made. Just like the society doesn't want to hear about it, the studios, or the executives that make decisions, don't want to hear about it—because they think or feel that the audience doesn't want to hear about it. But I say to you, and I submit to you, that the audience will hear about anything, if you put it to them in such a way that it touches them. They heard about *Roots* (1977), and it touched them. Why shouldn't it? They heard about *Schindler's List* (1993), and they felt it. So what is this whole thing?

I'll give you an example of what I find problematic. We have an industry that really either fears to make films with blacks in them, or fears to make films with subjects about blacks. But when Steven Spielberg does it and the film makes a lot of money, oh, that's different. It is only because Steven Spielberg, with Quincy Jones and the others, had enough power, or juice, or clout, or whatever you want to call it, to get *The Color Purple* (1985) made. And that movie was accepted. Of course it was a book first, but there are other books. There are other stories. And every single book and every single story can't go through Quincy Jones and Steven Spielberg.

When you have Quincy and Spielberg, then it's as if that power made the studio do a thing. That power enabled the studio to go along and cooperate. The studios then, I ask, don't have the ability to see the value in the stories that are out there—that touch and reach an audience? There is something wrong about the way things are going. If we all don't take a look at it, or we don't speak out about it, we're going to continually find the kids who are out there with guns—shooting at us—we're going to find that they are getting younger and younger and younger. We ourselves are going to produce a generation of murderers that become murderers for their own survival—the minute they come out of the womb. Hell of a concept. Hell of a concept.

DW: *I really want to talk about the misconception that there were no black filmmakers in the 1970s. There was you, and Bill Crain, Ivan Dixon, Michael Schultz, Lonne Elder, Gordon Parks Jr., Fred Williamson, and so many others. And of course there was Melvin [Van Peebles] and Gordon Parks Sr.*

OW: No one gives Gordon Parks—for instance—his just due. Or Melvin. Melvin is getting his just due now, because we are now realizing the value of Melvin Van Peebles. But Gordon Parks also has a similar value. Gordon was not only instrumental in having his views become films, but the way he did it, and the kind of quality of Gordon Parks's films—phenomenal. Phenomenal.

In most instances, you had black filmmakers, black writers, producers, directors, making these films. Most often the money and the way the film was distributed was not controlled by blacks. Most often the critics of the films were not blacks. And sometimes when you did have a black critic, he would try to ape a white critic to get a readership. When you have black critics only laying the term blaxploitation, and not the other value within those films, then those black critics also did a disservice to the black film-makers, the black writers, and the black producers.

If you were to talk about a film that was made by Charles Bronson—*Death Wish* (1974)—and we called it "whitesploitation," you'd laugh. Why then don't we laugh when we take a film that's made by Jim Brown or Fred Williamson and we call that blaxploitation? Both of those films are fantasies, going to an audience, and in those fantasies we have a star—an actor—going toward villains, and settling the situation, bringing normalcy back in area, in a place, through violence. Violence against violence to quell violence. When the black actor did it, or when the black film was made that way, it was a terrible thing. It was a negative thing, blah, blah, blah, blah. But when Clint Eastwood did it, it was "Hoorah!" There is a double standard, and a ridiculous double standard that's in our faces—in all our faces. The silence, or the addition to this madness, by the silence of the majority, is something I find troubling. Violence is violence. Why is it negative when a black character does it in a film, and why is it not negative when a white character does it in a film? *Scarface* (1983) was as violent as *Shaft* (1971). But *Shaft* is called blaxploitation, and *Scarface* is called a good film. It is madness. It is pure and simple nonsense.

DW: *I feel there's a definite value to the films of the 1970s. Am I wrong in believing that?*

OW: Look at it two ways. One, we got a chance to show young people that they can have a future in film, that they could make them. They could be writers. They could be directors. They could be actors. In those films of the 1970s, the young people who are making films today saw themselves up on screen—saw people who looked like them up on screen. And they saw a world that they thought wasn't available to them open up. That's one.

The studio saw the availability of making some money in those films, and with those films, at a time when the audience was really tired of the same old ordinary humdrum white knight on a white horse films—that's what we call it in the business. White knight comes in and saves the white princess on the white horse. So what? The stories are the same. You get tired of seeing them. And the audiences even get tired of seeing them, so you have to then try to put something else in them to make it a little different. But in terms of black films of the time, those films were a shot in the arm to an audience. We began to see a different side of the coin, a different side of life, a different side of what the American story is about. And it was good for them. We can do it again, and do different things rather than showing what we showed in the 1970s, and that was the black man, in the ghetto, running away from the police, or getting whitey. We're tired of that now. The audience is tired of that. These are things that we can go to, if the opportunities were there. Perhaps we have to create the opportunities ourselves.

I think that it is partially up to the black audience to step up and say, "We want to see different things. We want to see this and that. We don't want to see the ghetto story anymore." Maybe John Singleton did it definitively in *Boyz N the Hood* (1991). How many times is the studio going to ask you to make *Boyz N the Hood*? We as a group of black filmmakers, and the audience—both black and white—should ask to see something different, should demand to see something different. If that happens, we will see something different. Because after all, it is an art and it is a business. But the business part most often rules over the art.

DW: *Did you, as a filmmaker and as a black man, ever feel pressure? Pressure from political groups, or from studios, or from audiences?*

OW: There was more pressure to do something that was beneficial, even though you were often asked to do a film, or put a character in a film, that you thought was stereotypical or negative. You had more pressure trying to make that character sound, to make that character valuable, to make that character meaningful. I have worked on films where I had given the character a whole history, and the producers took the history out and just showed the character beating people up and shooting at people, and not showing why, and how the character came to that. That was where a lot of pressure was.

Also, we had pressure from our own black film critics. They would always hit us over the head with what we were doing, and not realize that in what we were doing there were some benefits to be derived, or benefits that were derived.

DW: *Why are there no more characters like Black Belt Jones or Truck Turner, or the films in which those characters existed?*

OW: The opportunity isn't there as much. When those films were made, the industry was in financial trouble, so they had to do something to hold, or stay, until they could get out of those problems. Now films are so much more expensive, and the audience has dwindled so much, that in order to get that kind of character out there, you need not only to create them, but you need the money to make the films that are gonna work. As much as we may think the film industry—Hollywood film industry—does different things, they really do the same thing with a slight difference in it. They really make the same films over and over again with a slight difference in them—with a new star in it. Whether the films are made as good or as bad as the previous film, that's for you and the audience to answer. I don't think so, but that's my personal feeling about it.

DW: *Tell me about the best experience you had as a filmmaker.*

OW: The film that I had the most fun making was *Five on the Black Hand Side*. Because at the time *Five on the Black Hand Side* was made, the financial interests in that film kept on asking this question, "Can a comedy about a black film make it, because it isn't what's being done now? What's being done now is the angry film, with the violent main character, going up against whitey in the community." So it was convincing the entities that

were putting the money into the film that it would work. And the film worked.

DW: *I've always believed that there is more of a market out there than the studios are willing to acknowledge. I know many filmmakers that feel frustrated that they cannot make the types of films that they believe an audience wants to see. How can this change?*

OW: Nowadays we need to have a vocal audience who says what they want. Who will say what they don't want. Who will say what they do want.

Who will say it profoundly. Because ultimately the films are made for an audience, and it's the audience who will decide whether a film is successful or not, or whether or not they want to see more films like this, or different kinds of films. We need to get the audience—especially the black audience—involved. If there is a black middle class, and that black middle class wants to see better films, or different kinds of films, say so. Say so by going to the box office. Or say so by not going to the box office. But say so. Do something. Don't just be silent and wish that changes would occur by your silence, because nothing happens in silence. Something always happens when we make it happen, when we move towards it. You take the smallest pebble and you start that pebble rolling down a hill, before you know it, it collects, and gets bigger, and eventually you have a boulder rolling down the hill.

I just want the black filmmakers to be bolder. Say more. Be more adventurous. And I want the black audience to speak up. I want the NAACP, CORE, and all those organizations to get involved when a black film opens. Get involved by supporting an opening. Get involved by speaking about a film—not only speaking about the films you like—speak about the films you don't like. Get involved. And speak about the films from a first-hand knowledge. Go see it and talk about it. Go see it and say, "I loved it. You ought to see it." Go and see it and say, "I hated it. Don't ever make a film like that again." But the audience needs to get involved. There are also blacks who could put money into films and make them, rather than just staying on the side and saying, "Well, I don't know anything about the filmmaking process. I don't want to lose my money." But yet, they still say we should see better films than that; better films than that should be made.

I have a feeling that films reflect the life that we live, reflect the place that we live in, and the time that we live in. So people who are living in that time should become involved in the films that are being made, and not just sit there like a lump.

CHAPTER 22

Fred Williamson

Fred Williamson is a modern legend. When one thinks of Williamson (or "the Hammer," as he's known in some circles), the immortal characters he played during the prolific 1970s come to mind: Nigger Charley, Black Caesar, and *No Way Back*'s (1976) Jesse Crowder are just a handful of the larger-than-life heroes he brought to life on the silver screen. It was in these roles, and in films such as *The Legend of Nigger Charley* (1972), *Hell up in Harlem* (1973), *Mean Johnny Barrows* (1976), and *Joshua* (1976) that Williamson did more than just carve out a niche for himself. Williamson was, and continues to be, far more than the typical Hollywood tough guy. Over the years, he has continued to survive as a viable force in the film industry by producing and directing his own films. While other black filmmakers have looked to the studio system for some type of artistic welfare, Williamson has gone outside the system to finance his films. And just as mavericks like Oscar Micheaux and Spenser Williams paved the way for those who would follow, Williamson also helped to clear a path for the independent black filmmaker. Perhaps some of his productions have been lacking in one area or another, but his impact is beyond measure. Fred has successfully raised financing for and produced films that have been distributed on a worldwide level. His movies have made money and disproved the myth that films with blacks cannot make money overseas.

Before Williamson would become the leading man of black action films, he was an equally impressive professional football player. It was during his 10-year career as an offensive lineman for the Oakland Raiders and then the Kansas City Chiefs that Williamson earned the nickname "the

Hammer." Like his contemporary Jim Brown, Williamson became a legend on the gridiron. But unlike Brown, he didn't retire from football to pursue a film career. After retiring from football, Williamson established an architectural firm. But it wasn't long before he grew restless for the attention and adoration that he'd known on the playing field. Packing his bags and moving to Los Angeles to take a crack at acting, Williamson soon found himself cast as Diahann Carroll's boyfriend on the sitcom *Julia*. He then landed supporting roles in films like *M*A*S*H* (1970) and *Tell Me That You Love Me, Junie Moon* (1970). When the blaxploitation cycle began, Williamson was in a unique position in that he was already a household name. His first starring role in these films was Al Adamson's *The Hammer*.

In the mid-1970s, as the flames of the blaxploitation cycle were quickly dying, Williamson took the initiative and formed his own company, Po' Boy Productions. His first films were *No Way Back* (1976) and *Adios Amigos* (1976). While the genre that had made him a screen star was dying, and with it the careers of many of his contemporaries, Williamson maintained a vital career. With more than 20 films produced by Po' Boy, Williamson has been more than successful.

DAVID WALKER: *I guess the best way to get started is to talk about the word blaxploitation itself. What does it mean to you? What do you think of the word?*

FRED WILLIAMSON: First of all, I never understood what it meant. Who was being exploited? Certainly not me. My checks cleared. And the people who worked for me, their checks cleared. So who the hell was being exploited? The people went to the show because they enjoyed what they were seeing.

DW: *Okay, fair enough. Let's talk about why the people enjoyed what they were seeing. The films of that era, whether you call them black action films, blaxploitation films, or whatever, were very popular. Why?*

FW: You have to look at the whole picture. The total picture is important. You have to understand that in the early 1970s and late 1960s, they were still siccing dogs on black people. More than eight people, more than 10 blacks on a corner constituted a riot, so it was time to call out the dog squad. So there was no way for the black public to fight back. They had no way to fight back without getting themselves into serious trouble. So what we brought them at the time was a guy who won the fight. When the smoke cleared, we were still standing. There wasn't no butlers. There wasn't no porters. There wasn't no shoeshine guy. And when I did do a shoeshine guy in *Black Caesar*, I was killin' somebody with the shoeshine box. [Laughs.] So we had images that were needed and necessary for that particular time and that particular era. It's unfair to compare that picture with where we are today, because the times have changed. We don't need to make "get whitey" pictures anymore, but that's what we needed at that time. We needed a way to fight back. We needed a way to pay back whitey. So we did that. We went through that evolution.

Now we want to stand up just as winners and fighters. Now I take down anybody. I'm an equal opportunity employer. I beat up white people, yellow people, pink people, black people, purple people. It don't matter what color they are; if you bad and you in my movie, you going down. I'm gonna be the only one standing. I'm gonna be the last one to go down in my movie, as is [Sylvester] Stallone, like [Arnold] Schwarzenegger, all of 'em. You know they're not gonna get killed in their movies. So you have to find a clever way to beat up the bad guys and leave you standin' at the end of the movie. The whole evolution has changed.

I have maintained my image, which has been very hard and difficult to do, because I've turned down a lot of work. They want me to play subservient roles, or go to jail right away, or be the crook or bad guy that gets locked up at the end of the movie. That's not what I want to do. That's not my thing. I want to be like Schwarzenegger. I want to be like Clint Eastwood. I want to be like Charles Bronson. I want to be the guy who takes the bad guy out.

One of my criteria when I first came to Hollywood, that I always wanted to do, because I always considered myself a he-man, so I wanted to star in movies just like all the guys I watched. Humphrey Bogart, George Raft, Edward G. Robinson, all those guys being heroes. So when I came to Hollywood, that's what I wanted to do. But then they started offering me all kinds of weird roles. I said, "Listen. You're not listening to me. I got three rules. One, you can't kill me. Two, I gotta win all the fights. And three, I want the girl at the end of the movie." They didn't listen. I started making my own movies. And I damn sure ain't gonna die in my own movie. And if I want the girl, I just write at the end line of the screenplay: "The Hammer gets the girl."

DW: *You talked about the difficulty in maintaining your image, and the types of roles others have wanted you to play versus what you want to play, and still* *your career has continued. Three decades you've been doing this. How do you account for your longevity?*

FW: Intelligence. I don't need pats on the back to make my life survive. I understood being used when I came into the movie business. I understood it from being a pro football player. When you get hurt, they drag you off to the side of the field and they replace you with somebody else, and they give you two weeks to get ready, and if you don't get ready, you've lost your job. So I understood being used. And I also understood that when people make more money off of me than me, then something's wrong with that picture.

So when I came into the motion picture business, I had a whole plan. I had a whole concept about marketability. If you understand my football career, you know that I understood marketability long before anybody else did. I was the first guy to wear white shoes. I was the first really controversial football player. The Hammer. The league fined me $100 a game for wearing white shoes, because they said I was breaking the dress code of professional football. I had pads on my arms and had an artist paint hammers on them, and so they fined me $100 a game for advocating violence in the league. But it doesn't really matter. Because when people came to the game, they knew I was there. They knew number 24 who wore the white shoes and played defensive back. You have to understand the whole picture. People who have favorite football teams never know the defensive backs. They know who runs the ball, throws the ball, and catches the ball. They can't name the defensive back. But when I played, they named the Hammer, Williamson, the guy who wore the white shoes. So I understood marketability.

When I came into the industry, I was giving them the opportunity to make me a marketable star. And they did. Rather quickly. Faster than I thought they would. Because when I came into show business, it took me three weeks to get a series. I was Diahann Carroll's boyfriend on the *Julia* show. While I was there, I did the movie *M*A*S*H* and then I said, "This is easy. Anybody can do this." Then I came up with an idea: "Let me make a western." So I went to Paramount, and this is all within two-and-a-half years, and so I went to Paramount and I said, "I want to make a black western." And they said, "What do you want to call it?" And I said, "I want to call it *The Legend of Nigger Charley*." And they about jumped out the window. They didn't understand terminology. They didn't understand that I wanted to use this dynamic impact. We took out a big billboard in New

York, and all it had was me with short sleeves and a gun, and it said, "Nigger Charley is here."

It was this impact, and this concept of marketability, that made me understand that sooner or later what was happening in the 1970s was going to run out. I started in 1970, and by 1973 I had formed my own company, Po' Boy Productions. The reason I call it Po' Boy is if you ever work for me, don't ask for no money, 'cause I got no cash to pay you. So by 1973, I had already done *Black Caesar*, *Hell up in Harlem*, and the *Legend* and *Soul of Nigger Charley* (1973). I had become a marketable commodity. People knew who I was. They knew my name on the marquee. So after 1973, I took myself away from Hollywood. I said from then on, if you want a Fred Williamson movie, you gotta come to Fred Williamson. And that's how I started doing my own films, and staying in the genre that I wanted to.

DW: *If other folks had your insights, maybe more of them would have survived the downfall of the genre.*

FW: You can't really say it was a downfall, because when they stopped making the movies, the movies were still making money; they were just not making enough money for the majors. Universal's light bill is 10 million bucks, and our films were grossing 10 to 15 million. They just weren't making enough money for the majors to stay interested in them; they wanted 40- and 50- and 60-million-dollar grosses, and that 10 and 15 million was just not enough for them. So it wasn't really a downfall; they just weren't making enough money.

DW: *Yeah, the economic side of it did have something to do with it, but what about the political backlash? You had guys like Tony Brown saying everyone involved with these films were race traitors and guilty of treason.*

FW: That doesn't make any sense. I don't really care who hires me as long as he's letting me do what I want to do, and as long as I'm not doing something that's destroying my image or going against what I believe as a person. It doesn't really matter who hires me. As long as I'm getting paid, and doing what I want to do, it doesn't really matter. Because every time I do a job, I get stronger. I get more powerful. And then I can really start doing the things I want to do.

It doesn't matter what you do. Somebody's not going to like everything you do anyway, man. Our people are strange when it comes to that anyway. We rarely stroke each other. We always have a lot of negative things to say about each other. But rarely do you hear a group stroke an individual. We always gotta find something bad to say. Something negative. I mean, if we're gonna do that, do it private. Don't do it public. That's one of our problems as a black race.

DW: *In-fighting and backstabbing.*

FW: As they always say, man, it's only crowded at the bottom. It ain't crowded at the top.

DW: *I want to go back to the longevity of your career. You've written, directed, produced, and starred in over 40 movies. How do you think your body of work and your accomplishments have affected those who have come after you?*

FW: It hasn't influenced it at all. Because as blacks come into the business, they grasp it like it's theirs. They grasp it like it's never been done before. All the new directors and producers that come in, it's like they discovered the black market. They don't take from the past. They don't reach back and bring people who've been through it all and try to gain anything from them. They accept it like it's theirs. So it really hasn't changed much.

As far as actors and talent are concerned, you see a lot more comedy, but it's the same old same old. All it is is an extension of comedy. If I saw any black families acting the way I see these black families acting on sitcoms, I'd call the police on 'em. I don't know any black families that act like that. But that's what's an easy sell, because it doesn't offend anybody. It's safe. It's middle-of-the-road comedy, and that's fine. Let 'em do it. But that's not what I'm going to succumb to, and you'll never see me doing any stuff like that.

DW: *So how can we start to change things? How, as black filmmakers, can we make a difference?*

FW: The power in anything is unity. The reality check is this: white Hollywood doesn't need any black actor at all. They can make films that will gross $100 million without any black actor. Now, if they want to make a film, and make it $120 million, then they give you [Wesley] Snipes. And they say, "Okay, with Snipes opposite a white star, now it's gonna make 120 or 115. So we give you Denzel, now it's gonna make $130 million. We give you Danny Glover, now it's gonna make 135."

Now what they don't understand is, these three guys have this much power to bring $20 million gross extra, or $30 million gross, why don't they unite? Why don't they form their own company and make their own

Fred Williamson looking tough as ever in *Hell up in Harlem*.

product and do their own thing? Let Hollywood do what they want to do, and they can do what they want to do. And if Hollywood adheres to their rules and gives them the $20 and $30 million that they give everybody else, then okay, fine. But if they don't, they don't need Hollywood. They don't understand that they don't need Hollywood. Hollywood needs them to get the gross up to $120 or $130 million.

All we have to understand is unity. As a people, again. I'm into this people thing, because we don't help each other. We don't reach back. And if they united and understood that, the industry would grow real fast as far as blacks are concerned.

DW: *It sounds like you're talking about a separate black Hollywood.*

FW: We can have separate but equal. You can work together and still be separate. It doesn't mean you have to ignore them. It doesn't mean you don't ever have to work in another film with a white star again. But you can certainly be separate and have the same power that they have. You can only live in one house at one time. You can't drive six cars at once. If you can drive six cars at one time, you're a better guy than I am.

DW: *On a closing note: out of all the things you've seen and done in the film business, what was the one thing that stands out the most in your mind?*

FW: Probably the most exciting thing I did was to make a film called *The Legend of Nigger Charley*, 'cause I'd stand back and watch the shock on people's faces. I watched Frank Yablans of Paramount try to explain at a Beverly Hills party how they made a movie that cost only $600,000 and made $30 million. And people asked, "What's your top grossing picture of the year, Frank?" "Well, it was a movie called (mumble, mumble) *Charley*." I loved that, because it was going against the grain, and it was making money and being successful. And watching them squirm was very pleasant. Putting that across was probably the most exciting thing in my career.

Blaxploitation from A to Z

This is an attempt to catalogue all known blaxploitation films. Some films, such as *In the Heat of the Night* (1967), predate 1970, which is generally believed to be the birth of the blaxploitation era. Others, such as *Penitentiary III* (1987), were released after 1976, which is generally considered the end of the blaxploitation era. However, these films still bear the characteristics of a blaxploitation film.

In some cases, next to nothing is known about a film in the blaxploitation genre other than its title, as many of these films have faded into obscurity. In other instances, films are rumored to exist but could not be substantiated.

When possible, we have provided the availability of these titles on either DVD or VHS (or both). Although the majority of these films have been released in one format or the other, not all titles remain in print (especially those on VHS). Also note that rampant bootlegging of these films and their frequent release under alternate titles make it impossible to provide a complete listing. However, most legitimate distributors are listed along with the format.

$6000 Nigger, a.k.a. *Super Soul Brother* (1978)
Director: Rene Martinez Jr.
Writers: Laura S. Martinez, Rene Martinez Jr.
Starring: Wildman Steve (Steve Gallon)
VHS: Xenon

Aaron Loves Angela (1975, Columbia)
Director: Gordon Parks Jr.
Writer: Gerald Sanford
Starring: Kevin Hooks, Irene Cara, Moses Gunn, Robert Hooks
VHS: Sony Pictures

Abar, the First Black Superman, a.k.a. *In Your Face* (1977)
Director: Frank Packard
Writers: James Smalley, J. Walter Smith
Starring: Tobar Mayo

Abby (1974, AIP)
Director: William Girdler
Writers: William Girdler, G. Cornell Layne
Starring: William Marshall, Carol Speed, Terry Carter, Austin Stoker
DVD: Televista

Across 110th Street (1972, United Artists)
Director: Barry Shear
Writer: Luther Davis
Starring: Anthony Quinn, Yaphet Kotto, Anthony Franciosa, Paul Benjamin, Ed Bernard, Richard Ward, Antonio Fargas
DVD and VHS: MGM

Adios Amigos (1975, Atlas)
Director: Fred Williamson
Writer: Fred Williamson
Starring: Richard Pryor, Fred Williamson, Thalmus Rasulala
VHS: Simitar Entertainment

AKA Cassius Clay, a.k.a. *Muhammad Ali a.k.a. Cassius Clay* (1970)
Director: Jim Jacobs
Documentary
DVD and VHS: MGM

Alabama's Ghost (1972)
Director: Fredric Hobbs
Writer: Fredric Hobbs
Starring: Christopher Brooks, Loni Freeman
VHS: Thriller Video

Amazing Grace (1973)
Director: Stan Lathan
Writer: Matt Robinson
Starring: Moms Mabley, Moses Gunn, Slappy White, Rosalind Cash, Butterfly McQueen, Stepin Fetchit
DVD: MGM

The Arena, a.k.a. *Naked Warriors* (1973, New World)
Director: Steve Carver
Writers: John William Corrington, Joyce Hooper Corrington
Starring: Pam Grier, Margaret Markov
DVD: New Concorde; VHS: MGM/UA

Bad, Black, and Beautiful (1972)
Director: Bobby Davis
Writer: Bobby Davis
Starring: Gwynn Barbee, Sammy Sams, Levi Balfour

The Bad Bunch, a.k.a. *Tom*; *Nigger Lover* (1976, Dimension)
Director: Greydon Clark
Writers: Greydon Clark, Alvin L. Fast
Starring: Greydon Clark, Tom Johnigarn, Aldo Ray, Jock Mahoney
VHS: United Home

Ball Buster, a.k.a. *San Francisco Ball Buster*

Bamboo Gods and Iron Men (1974, AIP)
Director: Cesar Gallardo
Writers: Ken Metcalfe, Joseph Zucchero
Starring: James Inglehart, Shirley Washington
DVD: HK Video

Bare Knuckles (1977)
Director: Don Edmonds
Writer: Don Edmonds
Starring: Gloria Hendry, Sherry Jackson, John Daniels
VHS: MGM/UA

The Baron, a.k.a. *Baron Wolfgang Von Tripps*; *Black Cue* (1975)
Director: Philip Fenty
Writer: Philip Fenty
Starring Calvin Lockhart, Richard Lynch, Charles MacGregor, Marlene
   Clark
DVD: Echo Bridge Home Entertainment

The Beast Must Die, a.k.a. *Black Werewolf* (1975)
Director: Paul Annett
Writer: Michael Winder
Starring: Calvin Lockhart, Marlene Clark, Peter Cushing, Charles Grey
DVD: Dark Sky Films; VHS: Image Entertainment

The Big Bird Cage (1972, New World)
Director: Jack Hill
Writer: Jack Hill
Starring: Pam Grier, Anita Ford, Carol Speed, Sid Haig
DVD and VHS: New Concorde

The Big Score (1983, Almi)
Director: Fred Williamson
Writer: Gail Morgan Hickman
Starring: Fred Williamson, John Saxon, Richard Roundtree, Ed Lauter,
   Nancy Wilson, D'Urville Martin
DVD: First Run Features; VHS: Vestron Video

Big Time (1977)
Director: Andrew Georgias
Writers: Anton Diether, Andrew Georgias, Lou Goss, Christopher Joy,
   Leon Isaac Kennedy, Smokey Robinson
Starring: Christopher Joy, Tobar Mayo, Jayne Kennedy, Art J. Evans, Roger
   E. Mosely

The Bingo Long Traveling All-Stars and Motor Kings (1976)
Director: John Badham
Writers: Hal Barwood, Matthew Robbins
Starring: Billy Dee Williams, James Earl Jones, Richard Pryor
DVD and VHS: Universal

Black Alley Cats (1974)
Director: Henning Schellerup
Writer: Joseph Drury
Starring: Sunshine Woods, Charlene Miles

Black Angels (1970, Merrick International)
Director: Lawrence Merrick
Writer: Lawrence Merrick
Starring: King John III, Des Roberts

Black Belt Jones (1974, Warner Bros.)
Director: Robert Clouse
Writers: Alexandra Rose, Alex Ross, Fred Weintraub, Oscar Williams
Starring: Jim Kelly, Gloria Hendry, Scatman Crothers, Alan Weeks, Eric
    Laneuville
VHS: Warner Home Video

The Black Bunch, a.k.a. *Super Sisters*; *Vicious Virgins* (1973)
Director: Henning Schellerup
Writer: Cherter Charlfi
Starring: Gladys Bunxer, Anita Cunningham, Rina Russell, Carmen Wiley

Black Caesar (1973, AIP)
Director: Larry Cohen
Writer: Larry Cohen
Starring: Fred Williamson, Gloria Hendry, Julius Harris, D'Urville Mar-
    tin, Don Pedro Colley
DVD and VHS: MGM

Black Chariot (1971, Goodwin)
Director: Robert L. Goodwin
Writer: Robert L. Goodwin
Starring: Bernie Casey

Black Cobra (1986, Almi)
Director: Stelvio Massi
Writer: Danilo Massi
Starring: Fred Williamson

Black Dragon (1974)
Director: Chin-ku Lu
Starring: Ron Van Clief

Blackenstein, a.k.a. *Black Frankenstein* (1973, Exclusive International)
Director: William A. Levy
Writer: Frank R. Saletri
Starring: Jon Hart, Ivory Stone, Joe DeSue
DVD and VHS: Xenon

Black Eye (1974, Warner Bros.)
Director: Jack Arnold
Writers: Mark Haggard, Jim Martin
Starring: Fred Williamson, Teresa Graves
VHS: Warner Home Video

Black Gestapo, a.k.a. *Ghetto Warriors* (1975, Bryanstone)
Director: Lee Frost
Writers: Wes Bishop, Lee Frost
Starring: Rod Perry, Charles P. Robinson
DVD: TGG Direct; VHS: United American Video

Black Girl (1972, Cinerama)
Director: Ossie Davis
Writer: J. E. Franklin
Starring: Leslie Uggams, Brock Peters

Black Godfather (1974, Cinemation)
Director: John Evans
Writer: John Evans
Starring: Rod Perry, Damu King
DVD: Vivendi; VHS: Xenon

Black Gunn (1972, Columbia)
Director: Robert Hartford-Davis
Writers: Franklin Coen, Robert Hartford-Davis, Robert Shearer
Starring: Jim Brown, Martin Landau, Brenda Sykes
DVD: Sony Pictures

Black Heat, a.k.a. *Murder Gang; U.S. Vice; Girl's Hotel* (1976)
Director: Al Adamson
Writers: John D'Amato, Bud Donnelly, Sheldon Lee
Starring Timothy Brown, Russ Tamblyn, Tanya Boyd
DVD: E.I. Independent; VHS: Xenon

Blackjack (1978, Cinemation)
Director: John Evans
Writer: John Evans
Starring: Damu King, Tony Burton

Black Jack, a.k.a. *Wild in the Sky; God Bless the Bomb* (1971)
Director: William T. Naud
Writers: Richard Gautier, Peter Marshall, William T. Naud
Starring: Georg Sanford Brown, Keenan Wynn

Black Jesus, a.k.a. *Seated at His Right* (1968)
Director: Valerio Zurlini
Writers: Franco Brusati, Valerio Zurlini
Starring: Woody Strode, Jean Servais
DVD: Eclectic; VHS: Ivy Classics

Black Klansman (1974)
Director: Terence Young
Writers: Millard Kaufman, Samuel Fuller
Starring: Lee Marvin, O. J. Simpson, Richard Burton
DVD: Miracle Pictures; VHS: Paramount

Black Lolita, a.k.a. *Wildcat Women* (1975, Parliament)
Director: Stephen Gibson
Writers: Mike Brown, Stephen Gibson
Starring Yolanda Love, Ed Cheatwood
DVD: Pathfinder Home Entertainment

Black Mama, White Mama, a.k.a. *Women in Chains* (1973, AIP)
Director: Eddie Romero
Writers: H. R. Christian, Jonathan Demme, Joe Viola
Starring: Pam Grier, Margaret Markov, Sid Haig
DVD and VHS: MGM

Black Rodeo (1972)
Director: Jeff Kanew
Writer: Jeff Kanew
Documentary featuring Woody Strode and Muhammad Ali

Black Samson (1974, Warner Bros.)
Director: Charles Bail
Writers: Daniel B. Cady, Warren Hamilton Jr.
Starring: Rockne Tarkington, Carol Speed, William Smith
VHS: Warner Home Video

Black Samurai (1977, B.J.L.J. International)
Director: Al Adamson
Writer: B. Readick
Starring: Jim Kelly
DVD and VHS: BCI/Eclipse

Black Shampoo (1976, Dimension)
Director: Greydon Clark
Writers: Greydon Clark, Alvin L. Fast
Starring: John Daniels, Tanya Boyd, Joe Ortiz
DVD: VCI Entertainment; VHS: United Home

The Black Six (1974, Cinemation)
Director: Matt Cimber
Writer: George Theakos
Starring: Gene Washington, Carl Eller, Lem Barney, Mercury Morris, Willie Lanier, Mean Joe Greene
DVD: TGG Direct; VHS: Miracle Pictures

Black Starlet, a.k.a. *Black Gauntlet* (1974)
Director: Chris Munger
Writers: Daniel Cady, Howard Ostroff
Starring: Juanita Brown, Eric Mason, Damu King, Rockne Tarkington
VHS: JTC, Inc.

Black Street Fighter, a.k.a. *Black Fist; Fist* (1977, Worldwide)
Director: Timothy Galfas
Starring: Richard Lawson, Dabney Coleman

Black the Ripper (rumored)

Black Voodoo, a.k.a. *The Possession of Nurse Sherri; Terror Hospital; Beyond the Living* (1978)
Director: Al Adamson
Writers: Michael Bockman, Gregg Tittinger
Starring: Jill Jacobson, Marilyn Joi
DVD: E.I. Independent Cinema; VHS: Xenon

Blacula (1972, AIP)
Director: William Crain
Writers: Raymond Koenig, Joan Torres
Starring: William Marshall, Vonetta McGee, Denise Nicholas, Thalmus Rasulala
DVD and VHS: MGM

Blind Rage (1976)
Director: Efren Piñon
Writers: Leon Fong, Efren Piñon, Jerry O. Tirazona
Starring: D'Urville Martin, Leo Fong, Fred Williamson

Blue Collar (1978, Universal)
Director: Paul Schrader
Writers: Leonard Schrader, Paul Schrader
Starring: Richard Pryor, Harvey Keitel, Yaphet Kotto
DVD: Starz/Anchor Bay; VHS: Universal

Body and Soul (1981, Cannon)
Director: George Bowers
Writer: Leon Isaac Kennedy
Starring: Leon Isaac Kennedy, Jayne Kennedy
DVD and VHS: MGM

Bogard, a.k.a. *Black Fist* (1975)
Directors: Timothy Galfas, Richard Kaye
Writers: Richard Kaye, Tim Kelly, Andrew Maisner
Starring: Richard Lawson, Philip Michael Thomas, Dabney Coleman
DVD: Phoenix Entertainment; VHS: United

Bone, a.k.a. *Housewife; Dial Rat for Terror; Beverly Hills Nightmare* (1970)
Director: Larry Cohen
Writer: Larry Cohen
Starring: Yaphet Kotto, Andrew Duggan, Joyce Van Patten
DVD: Blue Underground; VHS: Kino

Book of Numbers (1973, Avco Embassy)
Director: Raymond St. Jacques
Writer: Larry Spiegel
Starring: Raymond St. Jacques, Freda Payne, Philip Michael Thomas, D'Urville Martin

Boss Nigger, a.k.a. *Boss; Black Bounty Hunter; Black Bounty Killer* (1974, Dimension)
Director: Jack Arnold
Writer: Fred Williamson
Starring: Fred Williamson, D'Urville Martin, William Smith

Brotherhood of Death (1976, Downtown)
Director: Bill Berry
Starring: Michael Hodge, Ron David, Rick Ellis
DVD: Starz/Anchor Bay

Brother John (1971, Columbia)
Director: James Goldstone
Writer: Ernest Kinoy
Starring: Sidney Poitier, Will Greer, Bradford Dillman, Beverly Todd, Lincoln Kilpatrick, Paul Winfield
DVD and VHS: Sony Pictures

Brother on the Run, a.k.a. *Man on the Run; Soul Brothers Die Hard; Black Force II* (1973)
Directors: Edward J. Lakso, Herbert Strock
Writers: Edward J. Lakso, Herbert Strock
Starring: Terry Crater, Kyle Johnson, Gwen Mitchell, James B. Sikking

Brothers (1977, Warner Bros.)
Director: Arthur Barron
Writers: Edward Lewis, Mildred Lewis
Starring: Bernie Casey, Vonetta McGee, Ron O'Neal, Renny Roker, Stu Gilliam

Buck and the Preacher (1972, Columbia)
Director: Sidney Poitier
Writer: Ernest Kinoy
Starring: Sidney Poitier, Harry Belafonte, Ruby Dee, Cameron Mitchell
DVD and VHS: Sony Pictures

Bucktown (1975, AIP)
Director: Arthur Marks
Writer: Bob Ellison
Starring: Fred Williamson, Pam Grier, Thalmus Rasulala, Tony King, Bernie Hamilton
DVD and VHS: MGM

The Bus Is Coming, a.k.a. *Ghetto Revenge* (1971, William Thompson International)
Director: Wendell J. Franklin
Writers: Horace Jackson, Robert H. Raff, Mike Rhodes
Starring: Mike Simms, Stephanie Raulkner, Burl Bullock
DVD: Blax Film

The Candy Tangerine Man (1975, Moonstone)
Director: Matt Cimber
Writer: George Theakos
Starring: John Daniels, the "actual hookers and blades of Sunset Strip in Hollywood"

Carter's Army, a.k.a. *Black Brigade* (1970, ABC-TV)
Director: George McGowan
Writers: David Kidd, Aaron Spelling
Starring: Robert Hooks, Stephen Boyd, Rosy Grier, Moses Gunn, Richard Pryor, Glynn Turman, Billy Dee Williams
DVD: Westlake Entertainment; VHS: United American Video

Car Wash (1976)
Director: Michael Schultz
Writer: Joel Schumacher
Starring: Franklin Ajaye, Richard Pryor, Ivan Dixon, Bill Duke, Antonio Fargas, George Carlin
DVD: Universal; VHS: Good Times Home Video

Catch My Soul, a.k.a. *Santa Fe Satan* (1973)
Director: Patrick McGoohan
Writer: Jack Good
Starring: Richie Havens, Season Hubley

Change of Mind (1969)
Director: Robert Stevens
Writers: Seeleg Lester, Dick Wesson
Starring: Raymond St. Jacques

Charcoal Black, a.k.a. *Black Rage* (1972)
Director: Chris Robinson
Writers: Chris Robinson, Ted Cassidy
Starring: Chris Robinson, Ted Cassidy

Charley One Eye (1972, Paramount)
Director: Don Chaffey
Writer: Keith Leonard
Starring: Richard Roundtree, Roy Thinnes, Nigel Davenport

Claudine (1974)
Director: John Berry
Writers: Lester Pine, Tina Pine
Starring: Diahann Carroll, James Earl Jones, Lawrence Hilton-Jacobs
DVD and VHS: 20th Century Fox

Cleopatra Jones (1973, Warner Bros.)
Director: Jack Starrett
Writers: Max Julien, Sheldon Keller
Starring: Tamara Dobson, Bernie Casey, Shelley Winters, Brenda Sykes,
    Antonio Fargas
DVD and VHS: Warner Home Video

Cleopatra Jones and the Casino of Gold (1975, Warner Bros.)
Director: Chuck Bail
Writer: William Tennant
Starring: Tamara Dobson, Stella Stevens, Ni Tien (Tanny), Norman Fell
VHS: Warner Home Video

Coffy (1973, AIP)
Director: Jack Hill
Writer: Jack Hill
Starring: Pam Grier, Booker Bradshaw, Robert DoQui, William Elliot, Allan Arbus, Sid Haig
DVD and VHS: MGM

Combat Cops, a.k.a. *The Zebra Killer; Panic City* (1974)
Director: William Girdler
Writers: William Girdler, Gordon Cornell Lane
Starring: Austin Stoker, D'Urville Martin, Juanita Moore

Come Back, Charleston Blue (1972, Warner Bros.)
Director: Mark Warren
Writers: Peggy Elliott, Bontche Schweig
Starring: Godfrey Cambridge, Raymond St. Jacques, Philip Michael Thomas
VHS: Warner Home Video

Cool Breeze (1972, MGM)
Director: Barry Pollack
Writer: Barry Pollack
Starring: Thalmus Rasulala, Judy Pace, Jim Watkins, Lincoln Kilpatrick, Sam Laws, Margaret Avery, Wally Taylor, Raymond St. Jacques, Rudy Challenger

Cooley High (1975, AIP)
Director: Michael Schultz
Writer: Eric Monte
Starring: Glynn Turman, Lawrence Hilton-Jacobs, Garrett Morris, Eric Monte
DVD and VHS: MGM

Coonskin, a.k.a. *Street Fight* (1975, Bryanstone)
Director: Ralph Bakshi
Writer: Ralph Bakshi
Starring the voices of: Barry White, Scatman Crothers, Charles Gordone, Philip Michael Thomas
VHS: Academy Video

Cornbread, Earl, and Me (1975, AIP)
Director: Joe Manduke
Writer: Leonard Lamensdorf
Starring: Jamaal (Keith) Wilkes, Laurence Fishburne, Moses Gunn, Thalmus Rasulala, Bernie Casey, Madge Sinclair, Antonio Fargas
DVD and VHS: MGM

Cotton Comes to Harlem (1970, United Artists)
Director: Ossie Davis
Writers: Ossie Davis, Arnold Perl
Starring: Raymond St. Jacques, Godfrey Cambridge, Calvin Lockhart, Judy Pace, Redd Foxx
DVD and VHS: MGM

Countdown at Kusini, a.k.a. *Cool Red* (1976, Columbia)
Director: Ossie Davis
Writers: Ossie Davis, Al Freeman Jr., Ladi Labedo, John Storm Roberts
Starring: Ruby Dee, Ossie Davis, Greg Morris

Darktown Strutters, a.k.a. *Get Down and Boogie* (1975, New World)
Director: William Witney
Writer: George Armitage
Starring: Trina Parks, Edna Richardson, Bettye Sweet, Shirley Washington, Roger E. Mosely
VHS: Charter Entertainment

Death Dimension, a.k.a. *Black Eliminator, Kill Factor, Freeze Bomb* (1978, Movietime)
Director: Al Adamson
Writer: Harry Hope
Starring: Jim Kelly, Aldo Ray, Harold Sakata, Terry Moore, George Lazenby
DVD: Crash Cinema Media

Death Journey (1976, Atlas)
Director: Fred Williamson
Writer: Abel Jones
Starring: Fred Williamson, D'Urville Martin

Deliver Us from Evil, a.k.a. *Joey* (1977, Dimension)
Director: Horace Jackson
Writer: Horace Jackson
Starring: Marie O'Henry, Renny Roker, Juanita Moore

Detroit 9000, a.k.a. *Detroit Heat* (1973, General)
Director: Arthur Marks
Writer: Orville H. Hampton
Starring: Alex Rocco, Hari Rhodes, Vonetta McGee, Scatman Crothers,
    Herbert Jefferson
DVD: Miramax; VHS: Walt Disney

Disco 9000, a.k.a. *Fass Black* (1979)
Director: D'Urville Martin
Writer: Roland S. Jefferson
Starring: John Pool, Jeannie Bell, Shirley Washington
VHS: Xenon

Disco Godfather, a.k.a. *Avenging Disco Godfather, Avenging Godfather* (1979,
    Communications International)
Director: J. Robert Wagoner
Writers: Cliff Roquemore, J. Robert Wagoner
Starring: Rudy Ray Moore, Carol Speed, Jimmy Lynch, Lady Reed
DVD and VHS: Xenon

Dolemite (1974)
Director: D'Urville Martin
Writers: Jerry Jones, Rudy Ray Moore
Starring: Rudy Ray Moore, Lady Reed, D'Urville Martin
DVD and VHS: Xenon

Don't Play Us Cheap (1973)
Director: Melvin Van Peebles
Writer: Melvin Van Peebles
Starring: Melvin Van Peebles, Mabel King, Esther Rolle
DVD and VHS: Xenon

Dr. Black, Mr. Hyde, a.k.a. *The Watts Monster* (1976, Dimension)
Director: William Crain
Writers: Larry LeBron, Lawrence Woolner
Starring: Bernie Casey, Rosalind Cash, Ji-Tu Cumbuka
VHS: United Home

Drum (1976)
Director: Steve Carver
Writer: Norman Wexler
Starring: Ken Norton, Yaphet Kotto, Pam Grier, Brenda Sykes, Paula Kelly

Dynamite Brothers, a.k.a. *Stud Brown* (1975, Cinemation)
Director: Al Adamson
Writers: John D'Amato, Marvin Lagunoff, Jim Rein
Starring: Timothy Brown, James Hong, Alan Tang, Carol Speed
DVD: Rhino; VHS: BCI/Eclipse

Ebony, Ivory, and Jade, a.k.a. *American Beauty Hostages*; *Foxforce She Devils in Chains* (1976)
Director: Cirio Santiago
Writer: Henry Barnes
Starring: Rosanne Katon, Colleen Camp, Sylvia Anderson, Trina Parks
DVD and VHS: Starz/Anchor Bay

The Education of Sonny Carson (1974, Paramount)
Director: Michael Campus
Writer: Fred Hudson
Starring: Rony Clanton, Don Gordon, Joyce Walker, Paul Benjamin
DVD: VCI Video; VHS: Hollywood Select Video

El Condor (1970)
Director: John Guillerman
Writers: Larry Cohen, Steven W. Carabatsos
Starring: Jim Brown, Lee Van Cleef, Iron Eyes Cody
VHS: Warner Home Video

Embassy, a.k.a. *Target: Embassy* (1972)
Director: Gordon Hessler

Writers: John Bird, William Fairchild
Starring: Richard Roundtree, Max Von Sydow, Chuck Connors, Ray Milland, Broderick Crawford

Emma Mae, a.k.a. *Black Sister's Revenge* (1976, Pro International)
Director: Jamaa Fanaka
Writer: Jamaa Fanaka
Starring: Jerri Hayes, Ernest Williams II
VHS: Xenon

Fight for Your Life, a.k.a. *I Hate Your Guts; Held Hostage Stayin' Alive; Bloodbath at 1313; Getting Even; Fury Road* (1977)
Director: Robert Endelson
Writer: Straw Weisman
Starring: William Sanderson, Robert Judd
DVD: Blue Underground

Fighting Mad, a.k.a. *Fierce; Death Force* (1977)
Director: Cirio Santiago
Writer: Howard R. Cohen
Starring: Leon Isaac Kennedy, Jayne Kennedy, James Inglehart
VHS: JTC, Inc.

The Final Comedown, a.k.a. *Blast!* (1972, New World)
Director: Oscar Williams
Writer: Oscar Williams
Starring: Billy Dee Williams, Raymond St. Jacques, D'Urville Martin
DVD: BCI/Eclipse; VHS: Simitar Entertainment

Five on the Black Hand Side (1973)
Director: Oscar Williams
Writer: Charlie L. Russell
Starring: Leonard Jackson, Glynn Turman, D'Urville Martin
DVD and VHS: MGM

Force Four, a.k.a. *Black Force* (1975)
Director: Michael Fink
Starring: Malachi Lee, Owen Watson, Warhawk Tanzania
VHS: Simitar Entertainment

Fox Style (1973)
Director: Clyde Houston
Starring: Chuck Daniel, Juanita Moore

Foxtrap (1986, Snizzlefritz)
Director: Fred Williamson
Writer: Aubrey K. Rattan
Starring: Fred Williamson, Lela Rochon
VHS: MGM

Foxy Brown (1974, AIP)
Director: Jack Hill
Writer: Jack Hill
Starring: Pam Grier, Antonio Fargas, Peter Brown, Terry Carter, Kathryn
    Loder
DVD and VHS: MGM

Friday Foster (1975, AIP)
Director: Arthur Marks
Writers: Orville H. Hampton, Arthur Marks
Starring: Pam Grier, Yaphet Kotto, Godfrey Cambridge, Thalmus Rasulala,
    Eartha Kitt, Jim Backus, Scatman Crothers, Jason Bernard, Ted Lange
DVD and VHS: MGM

Gang Wars, a.k.a. *Devil's Express* (1975)
Director: Barry Rosen
Writers: Niki Patton, CeOtis Robinson, Barry Rosen
Starring: Warhawk Tanzania

Ganja and Hess, a.k.a. *Blood Couple*; *Double Possession*; *Black Vampire*;
    Blackout (1973, Kelly-Jordan Enterprises)
Director: Bill Gunn
Writer: Bill Gunn
Starring: Duane Jones, Marlene Clark, Bill Gunn
DVD: Image Entertainment; VHS: United American Video

Georgia, Georgia (1972)
Director: Stig Bjorkman

Writer: Maya Angelou
Starring: Diana Sands, Minnie Gentry, Dirk Benedict

Get Christie Love! (1974)
Director: William A. Graham
Writer: George Kirgo
Starring: Teresa Graves, Harry Guardino
DVD: BCI/Eclipse; VHS: Xenon

Getting Over (1976, Maverick International)
Director: Bernie Rollins
Writer: Bernie Rollins
Starring: John Daniels, The Love Machine

Golden Needles (1974)
Director: Robert Clouse
Writers: S. Lee Pogostin, Sylvia Schneble
Starring: Jim Kelly, Joe Don Baker

Gordon's War (1973, 20th Century Fox)
Director: Ossie Davis
Writers: Howard Friedlander, Ed Spielman
Starring: Paul Winfield, Carl Lee, Tony King, David Downing
VHS: Fox Home Entertainment

Greased Lightning (1977, Warner Bros.)
Director: Michael Schultz
Writers: Leon Capetanos, Lawrence DuKore, Melvin Van Peebles, Kenneth Vose
Starring: Richard Pryor, Beau Bridges, Pam Grier, Cleavon Little
DVD: Warner Home Video; VHS: Good Times Video

The Greatest (1977)
Director: Tom Gries, Monte Hellman
Writer: Ring Lardner Jr.
Starring: Muhammad Ali, Ernest Borgnine
DVD and VHS: Sony Pictures

The Great White Hope (1970)
Director: Martin Ritt
Writer: Howard Sackler
Starring: James Earl Jones, Jane Alexander
DVD and VHS: 20th Century Fox

The Guy from Harlem (1977)
Director: Rene Martinez Jr.
Writer: Gardenia Martinez
Starring: Loye Hawkins, Cathy Davis
VHS: Xenon

Halls of Anger (1970, United Artists)
Director: Paul Bogart
Writers: Al Ramrus, John Herman Shaner
Starring: Calvin Lockhart, Janet MacLachlan

Hammer (1972, United Artists)
Director: Bruce Clark
Writer: Charles Johnson
Starring: Fred Williamson, Bernie Hamilton, Vonetta McGee, William Smith
DVD: MGM

The Harder They Come (1973)
Director: Perry Henzell
Writers: Perry Henzell, Trevor D. Rhone
Starring: Jimmy Cliff, Janet Bartley
DVD: Xenon, Criterion; VHS: Polygram

Hell up in Harlem (1973, AIP)
Director: Larry Cohen
Writer: Larry Cohen
Starring: Fred Williamson, Julius Harris, Gloria Hendry, Margaret Avery,
    D'Urville Martin, Tony King
DVD and VHS: MGM

A Hero Ain't Nothin' But a Sandwich (1978)
Director: Ralph Nelson
Writer: Alice Childress

Starring: Cicely Tyson, Paul Winfield, Larry B. Scott
VHS: Paramount

Hickey and Boggs (1972, United Artists)
Director: Robert Culp
Writer: Walter Hill
Starring: Robert Culp, Bill Cosby, Rosalind Cash
DVD: AIP; VHS: Jef Films

Hit! (1973, Paramount)
Director: Sidney J. Furie
Writers: Alan Trustman, David M. Wolf
Starring: Billy Dee Williams, Richard Pryor
VHS: Paramount

Hit Man (1972, MGM)
Director: George Armitage
Writer: George Armitage
Starring: Bernie Casey, Pam Grier, Sam Laws

The Hitter (1979, Peppercorn-Wormser)
Director: Christopher Leitch
Writers: Ben Harris, Christopher Leitch
Starring: Ron O'Neal, Adolph Caesar, Sheila Frazier, Bill Cobbs

Honeybaby, Honeybaby (1974, Kelly-Jordan)
Director: Michael Schultz
Writers: Leonard Kantor, Brian Phelan
Starring: Diana Sands, Calvin Lockhart

Honky (1971, Jack H. Harris)
Director: William A. Graham
Writer: Will Chaney
Starring: Brenda Sykes, John Neilson, William Marshall

Hot Potato (1976, Warner Bros.)
Director: Oscar Williams
Writer: Oscar Williams
Starring: Jim Kelly, George Memmoli, Geoffrey Binney
VHS: Warner Home Video

House on Skull Mountain (1974, 20th Century Fox)
Director: Ron Honthaner
Writer: Mildred Pares
Starring: Victor French, Janee Michelle, Jean Durand, Mike Evans
DVD: 20th Century Fox; VHS: Fox Home Video

Human Tornado, a.k.a. *Dolemite II* (1976, Dimension)
Director: Cliff Roquemore
Writer: Jerry Jones
Starring: Rudy Ray Moore, Lady Reed, Jimmy Lynch, Ernie Hudson
DVD and VHS: Xenon

I Escaped from Devil's Island (1973, United Artists)
Director: William Witney
Writer: Richard L. Adams
Starring: Jim Brown, Christopher George

If He Hollers Let Him Go, a.k.a. *Dead Right* (1968, Cinerama)
Director: Charles Martin
Writer: Charles Martin
Starring: Raymond St. Jacques, Barbara McNair, Kevin McCarthy, Dana Wynter

In the Heat of the Night (1967, United Artists)
Director: Norman Jewison
Writer: Stirling Silliphant
Starring: Sidney Poitier, Rod Steiger
DVD: United Artists; VHS: MGM

Isaac Hayes: Black Moses of Soul
Director: Chuck Johnson
Concert film
DVD: Sofa

J.D.'s Revenge (1976, AIP)
Director: Arthur Marks
Writer: Jaison Starkes
Starring: Glynn Turman, Joan Pringle, Lou Gossett Jr.
DVD and VHS: MGM

Joshua, a.k.a. *The Black Rider* (1976, Lone Star)
Director: Larry Spangler
Writer: Fred Williamson
Starring: Fred Williamson
DVD: United American Video; VHS: Rhino

Lady Cocoa, a.k.a. *Pop Goes the Weasel* (1975, Moonstone)
Director: Matt Cimber
Writer: George Theakos
Starring: Lola Falana, Mean Joe Greene, Alex Dreier, Gene Washington

Lady Sings the Blues (1972, Paramount)
Director: Sidney J. Furie
Writers: Chris Clark, Suzanne De Passe, Terrence McCloy
Starring: Diana Ross, Billy Dee Williams, Richard Pryor
DVD: Paramount

The Landlord (1970)
Director: Hal Ashby
Writer: Bill Gunn
Starring: Beau Bridges, Diana Sands, Marki Bey, Lou Gossett Jr., Pearl
    Bailey
VHS: MGM

Last Fight (1983)
Director: Fred Williamson
Writer: Fred Williamson
Starring: Fred Williamson, Ruben Blades

Leadbelly (1976)
Director: Gordon Parks Sr.
Writer: Ernest Kinoy
Starring: Roger E. Mosely, Art J. Evans

The Legend of Nigger Charley (1972, Paramount)
Director: Martin Goldman
Writers: James Warner Bellah, Martin Goldman, Larry G. Spangler
Starring: Fred Williamson, D'Urville Martin, Don Pedro Colley

Let's Do It Again (1975, Warner Bros.)
Director: Sidney Poitier
Writers: Timothy March, Richard Wesley
Starring: Sidney Poitier, Bill Cosby, Calvin Lockhart, John Amos, Denise Nicholas, Lee Chamberlin
DVD and VHS: Warner Home Video

The Liberation of L. B. Jones (1970, Columbia)
Director: William Wyler
Writers: Jesse Hill Ford, Stirling Silliphant
Starring: Lee J. Cobb, Anthony Zerbe, Roscoe Lee Browne, Lola Falana, Yaphet Kotto
VHS: Columbia

The Limit (1972)
Director: Yaphet Kotto
Writers: Sean Cameron, Yaphet Kotto
Starring: Yaphet Kotto

Live and Let Die (1973, United Artists)
Director: Guy Hamilton
Writer: Tom Mankiewicz
Starring: Roger Moore, Jane Seymour, Yaphet Kotto, Gloria Hendry, Geoffrey Holder, Julius Harris
DVD and VHS: MGM

The Long Night, a.k.a. *Steely Brown* (1976)
Director: Woodie King Jr.
Writer: Julian Mayfield
Starring: Dick Anthony Williams, Peggy Kirkpatrick, Woodie King Jr.

Lord Shango, a.k.a. *The Color of Love* (1975)
Director: Ray Marsh
Writer: Paul Carter Harrison
Starring: Lawrence Cook, Marlene Clark

The Lost Man (1969, Universal)
Director: Robert Alan Arthur
Writer: Robert Alan Arthur

Starring: Sidney Poitier, Joanna Shimkus, Al Freeman Jr.
VHS: Universal

The Mack (1973, Cinerama)
Director: Michael Campus
Writer: Robert J. Poole
Starring: Max Julien, Richard Pryor, Roger E. Mosely, Carol Speed, Don Gordon, Dick Anthony Williams
DVD: New Line Home Video; VHS: Sony Pictures

Mahogany (1975)
Director: Berry Gordy
Writers: Toni Amber, John Byrum, Bob Merrill
Starring: Diana Ross, Billy Dee Williams, Anthony Perkins, Beah Richards
DVD and VHS: Paramount

The Man (1971)
Director: Joseph Sargent
Writer: Rod Serling
Starring: James Earl Jones, Martin Balsam, Georg Stanford Brown, Robert DoQui

Man and Boy (1972, Levitt-Pickman)
Director: E. W. Swackhamer
Writers: Harry Essex, Oscar Saul
Starring: Bill Cosby, Gloria Foster, Yaphet Kotto
DVD and VHS: Sony Pictures

Mandingo (1975)
Director: Richard Fleischer
Writer: Norman Wexler
Starring: James Mason, Perry King, Ken Norton, Brenda Sykes
VHS: Paramount

Man Friday (1975)
Director: Jack Gold
Writer: Adrian Mitchell
Starring: Peter O'Toole, Richard Roundtree
DVD: Lion's Gate

The McMasters, a.k.a. *The Blood Crowd; The McMasters . . . Tougher Than
the West Itself* (1970, Chevron)
Director: Alf Kjellin
Writer: Harold Jacob Smith
Starring: Brock Peters, Burl Ives, David Carradine, Nancy Kwan, Jack Palance
VHS: Starmaker Entertainment

Mean Johnny Barrows (1975, Dimension)
Director: Fred Williamson
Writers: Jolivett Cato, Charles Walker
Starring: Fred Williamson, Roddy McDowall, Stuart Whitman

Mean Mother (1973)
Directors: Al Adamson, León Klimovsky
Writers: Joy Garrison, Charles Johnson
Starring: Clifton Brown, Dennis Safren, Tracy King
DVD: EI Independent; VHS: Xenon

Melinda (1972, MGM)
Director: Hugh A. Robertson
Writers: Raymond Cistheri, Lonne Elder III
Starring: Calvin Lockhart, Rosalind Cash, Vonetta McGee, Rockne Tark-
ington, Jim Kelly

The Messenger (1986, Snizzlefritz)
Director: Fred Williamson
Writers: Brian Johnson, Conchita Lee, Fred Williamson, Anthony Wisdom
Starring: Fred Williamson, Christopher Connelly, Cameron Mitchell
DVD: MGM; VHS: Orion

Miss Melody Jones (1973)
Director: Bill Brame
Writer: Bill Brame
Starring: Philomena Nowlin, Ronald Warren
VHS: Xenon

Mister Deathman (1977)
Director: Michael D. Moore
Starring: David Broadnax, Stella Stevens

The Monkey Hustle (1976, AIP)
Director: Arthur Marks
Writers: Odie Hawkins, Charles Johnson
Starring: Rudy Ray Moore, Yaphet Kotto, Thomas Carter, Rosalind Cash
DVD and VHS: MGM

Mr. Mean (1977, Lone Star/Po' Boy)
Director: Fred Williamson
Writer: Fred Williamson
Starring: Fred Williamson
VHS: Rhino

The Muthers (1976, Dimension)
Director: Cirio Santiago
Writers: Cirio Santiago, Cyril St. James
Starring: Jeannie Bell, Rosanne Katon, Trinia Parks, Jayne Kennedy
VHS: United American Video

Norman, Is That You? (1976)
Director: George Schlatter
Writer: George Schlatter
Starring: Redd Foxx, Pearl Bailey, Michael Warren
VHS: MGM

No Way Back (1976, Atlas)
Director: Fred Williamson
Writer: Fred Williamson
Starring: Fred Williamson, Tracy Reed, Stack Pierce, Don Cornelius

The Obsessed One (1970s)

One Down, Two to Go (1981, Almi)
Director: Fred Williamson
Writer: Fred Williamson
Starring: Fred Williamson, Jim Brown, Jim Kelly, Richard Roundtree
DVD: Starz/Anchor Bay; VHS: Rhino

The Organization (1971, United Artists)
Director: Don Medford
Writer: James R. Webb
Starring: Sidney Poitier, Barbara McNair, Bernie Hamilton, Ron O'Neal
VHS: MGM

Passion Plantation (1977)
Director: Mario Pinzauti
Writer: Mario Pinzauti
Starring: Percy Hogan, Malisa Longo, Antonio Gismondo

Penitentiary (1979, Jerry Gross)
Director: Jamaa Fanaka
Writer: Jamaa Fanaka
Starring: Leon Isaac Kennedy, Thommy Pollard, Donovan Womack
DVD and VHS: Xenon

Penitentiary II (1982, MGM/United Artists)
Director: Jamaa Fanaka
Writer: Jamaa Fanaka
Starring: Leon Isaac Kennedy, Ernie Hudson, Mr. T, Glynn Turman
DVD and VHS: Xenon

Penitentiary III (1987, Cannon)
Director: Jamaa Fanaka
Writer: Jamaa Fanaka
Starring: Leon Isaac Kennedy, Anthony Geary
VHS: Warner Home Entertainment

Petey Wheatstraw, a.k.a. *The Devil's Son-in-Law* (1977)
Director: Cliff Roquemore
Writer: Cliff Roquemore
Starring: Rudy Ray Moore, Jimmy Lynch, Leroy Daniels, Ebony Wright
DVD and VHS: Xenon

A Piece of the Action (1977, Warner Bros.)
Director: Sidney Poitier
Writers: Charles Blackwell, Timothy March

Starring: Sidney Poitier, Bill Cosby, James Earl Jones, Denise Nicholas, Tracy Reed
DVD and VHS: Warner Home Video

Pipe Dreams (1976)
Director: Stephen Verona
Writer: Stephen Verona
Starring: Gladys Knight, Altovese Davis

A Place Called Today, a.k.a. *City in Fear* (1972)
Director: Don Schain
Writer: Don Schain
Starring: J. Herbert Kerr Jr., Timothy Brown, Lana Wood
VHS: Monterey Home Video

Putney Swope (1969)
Director: Robert Downey Sr.
Writer: Robert Downey Sr.
Starring: Arnold Johnson, Antonio Fargas
DVD: Home Vision; VHS: Rhino

Right On! (1971)
Director: Herbert Danska
Documentary about the Last Poets

Riot (1969, Paramount)
Director: Buzz Kulik
Writer: James Poe
Starring: Jim Brown, Gene Hackman

The River Niger (1976)
Director: Krishna Shah
Writer: Joseph A. Walker
Starring: James Earl Jones, Cicely Tyson, Glynn Turman, Lou Gossett Jr., Roger E. Mosely
DVD: Echo Bridge Home Entertainment; VHS: United American Video

Run, Nigger, Run, a.k.a. *Black Connection* (1974)
Director: Michael Finn
Starring: Bobby Stevens, Sonny Charles
VHS: Inner Visions Group

Savage!, a.k.a. *Black Valor, Black Savage* (1973, New World)
Director: Cirio Santiago
Writer: Ed Medard
Starring: James Inglehart, Carol Speed
VHS: Simitar Entertainment

Savage Sisters (1974)
Director: Eddie Romero
Writers: Harry Corner, H. Franco Moon
Starring: Gloria Hendry, Cheri Caffaro
DVD: BCI/Eclipse

Save the Children (1973)
Director: Stan Lathan
Writer: Matt Robinson
Concert film

Scott Joplin (1977)
Director: Jeremy Kagan
Writer: Christopher Knopf
Starring: Billy Dee Williams, Clifton James, Margaret Avery, Eubie Blake,
    Godfrey Cambridge
VHS: Universal

Scream, Blacula, Scream (1973, AIP)
Director: Bob Kelljan
Writers: Maurice Jules, Raymond Koenig, Joan Torres
Starring: William Marshall, Pam Grier, Richard Lawson, Don Mitchell,
    Michael Conrad
DVD and VHS: MGM

Shaft (1971, MGM)
Director: Gordon Parks Sr.
Writer: Ernest Tidyman

Starring: Richard Roundtree, Moses Gunn, Charles Cioffi, Christopher St. John, Antonio Fargas
DVD and VHS: Warner Home Video

Shaft in Africa (1973, MGM)
Director: John Guillermin
Writer: Stirling Silliphant
Starring: Richard Roundtree, Vonetta McGee
DVD and VHS: Warner Home Video

Shaft's Big Score (1972, MGM)
Director: Gordon Parks Sr.
Writer: Ernest Tidyman
Starring: Richard Roundtree, Moses Gunn, Drew Bundini Brown
DVD and VHS: Warner Home Video

Sheba, Baby (1975, AIP)
Director: William Girdler
Writers: William Girdler, David Sheldon
Starring: Pam Grier, Austin Stoker, D'Urville Martin, Rudy Challenger
DVD and VHS: MGM

Shoot It Black, Shoot It Blue (1974)
Director: Dennis McGuire
Writer: Dennis McGuire
Starring: Michael Moriarty, Eric Laneuville
VHS: Falcon Home Video

The Slams (1973, MGM)
Director: Jonathan Kaplan
Writer: Richard L. Adams
Starring: Jim Brown, Judy Pace

Slaughter (1972, AIP)
Director: Jack Starrett
Writers: Mark Hanna, Don Williams
Starring: Jim Brown, Stella Stevens, Rip Torn, Don Gordon, Marlene Clark
DVD and VHS: MGM

Slaughter's Big Rip-Off (1973, AIP)
Director: Gordon Douglas
Writer: Charles Johnson
Starring: Jim Brown, Ed McMahon, Brock Peters, Gloria Hendry, Don
  Stroud, Dick Anthony Williams
DVD and VHS: MGM

Solomon King, a.k.a. *Black Agent* (1974)
Directors: Jack Bomay, Sal Watts
Writers: Jim Alston, Sal Watts
Starring: Sal Watts, James Watts

The Soul of Nigger Charley (1973, Paramount)
Director: Larry Spangler
Writers: Larry Spangler, Harold Stone
Starring: Fred Williamson, D'Urville Martin, Denise Nicholas

Soul Patrol, a.k.a. *Black Trash*; *Death of a Snowman* (1980)
Director: Christopher Rowley
Writer: Bima Stagg
Starring: Ken Gampu, Nigel Davenport

Soul Soldiers, a.k.a. *Soul Soldier*; *The Buffalo Soldiers*; *Men of the Tenth*; *The
  Red, White, and Black*; *Black Calvary* (1970, Hirschman-Northern)
Director: John Cardos
Writer: Marlene Weed
Starring: Robert DoQui, Janee Michelle, Lincoln Kilpatrick, Isaac Fields,
  Rafer Johnson, Cesar Romero, Barbara Hale, Isabel Sanford

Soul to Soul (1971)
Director: Denis Sanders
Concert film
DVD: Rhino

Sounder (1972)
Director: Martin Ritt
Writer: Lonne Elder III
Starring: Cicely Tyson, Paul Winfield, Kevin Hooks
DVD: KOCH Vision; VHS: Paramount

Sounder, Part 2 (1976)
Director: William Graham
Writer: Lonne Elder III
Starring: Harold Sylvester, Ebony Wright, Taj Mahal

Space Is the Place (1974)
Director: John Coney
Writers: Sun Ra, Joshua Smith
Starring: Sun Ra
VHS: Rhapsody Films

Sparkle (1976)
Director: Sam O'Steen
Writers: Howard Rosenman, Joel Schumacher
Starring: Irene Cara, Lonette McKee, Dwan Smith, Philip Michael
    Thomas, Mary Alice, Dorian Harewood, Tony King
DVD and VHS: Warner Home Video

Speeding Up Time (1975, Cougman)
Director: John Evans
Writer: John Evans
Starring: Winston Thrash, Pamela Donegan

The Split (1968, MGM)
Director: Gordon Flemyng
Writer: Robert Sabaroff
Starring: Jim Brown, Diahann Carroll, Julie Harris, Ernest Borgnine, Gene
    Hackman, Jack Klugman, Donald Sutherland

The Spook Who Sat by the Door (1973, United Artists)
Director: Ivan Dixon
Writers: Melvin Clay, Sam Greenlee
Starring: Lawrence Cook, J. A. Preston, Paula Kelly, Janet League
DVD and VHS: Monarch Home Video

Street Sisters, a.k.a. *Black Hooker, Black Mama* (1974)
Director: Arthur Roberson
Writer: Arthur Roberson
Starring: Jeff Burton, Kathryn Jackson

Sugar Hill, a.k.a. *Zombies of Sugar Hill; Voodoo Girl* (1974, AIP)
Director: Paul Malansky
Writer: Tim Kelly
Starring: Marki Bey, Robert Quarry, Don Pedro Colley, Richard Lawson

Super Dude, a.k.a. *Hang Up* (1974, Dimension)
Director: Henry Hathaway
Writers: Lee Lazich, Albert Maltz (John B. Sherry)
Starring: William Elliot, Marki Bey, Cliff Potts

Super Fly, a.k.a. *Superfly* (1972, Warner Bros.)
Director: Gordon Parks Jr.
Writer: Phillip Fenty
Starring: Ron O'Neal, Carl Lee, Sheila Frazier, Julius Harris
DVD and VHS: Warner Home Video

Super Fly T.N.T (1973, Paramount)
Director: Ron O'Neal
Writers: Phillip Fenty, Alex Haley, Ron O'Neal, Sig Shore
Starring: Ron O'Neal, Sheila Frazier, Roscoe Lee Browne, Robert Guillaume
VHS: Paramount

Super Spook (1975, Levitt-Pickman)
Director: Anthony Major
Writers: Ed Dessisso, Leonard Jackson, Bill Jay, Tony King, Anthony Major
Starring: Leonard Jackson, Bill Jay, Tony King

Sweet Jesus Preacherman, a.k.a. *Sweet James Preacherman* (1973, MGM)
Director: Henning Schellerup
Writers: John Cerullo, Abbey Leitch, M. Stuart Madden
Starring: Roger E. Mosley, William Smith, Damu King, Marla Gibbs

Sweet Sweetback's Baadasssss Song (1971, Cinemation)
Director: Melvin Van Peebles
Writer: Melvin Van Peebles
Starring: Melvin Van Peebles, John Amos
DVD and VHS: Cinemation Industries

The Take (1974, Columbia)
Director: Robert Hartford-Davis
Writers: Franklin Coen, Del Reisman
Starring: Billy Dee Williams, Eddie Albert, Frankie Avalon, Sorrell Booke,
    Tracy Reed

Take a Hard Ride (1975, 20th Century Fox)
Director: Anthony Dawson (Antonio Margheriti)
Writers: Eric Bercovici, Jerrold L. Ludwig
Starring: Jim Brown, Fred Williamson, Jim Kelly, Lee Van Cleef, Cather-
    ine Spaak
DVD: Starz/Anchor Bay; VHS: 20th Century Fox

The Tattoo Connection, a.k.a *Black Belt Jones 2* (1978, World Northal)
Director: Lee Tso-Nam
Starring: Jim Kelly
DVD and VHS: World Northal

Tenafly (1973, NBC-TV)
Director: Richard Colla
Writers: Richard Levinson, William Link
Starring: James McEachin, Ed Nelson

That Man Bolt, a.k.a. *Thunderbolt*; *To Kill a Dragon* (1973, Universal)
Director: Henry Levin, David Lowell Rich
Writers: Charles Johnson, Ranald MacDougall
Starring: Fred Williamson
DVD and VHS: Universal

That's the Way of the World (1975)
Director: Sig Shore
Writer: Robert Lipsyte
Starring: Earth, Wind, and Fire, Harvey Keitel
DVD: BCI/Eclipse

They Call Me Mister Tibbs (1970, United Artists)
Director: Gordon Douglas
Writers: Alan Trustman, James R. Webb
Starring: Sidney Poitier, Martin Landau, Barbara McNair, Anthony Zerbe
DVD and VHS: MGM

The Thing with Two Heads (1972, AIP)
Director: Lee Frost
Writers: Wes Bishop, Lee Frost, James Gordon White
Starring: Ray Milland, Rosey Grier
DVD: MGM

Thomasine and Bushrod (1974, Columbia)
Director: Gordon Parks Jr.
Writer: Max Julien
Starring: Max Julien, Vonetta McGee, Glynn Turman, George Murdock

Three the Hard Way (1974, Allied Artists)
Director: Gordon Parks Jr.
Writers: Eric Bercovici, Jerrold L. Ludwig
Starring: Jim Brown, Fred Williamson, Jim Kelly, Sheila Frazier, Jay Robinson

Three Tough Guys, a.k.a. *Tough Guys* (1974, Paramount)
Director: Duccio Tessari
Writers: Nicola Badalucco, Georges Dutter, Luciano Vincenzoni
Starring: Isaac Hayes, Lino Venturo, Fred Williamson, Paula Kelly

tick . . . tick . . . tick (1969, MGM)
Director: Ralph Nelson
Writer: James Lee Barrett
Starring: Jim Brown, George Kennedy, Fredric March

TNT Jackson (1975, New World)
Director: Cirio Santiago
Writers: Ken Metcalfe, Dick Miller
Starring: Jeanne Bell, Stan Shaw
DVD: Echo Bridge Home Entertainment; VHS: United American Video

Together Brothers (1974, 20th Century Fox)
Director: William Graham
Writers: Jack DeWitt, Joe Greene
Starring: Ahmad Nurradin, Anthony Wilson, Nelson Simms, Kenneth Bell, Owen Page, Kin Dorsey, Ed Bernard, Lincoln Kilpatrick, Glynn Turman

Together for Days, a.k.a. *Black Cream* (1972)
Director: Michael Schultz
Writers: William B. Branch, Lindsay Smith
Starring: Clifton Davis, Lois Chiles, Woodie King, Leonard Jackson

Top of the Heap (1972, Fanfare)
Director: Christopher St. John
Writer: Christopher St. John
Starring: Christopher St. John, Paula Kelly

Tough, a.k.a. *Johnny Tough* (1974)
Director: Horace Jackson
Writer: Horace Jackson
Starring: Dion Gossett, Renny Roker

Train Ride to Hollywood (1975)
Director: Charles Rondeau
Writer: Dan Gordon
Starring: Bloodstone
DVD and VHS: Starz/Anchor Bay

Trick Baby, a.k.a. *Double Con* (1973, Universal)
Director: Larry Yust
Writers: A. Neuberg, T. Raewyn, Larry Yust
Starring: Kiel Martin, Mel Stewart
DVD and VHS: Universal

Trouble Man (1972, 20th Century Fox)
Director: Ivan Dixon
Writer: John D.F. Black
Starring: Robert Hooks, Paul Winfield, Ralph Waite, Paula Kelly, Julius
    Harris
DVD: 20th Century Fox

Truck Turner (1974, AIP)
Director: Jonathan Kaplan
Writers: Michael Allin, Leigh Chapman, Jerry Wilkes, Oscar Williams
Starring: Isaac Hayes, Yaphet Kotto, Alan Weeks, Annazette Chase,
    Nichelle Nichols
DVD and VHS: MGM

Up Tight! (1968, Paramount)
Director: Jules Dassin
Writers: Jules Dassin, Ruby Dee, Julian Mayfield
Starring: Raymond St. Jacques, Ruby Dee, Frank Silvera, Roscoe Lee
    Browne, Julian Mayfield, Janet MacLachlan, Max Julien, Juanita
    Moore, Dick Anthony Williams

Uptown Saturday Night (1974, Warner Bros.)
Director: Sidney Poitier
Writer: Richard Wesley
Starring: Sidney Poitier, Bill Cosby, Harry Belafonte, Flip Wilson, Richard
    Pryor, Rosalind Cash, Roscoe Lee Browne, Paula Kelly
DVD and VHS: Warner Home Video

Velvet Smooth (1976, Howard Mahler)
Director: Michael Fink
Writers: Leonard Michaels, Jan Weber
Starring: Johnnie Hill, Owen Watson

A Warm December (1973)
Director: Sidney Poitier
Writer: Lawrence Roman
Starring: Sidney Poitier
VHS: Warner Home Video

Watermelon Man (1970, Columbia)
Director: Melvin Van Peebles
Writer: Herman Raucher
Starring: Godfrey Cambridge, Estelle Parsons
DVD and VHS: Sony Pictures

Wattstax (1973)
Director: Mel Stuart
Concert documentary
DVD: Warner Home Video

Welcome Home, Brother Charles, a.k.a. *Soul Vengeance* (1975)
Director: Jamaa Fanaka

Writer: Jamaa Fanaka
Starring: Monte Moore
DVD and VHS: Xenon

Which Way Is Up? (1977)
Director: Michael Schultz
Writers: Cecil Brown, Carl Gottlieb, Lina Wertmuller
Starring: Richard Pryor, Lonette McKee, Margaret Avery
DVD and VHS: Universal

The Wilby Conspiracy (1975)
Director: Ralph Nelson
Writers: Rodney Amateau, Harold Nebenzal
Starring: Sidney Poitier, Michael Caine
DVD and VHS: MGM

Willie Dynamite (1973, Universal)
Director: Gilbert Moses III
Writers: Ron Cutler, Joe Keyes Jr.
Starring: Roscoe Orman, Diana Sands, Thalmus Rasulala, Joyce Walker
DVD and VHS: Universal

Youngblood (1978, AIP)
Director: Noel Nosseck
Writer: Paul Carter Harrison
Starring: Lawrence Hilton-Jacobs, Bryan O'Dell

Zebra Force (1976)
Director: Joe Tornatore
Writers: Robert Leon, Annette Lombardi
Starring: Rockne Tarkington, Timothy Brown
VHS: Media Home Entertainment

Index

About the Authors

David Walker is an award-winning journalist, filmmaker, comic book writer, and the creator of the pop culture magazine *BadAzz MoFo* (www.badazzmofo.com). Walker is recognized as a leading expert on the blaxploitation films of the 1970s and has appeared on American Movie Classics, E!, and VH-1 discussing those films. His publication *BadAzz MoFo* has become internationally known as the indispensable resource guide to black films of the 1970s, and his documentary *Macked, Hammered, Slaughtered, and Shafted* offers an in-depth examination of the films of that era and the people who made them. His other films include *Black Santa's Revenge*, *Damaged Goods*, and *Uncle Tom's Apartment*.

Andrew J. Rausch is the author of numerous books on cinema, including *Turning Points in Film History*, *Fifty Filmmakers: Conversations with Directors from Roger Avary to Steven Zaillian*, and (with Gary Graver) *Making Movies with Orson Welles*. He has worked on a number of films in various capacities, including executive producer, screenwriter, cinematographer, actor, and composer. He resides in Parsons, Kansas, where he is the resident film critic for his local newspaper, the *Parsons Sun*.

Chris Watson is the director of the films *Zombiegeddon* and *Dead in Love*. He has also produced numerous films, including *Slaughter Party*, *Minds of Terror*, and *Evil Ever After*. *Reflections on Blaxploitation* is his first book.